The Anthropology of Food and Body

Gender, Meaning, and Power

CAROLE M. COUNIHAN

Routledge
New York and London

Published in 1999 by
Routledge
29 West 35th Street
New York, NY 10001

Published in Great Britain by
Routledge
11 New Fetter Lane
London EC4P 4EE

Copyright ©1999 by Routledge

Printed in the United States of America on acid-free paper.

Library of Congress Cataloging-in-Publication Data

Counihan, Carole, 1948–
    The anthropology of food and body : gender, meaning, and power / Carole
M. Counihan.
      p.   cm.
    Includes bibliographical references and index.
    ISBN 0-415-92192-9 (hb : acid-free paper). — ISBN 0-415-92193-7
(pb : acid-free paper)
      1. Food habits—Cross-cultural studies.   2. Food habits—Italy.
    3. Food habits—United States.   4. Sex role—Cross-cultural studies.
    5. Women—United States—Social conditions.   6. Women—Italy—social
    conditions.   I. Title.
    GT2850.C68   1999
    394.1—dc21   98-49970
                                                                       CIP

The Anthropology
of Food and Body

Contents

Acknowledgments

There are many people I must thank who have inspired me and taken an interest in my work over the years. First, I must thank all the Italians who told me their food stories: the men and women of the Italian town of Bosa on the island of Sardinia and the members of one extended Florentine family whom I knew intimately for over a decade in the 1970s and 1980s. *A voi, grazie delle tante belle parole and dei tanti piatti gustosi!* I thank the college students at Franklin and Marshall College, Richard Stockton College, and Millersville University who have taken my Food and Culture class. I thank you for your candor and trust in sharing your stories about food and body. I write in part out of my sense of outrage at the pain and self-hatred many of you recount in your relationships to food and body. I thank you rare few who feel good about yourselves, your bodies, and your eating—keep the faith and tell your stories.

I thank the pregnant women in Lancaster, Pennsylvania, who participated in my study of pregnant and postpartum women's attitudes toward food and body—I loved hearing your rich stories. I thank the children who told me tales at two day-care centers and your parents who let me tape-record you—your wild imaginations made my head spin and gave me boundless food for thought.

I thank many scholars and writers about food for inspiration. During graduate school in anthropology at the University of Massachusetts, Dr. Sylvia Helen Forman and Dr. George Armelagos pioneered a course called Food and Culture. Their intellectual interests meshed with life as I saw it in Italy and legitimized my focus on foodways. The noted historian of French foodways, Dr. Steven Kaplan of Cornell University, invited me to join the *Food and Foodways* editorial staff in 1981 and my years of association with him and the journal have stretched my thinking in immeasurable ways. Cornell University Historian Dr. Joan Jacobs Brumberg, author of *Fasting Girls* (Harvard 1988) and *The Body Project* (Random House 1997), has been an unfailingly generous and supportive mentor as well as a fine friend for years.

Many friends and colleagues have spurred my thinking about food and body over the years, including: Kristen Borre, Carole Browner,

Claire Cassidy, Barbara Collins, JoAnn D'Alisera, Lin Emmons, Renate Fernandez, Pam Frese, Christine Hastorf, Rebecca Huss-Ashmore, Sue Ketler, Beppe Lo Russo, Liz Mathias, Ellen Messer, Mimi Nichter, Phyllis Passariello, Peggy Ratcheson, Nicole Sault, David Sutton, Nickie Teufel, Penny Van Esterik, and Barbara Welles-Nystrom. I have been greatly animated by the food and body writings of scholars Carol Adams, Anne Becker, Susan Bordo, Caroline Bynum, Miriam Kahn, Frances Moore Lappé, Anna Meigs, Sidney Mintz, and M. J. Weismantel.

I thank my women's studies colleagues at Millersville University—especially Jen Miller, Jeri Robinson, Nancy Smith, Tracey Weis, Darla Williams, and my feminist-avenger partner Barb Stengel—you all have filled my professional life with strength, support, and fun! I thank everyone who has helped bring this book to fruition—at Routledge, Deanna Hoak, Liana Fredley, Bill Germano, and Nick Syrett, and at Millersville University, Barb Dills, Nicole Keiper, Becky Newman, Tricia Wolfe, the Faculty Grants Committee, and my Sociology-Anthropology department colleagues, especially Sam Casselberry, department chair. I thank all my students for thinking and I especially thank the following students whose tenacious pursuit of ideas has made teaching a joy: Betsy Fischer, Jeannine Giffear, Karen Lindenberg, Paula Miller, and Liz Richards.

I thank my many friends who love to talk about food and ideas, especially Bill Fratus, Christine Streit Guerrini, Angela Jeannet, Ruthie Miller, Jane Rossetti, and Martha Schley. I thank my brothers Ted, Chris, and Steve for always eating my cooking with great gusto and my sister Susan for being the best. I thank Ben and Willie Taggart for being wonderful sons—you ask great questions; I wish you were as good at eating! I thank my husband Jim Taggart for being there for me in so many ways—you are my anthropological interlocutor, my partner, and my soul-mate.

Introduction

This book tells the story of my evolving interest in the anthropological study of food and culture over the past twenty years. Anthropologists admit that while we travel to far-off lands and spend long periods of time listening to diverse people tell us about their lives, we are also studying ourselves. And so it is with me and food.

My story with food runs deep. It runs through my childhood filled with physical activity and the consumption of enormous amounts of candy and sugar, a story I have yet to tell. It runs through my body image in contrasting ways: the solace of eating battling with a fear of fat. My story with food runs through the six years I spent living and doing fieldwork in Italy—in the town of Bosa on the island of Sardinia and in the city of Florence in the region of Tuscany. In both places people made delicious food, loved to eat, and continually re-created relationships at the table. They taught me to enjoy food and to prioritize the pleasure of eating over the image of thinness, an invaluable gift. Food runs through my current family life: the many good meals my husband and I make for each other and the eccentric and occasionally exasperating appetites of our two sons. Finally, food runs through my intellectual life. Over the past two decades I have been studying the relationship between food, culture, and gender and have written the essays collected here.

My approach to food has been anthropological and feminist. For me to be feminist means to focus on gender, to pay particular attention to the contributions and perspectives of women, and to point toward gender equality. For me, to be an anthropologist means to combine data, analysis, philosophy, and writing. Cultural anthropologists, or ethnographers, collect data about how people in diverse cultures live, as often as possible in the words of our subjects, tape-recorded and transcribed. We gather data by living with people, observing their lives, and asking them questions about what they do and what it means to them. Cultural anthropologists then try to make sense out of, or interpret, the data they gather about human behavior. Here analysis and philosophy enter. In data analysis we explore the connections and conflicts in people's diverse ways of behaving and relate them to other

1

things we know about the culture and about human behavior in general. Then we philosophize—we seek ways of explaining the data by looking at ideas of other social scientists and ultimately coming up with our own interpretation. Finally comes the writing, the communication of our ideas to others.

In my research and reading, I have focused on foodways—the beliefs and behavior surrounding the production, distribution, and consumption of food. Study of food led directly to the consideration of the meanings given to the feeding body, especially gendered ones. I have wondered about specific food behaviors and body conceptions in Italy and the United States. I have used the cross-cultural perspective fundamental to anthropology to explain some of our own foodways here in the United States. I have found that feeding and eating are profoundly meaningful in all cultures and are deeply entwined with gender relations. The search to find and move toward more equal and mutually empowering gender relationships in regard to food animates this book.

The chapters chronicle the evolution of my thinking about foodways, power, and gender. The essays are comparative, using fieldwork data collected globally by others and by myself in Sardinia, Florence, and the United States. The chapters are organized in roughly chronological order, but since they were written as discrete essays they may be read in any sequence. I have organized the essays chronologically because there is a certain intellectual logic in how I moved from one question to another. The essays become more explicitly feminist and more directly concerned with gender over time. They also evolve in writing style. The earlier essays are more analytical, the later ones more narrative. The earlier essays prioritize my own words about anthropological subjects, whereas the later essays highlight subjects' words. I have moved increasingly toward a more narrative style in writing because I believe it is more interesting, more revealing, and more directly true to the people I study. I have tried to write in a clear and flowing manner so that essays would appeal to general readers, but I have also included an extensive list of references so that scholars and students can use this book to further their own research.

Chapters 2 through 7 have been previously published and are reprinted here with very minor revisions. I have added footnotes to update the references but otherwise left them as they were when published. Chapters 1, 8, 9, 10, and 11 are either entirely new or substantially revised and represent my most recent work. In addition to the developmental logic in the essays, there are other organizing forces — geographic, for example. Chapters 2, 3, 9, and 10 focus on my research in Italy, whereas chapters 5, 6, 7, 8, and 11 focus on the United States. But all the chapters are immersed in the cross-cultural perspective that challenges the taken-for-grantedness of our own foodways.

Essays ask from a variety of perspectives how foodways reinforce or challenge social and economic inequality in family and society. Chapter 1, "Food, Culture, and Gender," is an overview of the field and a review of the literature; it describes the social and symbolic uses of food. Food studies provide many insights into gender, family, community, sexuality, and language that offer insights into broad cultural questions about power and control. From the exploration of this literature, I fashioned a food and culture study for my doctoral dissertation research in the town of Bosa on the west coast of Sardinia. Chapter 2, "Bread as World," describes this research by chronicling the effects of modernization on social relations through a study of the beliefs, behaviors, and relationships surrounding bread.

When I finished my Sardinian research, I inaugurated a study of gender in Florence by conducting food-centered life histories from twenty-five members of one family that I had known for over a decade. I began to look specifically at how women and men constructed gender around giving, receiving, and making food. Chapter 3, "Female Identity, Food, and Power in Contemporary Florence," shows how Florentine women's identity and power have traditionally been attained and wielded through control of food provisioning. Today they increasingly take on wage labor jobs and can no longer cook and feed in culturally expected ways. This chapter explores the dilemmas in gender relations that result.

Chapters 4 through 7 focus on how food is a source of both power and oppression for women, especially in the United States. Chapter 4 investigates the connections between food, sex, reproduction, and gender across cultures and uses them to make some suggestions about gender and power in our own culture. I specifically investigate men's and women's relationships and power as revealed through meanings about bodily penetration through sex and eating. Chapter 5 examines the pathological relationship between women and food in the United States marked by compulsive eating, obsession with slenderness, and bodily objectification. It examines the cultural dimensions of eating problems in the United States and their relationship to gender definitions—particularly women's self-oppression through body loathing and denial. In chapter 6, I look at women's prodigious fasting across cultures and time. I examine the relationship between medieval Western European "holy anorexia" and contemporary anorexia nervosa in the West and compare them to kinds of fasting practiced by non-Western peoples. Women's fasting in the West is more relentless, total, and never-ending than that practiced in any other culture. This essay underscores the centrality of female self-denial and bodily objectification to Western patriarchal culture.

At the same time as I was studying the literature on food, body, and gender in the United States, I also began to conduct research by collecting food journals from college students in my Food and Culture course. In Chapter 7, I show how students' writings about food, hunger, fat, thin, good foods, and bad foods reveal an ideology of individualism, control, and hierarchy. Students adhere to beliefs and practices around eating that exalt men and whites over women and people of color. Morality demands self-control for women but allows indulgence to men. Women and men both hold standards of thinness for women that continually reproduce female oppression.

Eventually I got tired of studying women's victimization through food and body, and so I began to look for the origins of that victimization by studying children. I wanted to see if preschool boys and girls exhibited beliefs or behaviors surrounding food that disadvantaged one or the other gender. The only way I could get information from children was to collect stories from them, so I looked at food symbolism in their made-up stories to see if they exhibited gender similarities or differences. Chapter 8, "Fantasy Food," examines how boys and girls use metaphors of devouring, being hungry, eating, and feeding in both similar and different ways to cope with central issues of childhood: establishing gender identity and autonomy. The children's stories revealed no serious concerns with body image by either sex and indicated that preschool girls may be more empowered by their relationship to food than boys.

Chapter 9, "Food as Tie and Rupture," continues the search for empowering models of food-centered relationships by examining how two mother-daughter pairs in Florence negotiate their connection across the life cycle through giving and receiving food. One pair has reached a successful mutuality; the other has broken apart over the inability to attain mutual respect and reciprocity around food. Chapter 10, "The Body as Voice of Desire and Connection in Florence, Italy," examines Florentine conceptions of eating and the body and their relationship to women's self-concept and power. Florentines define the body as given by nature and family, as active, and as a source of legitimate gustatory pleasure called *gola*. These definitions serve as a buffer between Florentine women and the objectification of the female body so central to patriarchal commodity capitalism. They provide a way to think about the body that gives women self-respect and agency. Unfortunately, however, there is evidence that the "tyranny of slenderness" may be making inroads into Italy, hand in hand with Italy's fixation with fashion.

The final essay concludes the book with a direct focus on how women may be able to overcome body oppression in the United States. It suggests that women's empowerment depends on challenging the objectification of the female body and redefining it as a subject. It looks at women's conceptions of food, eating, and the body during pregnancy and the postpartum period as expressed in ethnographic interviews with fifteen women in eastern central Pennsylvania. The chapter focuses on two women's narratives to show how pregnancy and birth under certain conditions can transform women's relationship to the body into an empowering one. Their stories tell us that overcoming the objectification of women's bodies is not only a necessary step in the move toward gender equality but also a possible one.

The essays presented here hope to pose some interesting questions and illuminate them with reference to some fascinating cross-cultural data. They are filled with hypotheses and interpretations that I hope will stimulate readers to think further about how cooking, eating, and feeding—activities we so often take for granted—define our identities and relationships as men and women.

1

Food, Culture, and Gender[1]

INTRODUCTION

Food is a many-splendored thing, central to biological and social life. We ingest food over and over again across days, seasons, and years to fill our bellies and satisfy emotional as well as physical hungers. Eating together lies at the heart of social relations; at meals we create family and friendships by sharing food, tastes, values, and ourselves. Festive meals celebrate festive occasions and enlarge the social group at office picnics, church suppers, barbecues, and potluck dinners. Because eating good food when hungry causes a euphoric feeling, feasts and meals are a wonderful way to create positive social relations. Similarly, when social relations are bad, eating can be painful and unpleasant.

Food is a primary focus of much economic activity (though less in industrial societies and wealthy classes than in preindustrial societies and poorer classes). Food is a product and mirror of the organization of society on both the broadest and most intimate levels. It is connected to many kinds of behavior and is endlessly meaningful. Food is a prism that absorbs and reflects a host of cultural phenomena. An examination of foodways—behaviors and beliefs surrounding the production, distribution, and consumption of food—reveals much about power relations and conceptions of sex and gender, for every coherent social group has its own unique foodways.

Foodways influence the shaping of community, personality, and family. The study of foodways contributes to the understanding of personhood across cultures and historical periods. Foodways also share a loose structure and organization across the population, though variations on themes are constant. Florentines, for example, eat a light breakfast and then a large three-course meal at lunch and dinner. The first course of pasta, rice, or soup is regularly followed by a second course of meat and vegetables and a third course of fruit. Although

Florentines will banter endlessly about the "right" way to cook a basic dish like spaghetti with tomato sauce,[2] they recognize that their cuisine is different from all others in Italy. Their cuisine is simple but delicious, they say, based on the strong flavors of garlic, onion, basil, parsley, and pepper. Their food is rooted in a centuries-old sharecropping farming system that enabled intensive agricultural production on fields near enough to the city to ensure extremely fresh produce all year round. Florentines are passionate about their own cooking and establish their cultural identity through attachment to it.

People articulate and recognize their distinctiveness through the medium of food. The English call the French "Frogs" because of their habit, wildly barbaric to the English, of eating frogs' legs (Leach 1964, 31). In the Amazon, Indian tribes distinguish themselves from each other in part through their different habits, manners, or conceptions of eating; the maligned other is defined as eating people or animals thought disgusting, for example, "frogs and snakes and mice" (Gregor 1985, 14). Food systems are of course intimately related to the local environment, but in most cultures people define as edible only certain products and execrate many other potentially edible substances. North Americans, for example, do not eat dogs, but gobble up hot dogs by the millions; Jews and Muslims, though, abominate pork in any form. Leach tells us, "Such classification is a matter of language and culture, not of nature" (1964, 31). Even people in cultures in the process of disintegration due to famine reveal their plight in the ways they deal with and think about eating.[3] The study of foodways enables a holistic and coherent look at how human beings mediate their relationship with nature and each other across cultures and through history.

FOOD AND POWER

Food is essential to life and must enter our bodies daily in substantial amounts if we are to live. Because of our dire need for it, Arnold suggests that "food was, and continues to be, power in a most basic, tangible and inescapable form" (1988, 3). Lappé and Collins make a strong argument that there is no more absolute sign of powerlessness than hunger (1986); it is a stark indication that one lacks the ability to satisfy one's most basic subsistence need. Food is a central concern in the politics of nation-states (Burbach and Flynn 1980). Whereas Camporesi argues that chronic hunger and malnutrition were part of a calculated strategy of early modern political elites to maintain their power by keeping the poor debilitated and dazed (1989, 137), Arnold and others point out that extreme hunger causes popular protest and can seriously threaten a government's stability.[4] "The fortunes of the state, whether in Europe or in Africa or Asia, have long been closely bound up with the containment or prevention of famine and, more generally, with provisioning the populace" (Arnold 1988, 96).

Class, caste, race, and gender hierarchies are maintained, in part, through differential control over and access to food. One's place in the social system is revealed by what, how much, and with whom one eats. As Goody says, "the hierarchy between ranks and classes takes a culinary form" (1982, 113). In India, caste is marked quite conspicuously by different food habits and prohibitions against eating with those of lower caste (Goody 1982, 116 ff; Khare and Rao 1986). Different consumption patterns are one of the ways the rich distinguish themselves from the poor. According to Adams, for example, the consumption of meat protein reveals "the white Western world's enactment of racism" in claiming thousands of acres of land in the Third World for grazing cattle to produce meat for the First World and in claiming the choicest cuts and largest quantities of meat as well (1990, 30).

Sugar is another example of how food reproduces and sustains hierarchy. It was at first only a food of the rich, who used it to create fabulous ostentatious sculptures that proclaimed their wealth and power through extravagance with the precious and desirable commodity (Mintz 1985). Eventually, as ever greater areas of the world were colonized and ever greater numbers of Africans were enslaved to produce sugar, the poor were increasingly able to eat it; they did so, in part, to emulate the rich. Sugar consumption conveyed "the complex idea that one could *become* different by *consuming* differently" (Mintz 1985, 185). But to eat sugar, the poor sacrificed other foods, and their diet suffered, while the rich could eat sugar *and* other foods, and simply chose new icons to proclaim their difference. As historian Stephen Mennell concludes his study of France, "Likes and dislikes are never socially neutral, but always entangled with people's affiliations to class and other social groups. Higher social circles have repeatedly used food as one of many means of distinguishing themselves from lower rising classes. This has been manifested in a succession of styles and attitudes towards food and eating" (1985, 331–32).

In stratified societies, hunger—like poverty—is far more likely to strike people in disadvantaged and devalued social categories: women, people of color, the mentally ill, the handicapped, and the elderly.[5] Women, for example, very often suffer hunger and famine more severely than men because of their socioeconomic and political subordination in many countries of the world (Leghorn and Roodkowsky 1977; Vaughn 1987). Food scarcity mirrors and exacerbates social distinctions; famine relief goes first to groups with power and, in times of economic crisis, the rich get richer by buying the land and other resources of the poor as the latter give up everything in the struggle to eat.

Race, class, and gender distinctions are manifest through rules about eating and the ability to impose rules on others. In the United States, for example, we value thinness.[6] The dominant culture—manifest in advertising, fashion, and most especially the media—projects a belief that thinness connotes control, power, wealth, competence, and success (Dyrenforth, Wooley, and Wooley 1980). Not surprisingly, standards are more strict for women than for men, which means more women fall outside prescribed norms and feel less valued. Furthermore, obesity for women varies directly with class status and ethnicity. Whiteness and greater wealth go along with thinness; poor Puerto Rican, black, and Native American women have greater obesity rates and lower status than well-off Euro-American women. The standard of thinness upholds a class structure where men, whites, and the rich are superior to women, people of color, and the poor.[7]

FOOD, SEX, AND GENDER[8]

One of the most significant domains of meaning embodied in food centers on the relation between the sexes, their gender definitions, and their sexuality. In many cultures, eating is a sexual and gendered experience throughout life. Food and sex are metaphorically overlapping. Eating may represent copulation, and food may represent sexuality. For example among the Mehinaku Indians, "to have sex" is defined literally as "to eat to the fullest extent. . . . The essential idea is that the genitals of one sex are the 'food' of the other's" (Gregor 1985, 70). The poet George Herbert captured this relation in the early seventeenth century: "'You must sit down,' says Love, 'and taste my Meat.'/ So I did sit and Eat."[9] In many cultures, particularly those with food scarcity, food gifts may be an important path to sexual liaisons, as both Holmberg (1969) and Siskind (1973) have noted for Amazonian Indians. About the food-scarce Siriono of eastern Bolivian lowlands, Holmberg says, "Food is one of the best lures for obtaining extra-marital sex partners, and a man often uses game as a means of seducing a potential wife" (1969, 64).

In many cultures there are associations between eating, intercourse, and reproduction, which chapter 4 explores in detail. Eating and intercourse both involve passage across body boundaries of external substances that are then incorporated into the body. Both are essential to life and growth. The instinctive drives for food and sex are similar, and they often take on overlapping symbolic associations. There is a life-long connection between oral and sexual gratification (Freud 1962). Eating together implies intimacy, both sexual intimacy and kinship (Freud 1918, 175; Siskind 1973, 9). Both eating and copulation cause and symbolize social connection.

Precisely because eating and intercourse involve intimacy, they can be dangerous or threatening when carried out under adverse conditions or with untrustworthy people. Hence all cultures have rules and taboos to regulate food and sex and to define appropriate bed and table mates. In many cultures people with whom one can eat are those with whom one can have sex and vice versa (Tambiah 1969). Among the Wik Mungkan of Australia, the symbolic overlap between food and sex acts to balance relationships between groups around marriage, for in this group, "wife-givers are food-receivers, and wife-receivers are food givers" (McKnight 1973, 196). Among the Trobriand Islanders, "two people about to be married must never have a meal in common. Such an act would greatly shock the moral susceptibility of a native, as well as his sense of propriety. To take a girl out to dinner without having previously married her—a thing permitted in Europe—would be to disgrace her in the eyes of a Trobriander" (Malinowski 1929, 75). In fact the act of eating yams together in public is the equivalent to announcing a Trobriand marriage (Weiner 1988, 77).

Maleness and femaleness in all cultures are associated with specific foods, and rules often exist to control the consumption of those foods (Brumberg 1988, 176–78; Frese 1991). The Hua of Papua New Guinea reveal complex gender relations in their elaborate conceptions about *koroko* and *hakeri'a* foods. The former are cold, wet, soft, fertile, fast-growing foods associated with females; the latter are hot, dry, hard, infertile, and slow-growing foods associated with males. Women can become more like men by consuming *hakeri'a* foods; in particular they believe that these help minimize their menstrual flow. Men, on the other hand, proclaim publicly that female foods and substances are "not only disgusting but also dangerous to the development and maintenance of masculinity." But they secretly eat foods associated with females to gain their vitality and power (Meigs 1984, xv and passim).

Chapters 5, 6, and 7 compare the attitudes toward food and body of men and women in the United States to those prevailing in other times and places. This comparison reveals in stark outline how male power and female subordination are reproduced through food and body beliefs and practices. Carol Adams argues that patriarchal power in Western society is embodied in meat consumption, which involves the linking of women and animals and their objectification and subordination (1990). Women, Adams suggest, can rebel through vegetarianism, which she interprets as rejecting patriarchal values of domination and affirming female power and respect for nature. American college students associate "light" foods like salad, chicken, or yogurt with women, and "heavy" foods like beef, beer, and potatoes with men. Their rules about appropriate food consumption define men as powerful and women as weak. U.S. women report that men denigrate and gain power over them by saying they eat too much or are too fat. Many women feel ashamed to eat in front of men, so they may offer food but not eat it, giving pleasure to males but denying it to themselves (Millman 1980; Orbach 1978; Chernin 1981).

The pathological and misogynistic nature of American women's obsessive fear of fat and restrictive eating shows up sharply when contrasted with the more empowering attitudes and habits prevailing in other cultures. In the majority of cultures for which data exist, plumpness is preferred, especially for women, because it is associated with fertility, hardiness, power, good nurturance, and love.[10] Jamaicans define a fat body as juicy, flowing with fertility and sexiness (Sobo 1997). In contrast to the way Americans cultivate their bodies as reflections of individuality and focus on thinness as symbol of self-control and power, Fijians prefer a plump body because they define it as a product and symbol of care, generosity, and social cohesion (Becker 1995). In many cultures, similar standards of body morphology apply to both men and women, but in the United States women are held to more stringent standards of thinness than men even though women have greater biological propensity to be fat (Beller 1977). For U.S. women, dissatisfaction with their body size and shape is yet another expression of and contributor to their subordination. Women's internalized oppression is manifest in the self-hatred directed at the body and the enormous amount of female energy devoted to improving the body, energy that could be spent in many other positive and productive ways. In other cultures, however, such as that in Florence discussed in chapter 10, women and men both are allowed greater latitude in body morphology and an easier path to self-satisfaction through the body.

The power relations around food mirror the power of the sexes in general.[11] Control of money and food purchases is a key index of husband-wife balance of power. Men may wield power by controlling food purchases and claiming the authority to judge the meals women cook. They can disparage the food or demand certain dishes. Men can refuse to provide food or to eat. Husbands often legitimate wife abuse by citing meal failures (Adams 1990; Charles and Kerr 1988; DeVault 1991). Women can exert power over men by refusing to cook, cooking food men dislike, forcing them to eat, or manipulating the status and meaning systems embodied in foods. Women in eighteenth-century Mexico tamed husbands' abusive behavior by ensorcelling food with bits of menstrual blood or other "magical" matter and "tying them up"; not only village men and women believed some women had this power, but church and state believed it as well (Behar 1989). Among Zumbaguan Indians of Andean Ecuador, the senior female is in charge of preparing and serving meals. This gives her the ability to determine hierarchies by the order in which she serves people and the contents of the plate she gives them; important people get chunks of meat while others get only vegetables. A woman can also exert power over her errant husband when he finally returns from a drinking spree by serving him massive quantities of rich food which the husband, by force of etiquette, has to eat—with extremely unpleasant physical results (Weismantel 1988).

In Western societies, for at least eight centuries, some women have used food in symbolic ways as a path to power.[12] Today, modern anorexics starve themselves, sometimes to death, to achieve what they believe is physical and spiritual perfection. Chapter 6 notes that their behavior is strikingly similar to that of medieval holy women in the fourteenth, fifteenth, and sixteenth centuries, although the meanings of their behaviors are rather different because of the different cultural contexts in which they occur (Bell 1985; Bynum 1987; Brumberg 1988). Medieval holy women fasted for religious and spiritual perfection—holiness. They used eating or fasting as a path to reach God and to circumvent patriarchal familial, religious, and civil authority. Some women achieved sainthood by virtue of the spirituality they revealed through fasting and other food-centered behaviors such as multiplying food in miracles, exuding holy oils or milk from their own bodies, and giving food to the poor (Bynum 1987). Contemporary anorexics attempt to achieve perfection through self-control and thinness. They receive pitying recognition only from family, friends, and medical professionals and may die unless they find a path to the self-esteem, sense of control, and autonomy they so desperately seek through fasting (Bruch 1973, 1978; Brumberg 1988; Lawrence 1984).

Modern and medieval fasting behaviors have been practiced almost exclusively by women, who used food as their distinctive voice. Between men and women in many cultures, food is both a means of differentiation and a channel of connection. By claiming different roles in regard to food and distinct attributes through identification with specific foods, men and women define their masculinity and femininity, their similarity and difference. Among Wamirans of Papua New Guinea, men and women define gender through their relation to taro, the most important food both symbolically and nutritionally (Kahn 1986). Taro plants are men's "children," and they represent male status and virility. Yet men cannot grow taro without women making essential contributions to the planting and weeding of it. Women's essential contributions to taro production reinforce their needed role in Wamiran economy and culture, just as men's recognized role in reproducing children reinforces their importance in social reproduction. By making a symbolic parallel between taro and children, and involving men and women in the production of both, Wamirans equalize male and female powers (Kahn 1986, 1988).

Among the Culina of the western Amazon, men and women similarly establish distinctive identities as well as social and economic interdependence through the production and distribution of food. A clear sexual division of labor allocates most of the gardening to women and the hunting to men. The sexes are identified with the different products of their labor: women with vegetables and men with meat. Marriage involves the reciprocal exchange of "food for food: meat for cultivated garden products" (Pollock 1985, 33). In this egalitarian culture, male and female differential control over diverse aspects of the food system is explicitly balanced in exchanges and in beliefs.

Food is often a medium of exchange, connection, and distinction between men and women, but exchanges must be reciprocal to maintain equality. McIntosh and Zey point out the lack of reciprocity in men's and women's food exchanges in the United States (1998). They explore Lewin's (1943) concept of women as "gatekeepers" of food into the home, which implies that women hold much power over food distribution. They suggest that while women may have responsibility over provisioning food, "responsibility is not equivalent to control" which may in fact reside with men (1988, 126). Food provisioning often reproduces female subordination by requiring women to serve, satisfy, and defer to husbands or boyfriends who do not feel a similar need to serve their women (DeVault 1991). Reciprocity of giving and receiving, of cooking and eating, makes for equality among partners, and its lack contributes to power imbalances. In many ways, food establishes and reflects male and female identity and relationships.

FOOD AND COMMUNITY

Manners and habits of eating are crucial to the very definition of community, the relationships between people, interactions between humans and their gods, and communication between the living and the dead. Communal feasts involve a periodic reaffirmation of the social group. As Freud noted, "To eat and drink with some one was at the same time a symbol and a confirmation of social community and of the assumption of mutual obligations" (1918, 174).

Sharing food ensures the survival of the group both socially and materially. A companion is literally a person one eats bread with (Farb and Armelagos 1980, 4). Refusal to share food is a sign of enmity and hostility. Among Brahmins, for example, "A man does not eat with his enemy" (Mauss 1967, 58). For eating together is a sign of kinship, trust, friendship, and in some cultures, of sexual intimacy as well.

On a day-to-day basis, food exchanges are crucial in maintaining

good relations between individuals. In Sardinia, there are many prov-
erbs like the following: *"Si cheres chi s'amore si mantenzat, prattu chi
andet prattu chi benzat"*—"If you want love to endure, for a plate that
goes, let a plate return" (Gallini 1973, 60). This is very similar to "what
goes around comes around," a central belief among the poor urban
black families studied by Carol Stack (1974). Mauss has shown the pervasive cultural power of the gift, which keeps individuals constantly
indebted to each other and continuously engaged in positive interaction through giving and receiving (1967). Sahlins has said, "The gift is
alliance, solidarity, communion, in brief, peace" (1972, 169). Food is an
extremely important component of reciprocal exchanges, more so than
any other object or substance, and is subject to strong prescriptions of
sharing across most cultures (Sahlins 1972, 215). In fact, the collapse
of food sharing is often linked to the breakdown of social solidarity
(Turnbull 1972, 1978; Vaughn 1987).

In Melanesia, feasting both joins people in community and establishes power relations.[13] Kahn (1986, 1988) describes two different
kinds of feasts held by the Wamirans of Papua New Guinea, the "trans-
action" feast, which reinforces male power ranking by allowing some
men to attain power by giving away food that they do not consume
themselves, and the "incorporation" feast, which strengthens community solidarity through collective food consumption. Similarly, in the
Sardinian community of Tresnuraghes discussed in chapter 2, the
annual Saint Mark celebration involves a collective feasting on mutton
donated by wealthy shepherds and bread donated by villagers seeking
or reciprocating divine assistance. This redistributive feast serves
simultaneously to bring the community together, to make abundant
food available to the poor, and to display the wealth and prestige of
those able to sponsor the feast. Similar redistributive celebrations
occur in a wide range of peasant and tribal societies and are central to
the maintenance of community and political organization.[14]

In many cultures, food is instrumental in maintaining good relations
between humans and their gods. Among the Atimelangers of Indonesia
studied by Cora DuBois, sacrifice "is a matter of almost daily experience, representing practically all relationships to the supernatural. The
word for sacrifice means literally 'to feed,' and every supernatural
object is so placated. . . . It is, in fact, difficult to find any aspect of religious or social ceremonial which does not involve 'feeding'" (1941, 278).
Offering food is a major form of supplicating the gods in most religions.
In Christianity, a central symbolic act is the consumption of bread, both
by Christ and his disciples at the Last Supper, and regularly by the
faithful in the Communion ritual. The bread, or host, is the body of
Christ; it stands for redemption, holiness, and salvation. The faithful

literally eat their God, and in so doing incorporate the values and messages of their religion (Bynum 1987; Feeley-Harnik 1981). Ancient Greeks, and many other peoples, use food sacrifices as a means of propitiating their gods (Détienne and Vernant 1989; Mauss 1967). Tibetan Buddhist Sherpas consciously cajole their gods with food offerings and say, "I am offering you the things which you eat, now you must do whatever I demand" (Ortner 1975, 147). By consciously employing with the gods the mechanisms of hospitality that facilitate human interaction, Sherpas hope that "aroused, pleased, and gratified, the gods, like one's neighbors, will feel 'happy' and kindly disposed toward the worshipper/hosts and any requests they might make" (Ortner 1975, 146–47).

In patriarchal cultures, men claim exclusive mediating powers with the supernatural. In Catholic ritual, for example, only male priests can perform the ritual of transubstantiation, where the bread and wine are converted into the body and blood of Christ. Interestingly, medieval holy women sometimes subverted male clerical authority by manipulating food. Some challenged the legitimacy of priests by vomiting the host and thus claiming it unconsecrated. Others exuded miraculous holy foods from their own bodies, and still others emulated Christ directly by giving food to the poor (Bell 1985; Bynum 1986).

In more egalitarian cultures, women's control over food carries over into an essential mediating role in rituals supplicating gods and spirits. March discusses Sherpa and Tamang Buddhists who live in the highlands of Nepal (1998). Among both populations, hospitality, especially in the form of commensalism, is central to maintaining relations between humans and gods. March points out that women have a significant role in supplicating deities because of their central role in food and beer production and their symbolic association with "the many blessings—of health, strength, fertility, prosperity, plenitude, and general increase—that fermented and distilled offerings are thought to secure" (1998, 62). Van Esterik underlines the significance of Thai women's role in feeding the deities through sacrificial gifts because women are the primary food preparers (1998). They underscore the "'connectedness' of the living and the dead" (1998, 86) by preparing food for the ancestors; they are also in charge of giving food to the Buddhist monks and deities, thus playing a central role in religious expression.

Offerings of food to the deceased are a common cultural means of ensuring good relations with them.[15] On All Souls' Day or Eve, throughout the Christian world, people make food offerings and sometimes prepare entire meals for the dead. Some Sicilians eat fava beans; others consume cooked cereals (De Simone and Rossi 1977, 53–54).

Two examples of *sa mesa,* the meal set out for the dead on All Souls' Eve in Bosa (Sardinia), Italy. Note that both displays contain spaghetti, the centerpiece of the meal, and the special All Souls' Day cookies called *pabassini.* Both meals also contain nuts, seasonal fruit, bread, and tobacco. They were set out specifically for the father of the family who in both cases had recently died. (Photos by Carole M. Counihan.)

On All Souls' Day, Sardinians in the town of Bosa prepare *sa mesa*, literally, "the table," a meal for the deceased that they lay out as they are going to bed (Counihan 1981, 276–79). They always include spaghetti and *pabassini*, a frosted cookie made specially for All Souls' Day, as well as many other foods, including bread, nuts, and fruit; they sometimes include wine, beer, coca cola, juice, coffee, snuffing tobacco, or cigarettes. The meal is destined specifically for one's own dead relatives, and often the optional food items reflect a specific deceased person's preferences in life. The meal serves to communicate and maintain good relations with the dead, just as food exchanges regularly do with the living.

In some cultures, the living actually eat the dead to honor them and gain some of their powers (Arens 1979; Sanday 1986; Walens 1981). Freud argued that consumption of the deceased is based on the belief that "by absorbing parts of the body of a person through the act of eating we also come to possess the properties which belonged to that person" (1918, 107). The Yanomamo Indians of the Venezuelan Amazon eat the ashes of their deceased loved ones to ensure a successful afterlife. When ethnographer Kenneth Good was deathly sick with malaria, his informants expressed their affection by assuring him, "Don't worry, older brother. Don't worry at all. We will drink your ashes" (Good 1991, 133). Food offerings connect the living and the dead, humans and their gods, neighbors and kin, and family members.

FOOD AND FAMILY

In some cultures, the family may be most effectively conceptualized as those people who share a common hearth (Weismantel 1988, 169). As Siskind says of the Sharanahua Indians of the Peruvian Amazon, "Eating with people is an affirmation of kinship" (1973, 9). So important is feeding to the establishment of parent-child relations in Kalauna, Goodenough Island, that "fosterage . . . is wholly conceived in terms of feeding" (Young 1971, 41). Young goes on to note that this same "identification is buried in our own language: Old English 'foster' means 'food'" (1971, 41). In Kalauna, the father establishes his paternity by providing food for his pregnant wife. "While the role of the mother in producing the child is self-evident, the father must reinforce his own role by feeding his wife during pregnancy. This is explicitly seen as nurturing the foetus, and it is a principal element in the ideology of agnatic descent" (Young 1971, 40).

Feeding is one of the most important channels of infant and child socialization and personality formation.[16] The Pacific Atimelangers represent this belief literally by professing that the original human beings were "created from molded rice and corn meal"; they are literally "made from food" (Du Bois 1941, 278–79). According to Freud (1962), the child's earliest experiences of eating are the stage for important developmental processes and shape his or her lifelong personality. Margaret Mead suggested that through the infant feeding relationship, "every child learns something about the willingness of the world to give or withhold food, to give lavishly or deal out parsimoniously" (Mead 1967, 70). Furthermore, breast-feeding becomes part of the process of individualization for the child. As it recognizes gradually that the mother is other, and that its source of food is outside of itself, the child begins to establish an autonomous, bounded, and subjective identity (see chapter 8).

Problematic feeding can lead to personality disturbances in children, and children's eating problems may erupt in dysfunctional families (Palazzoli 1971; Bruch 1973). Anna Freud suggests that disturbed eating patterns may be "symbolic of a struggle between mother and child, in which the child can find an outlet for its passive or active, sadistic or masochistic tendencies towards the mother" (1946, 121). D. Shack (1969) and W. Shack (1971) attribute a host of negative personality characteristics of the Gurage of Ethiopia to their inconsistent early childhood feeding habits and later patterns of want and glut, which reveal severe "dependency-frustration" (Shack 1971, 34). Gurage children are often neglected when hungry and then finally fed to excess after crying for hours (Shack 1969). Adults eat sparingly and quickly on normal occasions, but occasionally find themselves forced to eat when not hungry at feasts or as a guests (Shack 1971). D. Shack argues that such eating patterns contribute to the development of personality traits including selfishness, emotional detachment, and insecurity (1969, 298).

W. Shack suggests that because food supply is particularly unreliable for low-status men, they are susceptible to *awre* spirit possession, marked by "loss of appetite, nausea and intermittent attacks of severe stomach pains" (1971, 35). The affliction is cured through a collective ritual where the victim is covered by a white shawl, seated in a smoky room, and given special food called *bra-brat*. With this, he "begins greedily and ravenously stuffing his mouth" and continues to do so until the spirit, "speaking through the possessed person, utters with a sigh, several times—'*tafwahum*'—'I am satisfied'" (Shack 1971, 36). The rite of *awre*-spirit exorcism allows a low-status man deprived of both food and prestige to gain both. It is a temporary overcoming of the dependency-frustration embedded in the cultural foodways that produce a chronic anxiety in those most often hungry. The Gurage exemplify how feeding patterns can influence personality formation and show how different cultures have distinct ways of using food to handle psychic distress.

Cookies before being baked in a wood oven in Bosa (Sardinia). These cookies indicate some of the ways food can be a symbol. The patterned beauty of the cookies in the hand-woven reed baskets is an essential facet of their production and demonstrates the bakers' competence as much as their taste. The cookies are in the bedroom awaiting the oven, and are juxtaposed against two other important purveyors of cultural meaning, the crucifix and the television. (Photo by Carole M. Counihan.)

FOOD AS MEANING, SYMBOL, AND LANGUAGE

In every culture, foodways constitute an organized system, a language that—through its structure and components—conveys meaning and contributes to the organization of the natural and social world. "Food . . . is not only a collection of products that can be used for statistical or nutritional studies. It is also, and at the same time, a system of communication, a body of images, a protocol of usages, situations and behavior" (Barthes 1975, 49–50). Foodways are a prime domain for conveying meaning because eating is an essential and continuously repeated activity. Foods are many, and they have different characteristics of texture, taste, color, and modes of preparation that are easy labels for meaning. Food constitutes a language accessible to all.

In examining the meaning of food, social scientists have studied *cuisine*, the food elements used and rules for their combination and preparation; *etiquette and food rules*, the customs governing what, with whom, when, and where one eats; *taboo*, the prohibitions and restrictions on the consumption of certain foods by certain people under certain conditions; and *symbolism*, the specific meanings attributed to foods in specific contexts.[17] There is of course much overlap between these four domains. For example, the study of Jewish dietary law involves examination of foods eaten and not eaten and the legitimate bases of their combination: cuisine. It involves the study of meals, the arrangement and sequence of foods, people's roles in preparation and serving of food, and people's placement at the table: etiquette. It involves the study of foods not eaten and why: taboo. And of course, to make sense out of all this, it involves the study of the complex and multivocal meanings of the foods and the behaviors centered around them.[18]

Food functions effectively as a system of communication because everywhere human beings organize their foodways into an ordered system parallel to other cultural systems and infuse them with meaning. "The cuisine of a people and their understanding of the world are linked" (Soler 1973, 943). It is to this cultural association between food and meaning that Lévi-Strauss (1963a, 89) was referring in his oft-quoted statement that certain animal species are chosen as totems "not because they are 'good to eat' but because they are 'good to think.'" Foods have and convey meanings because they are part of complex systems; "food categories ... encode social events" (Douglas 1974, 61). Soler suggests that a food taboo "cannot be understood in isolation. It must be placed in the center of the signs of its level, with which it forms a system, and this system must itself be connected to systems of other levels, with which it articulates to form the socio-cultural system of a people" (1973, 946).

Structuralists emphasize that food and cuisine stand between and mediate nature and culture (Lévi-Strauss 1966; Verdier 1969). The process of naming a wild product as food and transforming it into something edible involves the "culturizing" of nature. And cuisine, because it is a "means of transformation, must facilitate at least metaphorically all transformation" (Verdier 1969, 54). Hence, foods are very often used in rites of passage (see Goody 1982, 79–81). Among the Mehinaku Indians of the Amazon, initiation ceremonies for girls focus on the first menses, for boys on the ear-piercing ceremony. These rituals and the related blood flow are seen as parallel and involve the same restrictions on eating:

> Both boys and girls must follow certain food taboos to ensure the rapid cessation of the flow of blood and a favorable dream. Initially, the children are subject to a fast; they are allowed to drink water after twenty-four hours. . . . Following the fast, they may eat all foods but fish, which would prolong the blood flow. "Fish," it is said, "eat other fish and therefore are filled with blood." Monkeys and birds eat only fruit and have a

"different kind of blood" and are therefore acceptable to "menstruating" boys and girls. . . . With the total cessation of the flow of blood, a ceremony reintroduces fish to the diet. The boys are led outside, taste a small amount of fish, and spit it onto a fiber mat. The girls follow the same ritual inside the house. . . . Fish are now permissible. . . . (Gregor 1985, 189)

Here food is used to signify the transformation of boys to men and girls to women while it simultaneously marks the similarity of the maturation of boys and girls.[19]

Food can be used metaphorically to convey just about any imaginable condition, thought, or emotion. Chapter 7 explores how American college students express feelings of love, anger, anxiety, depression, sorrow and joy through their eating habits. After a satisfying meal, Sardinians say, *"consolada(o) soe"*—"I am consoled"—and imply the metaphorical and physical overlap between good food and good feelings (Counihan 1981). Because of the strong visceral pleasure of eating and pain of hunger, food readily adopts powerful connotations and is a rich symbol in written and oral literature.

FOOD IN FOLKLORE AND LITERATURE

Food meanings are paramount in Claude Lévi-Strauss's monumental study of mythology (1963b, 1966, 1969, 1971). He uses mythology to investigate the structure of the human mind. According to Lévi-Strauss, binary oppositions are embedded in our brains and appear in many levels of our thinking. The oppositions in the human relationship to nature mediated through food—e.g. "the raw and the cooked," nature and culture, or human and animal—reveal universals in human thinking.

In stories told to children, proper eating represents humanness and effective socialization, while out-of-control eating and cannibalism stand for wildness and incomplete socialization (see chapter 9). The widely known European folktale "Hansel and Gretel" is a good example of these themes; it is about "conflicting family loyalties expressed in terms of sharing and hoarding food" (Taggart 1986:435). Bettelheim interprets the food themes of the story as being about children's struggle to outgrow oral dependency and symbiosis with the mother (1977, 159–66). Hansel and Gretel are forced from home due to food scarcity, and they subsequently gobble up the candy house without thought or restraint. This regression to "primitive incorporative and hence destructive desires" only leads to trouble: being trapped by the wicked witch, "a personification of the destructive aspects of orality" (1975, 160–62). Eventually, the children use reason to dominate their oral urges and refuse food so as to be able to kill the witch. Then they inherit her jewels and become reunited with their family in a new status. "As the children transcend their oral anxiety, and free themselves of relying on oral satisfaction for security, they can also free themselves of the image of the threatening mother—the witch—and rediscover the good parents, whose greater wisdom—the shared jewels—then benefit all" (1975, 162). Their struggle with food in essence represents stages in their maturation.

The same theme about the power of food in family relations is beautifully depicted in Maurice Sendak's Caldecott Medal–winning children's story *Where the Wild Things Are* (1963).

> The night Max wore his wolf suit and made mischief of one kind and
>   another
> his mother called him "WILD THING!"
> and Max said "I'LL EAT YOU UP!"
> so he was sent to bed without eating anything.

A forest grew in Max's room, a boat appeared, and he sailed off to "where the wild things are." He tamed the wild things, and they "made him king of all the wild things." They had a wild rumpus until the following thing happened:

> "Now stop!" Max said and sent the wild things off to bed
> without their supper. And Max the king of all wild things was lonely
> and wanted to be where someone loved him best of all.
> Then all around from far away across the world
> he smelled good things to eat
> so he gave up being king of where the wild things are.
> But the wild things cried, "Oh please don't go—
> we'll eat you up—we love you so!"
> And Max said, "No!"
> The wild things roared their terrible roars and gnashed their terrible
> teeth
> and rolled their terrible eyes and showed their terrible claws
> but Max stepped into his private boat and waved good-bye
> and sailed back over a year
> and in and out of weeks
> and through a day
> and into the night of his very own room
> where he found his supper waiting for him
> and it was still hot.

Sendak's story shows how food is a source of love, power, socialization, and connection between parents and children. In the story, Max is a "wild thing," an incompletely socialized child. His wildness is shown by the wolf suit and his desire to eat his mother up. This incorporative desire also expresses the incomplete separation of the child from the mother. This theme of eating as incorporation is re-created later in the story when the wild things want to eat Max up, to keep him from leaving them. But Max does not stay with the wild things who represent his untamed nature. He feels the pull of love and maternal nurturance in the smells of "good things to eat" that come from the place "where someone loved him best of all." He takes the long journey home, where love awaits him in the form of the supper that was previously denied him due to his bad behavior. The fact that "it was still hot" symbolizes that the mother's love it represents persists and is there to facilitate his socialization.

Food plays an important symbolic role in stories not only for children, but for adults as well.[20] Laura Esquivel's magnificent *Como agua para chocolate—Like Water for Chocolate* (1989) is a wonderful novel about "the secrets of love and life as revealed by the kitchen" (1989, 239). The main character, Tita, is oppressed and silenced by her overbearing mother, Elena, who prohibits Tita from marrying Pedro, her true love, and forces her to serve Elena her whole life. Tita attains a voice through her rich cooking, which expresses powerful emotions and influences others deeply. One day, after receiving roses from Pedro, rather than throw the roses away as ordered by her mother, Tita uses them to cook "quail in rose petal sauce" which has a powerful effect on everyone at the table, Tita included:

> It was as if a strange alchemical process had dissolved her entire being in the rose petal sauce, in the tender flesh of the quails, in the wine, in every one of the meal's aromas. That was the way she entered Pedro's body, hot, voluptuous, perfumed, totally sensuous. . . .
>
> Pedro didn't offer any resistance. He let Tita penetrate to the farthest corners of his being, and all the while they couldn't take their eyes off each other. (52)

Throughout the novel, Esquivel uses food as a vehicle for conveying deep emotions of love, nurturance, and rage. The novel is organized around twelve chapters representing the twelve months, and each one has a key recipe that carries the plot and provides a sensual medium for conveying the complexities of human relationships. Esquivel's great contribution is to underline that food is powerful because it is so intimately connected with our physical, sensual selves—with our strongest feelings of hunger, desire, greed, delectation, and satiety.

CONCLUSION

Food is indeed a many-splendored thing. Essential to biological survival, it takes on myriad meanings and roles in the ongoing constitution of society and culture. As humans construct their relationship to nature through their foodways, they simultaneously define themselves and their social world. Through producing, distributing, and consuming food, they act out some of their most important relationships to family, friends, the dead, and the gods. Food provides order to the world and expresses multiple meanings about the nature of reality. The social and cultural uses of food provide much insight into the human condition.

2

Bread as World

Food Habits and Social Relations in Modernizing Sardinia[1]

This chapter is about contemporary social and economic change in the town of Bosa in the peripheral Italian region of Sardinia. During the twentieth century Bosa has undergone an experience, shared by many rural Mediterranean regions, that Schneider, Schneider, and Hansen have called "modernization without development" (1976) characterized by the stagnation of local production and the increasing emulation of Western industrial consumption patterns. These large-scale economic trends are accompanied by changes in social relations. One of these, this chapter argues, is a process of individualization, where decisions and actions gradually become more independent of community ties. Description and analysis of the production, distribution, and consumption of bread—-the most important food in the Sardinian diet— illustrate these transformations in Bosan economy and society and enable consideration of their qualitative impact on the Bosan people.

The chapter begins with the belief that human nature is a product of history and society (Geertz 1973; Gramsci 1957; Marx and Engels 1970; Sahlins 1976). Thus the extent to which a society is characterized by an individualistic conception of human nature varies a great deal. Individualism refers to a reduction in dependence on others for survival and to an increasing autonomy of action and decision making. The "Western conception of the person as a bounded, unique," autonomous individual is by no means universal (Geertz 1975, 48). Anthropologists have consistently drawn our attention to the fact that members of foraging, tribal, and peasant societies are much more closely interdependent in behavior and ideology than citizens of modern Western states. They work together, continuously practice generalized reciprocal exchange, and conceptualize their identities not primarily as individuals,

25

but as members of a group, a lineage, or a family (e.g., for Italy see Banfield 1958; Belmonte 1979; Pinna 1971).

Beginning with Marx, many social scientists have argued that individualism is created by the production system and market exchange typical of the capitalist economy (Gramsci 1957; Marx and Engels 1970; Sahlins 1972). Mauss's brilliant book *The Gift* (1967) gives further support to this thesis. He shows not only the importance of gifts in tying people together in "archaic" societies, but also the fragmentation of social relations in the France of his day resulting from the increase in market exchange and the decline of gift giving. This chapter continues this line of inquiry. It describes changes in Sardinian bread habits, links them to large-scale economic processes, and examines through them the atomization of social relations.

THE CONTEXT

Geographical isolation, scarce natural resources, and low population density traditionally have made Sardinia one of the poorest regions of Italy (Counihan 1981, 31–80). Up until the 1950s, malaria was endemic (Brown 1979, 1981), and population density was the lowest in the nation: 111 per square mile. In 1930 there were one million people and two million sheep on the island's 24,000 square kilometers (Great Britain 1945, 578, 605). The population was concentrated in villages in the interior where extensive wheat cultivation and animal herding were the mainstays of the largely subsistence economy (Le Lannou 1941).

Since the Second World War, Sardinia has undergone massive cultural and economic changes fostered by governmental development measures like the *Cassa per il Mezzogiorno* (Fund for the South), the *Piano di Rinascita* (Plan of Rebirth) and the European Economic Community Mansholt Memorandum (Di Giorgi and Moscati 1980; Graziani 1977; King 1975; Lelli 1975; Orlando et al. 1977). These measures have instigated industrial development in a few scattered areas—what Lelli calls "development poles" (1975)—and the capitalization of agriculture, principally in the rich Campidano valley. Subsistence agriculture has declined radically over much of the island. Animal herding continues in the same small-scale and free-grazing style that it has followed for centuries. The Sardinian standard of living as measured through education, hygiene, and consumer goods has greatly improved (Musio 1969), and malaria has been eradicated (Brown 1979, 1981). This increased standard of living has been achieved through increases in available goods and cash. Consumer goods are largely imports, for Sardinian industry has concentrated on capital-intensive petrochemical conversions rather than on consumer products (Lelli 1975). People have greater access to cash largely through funds brought to Sardinia

Panorama of the city of Bosa, population 9,000, taken from a hill south of town looking north. The Temo River runs through town at the center of the photo toward the Mediterranean Sea two kilometers to the west. (Photo by Carole M. Counihan.)

by vacationing tourists; by emigrants working in northern Italy and northern Europe; and by the state in the form of pensions, unemployment compensations, family assistance checks, and short-term public works projects. Sardinia has undergone modernization—cultural changes produced by the influx of models and practices "from already established centers," without development—"an autonomous and diversified economy on its own terms" (Schneider, Schneider, and Hansen 1972, 340).

Bosa is situated about two-thirds of the way up the west coast of Sardinia, on a small hill, about 3 kilometers inland on the north bank of the Temo river. Although it has never had more than the roughly nine thousand inhabitants it has today, Bosa has always had an urban character that has differentiated it from its hinterland and from the small Sardinian villages of the mountainous interior and the plains (Anfossi 1968; Angioni 1974, 1976; Barbiellini-Amidei and Bandinu 1976; Bodemann 1979; Mathias 1979, 1983; Musio 1969; Pinna 1971). It has highly stratified classes, has acted as a market and political center, and has had some rudimentary industry. Its unique ecological setting in the river valley near the coast surrounded by hills and highland plateaus made possible a productive agro-pastoral and fishing economy. A small elite controlled most of the land, tools, animals, and fishing boats, as well as the machines of the mills, tanneries, and canneries. The majority of the population consisted of primary producers who were poor, dependent, and economically precarious, although the town itself was the scene of a certain economic bustle and a relative cultural opulence that are the more notable today by their absence (Anfossi 1968; Counihan 1981). In the extent of its stratification, urbanity, and relative wealth, Bosa was somewhat unique in Sardinia, but its recent history has much in common with that of rural Sardinia and the Italian South (Davis 1977; Weingrod and Morin 1971).

In the past thirty years Bosa and its hinterland have been increasingly tied to the capitalist world system by sending emigrants to work in the industrial north of Italy and Europe and by serving as a growing market for imported consumer goods. Reliable figures on emigration do not exist, but in 1971 the government census listed 951 Bosans "absent for reasons of work"—11 percent of the total population, 36 percent of the employed. Agriculture, pastoralism, and fishing have declined dramatically in Bosa, from involving 52 percent of the employed in 1951 to 19 percent in 1971. During the same period, the number of those employed by the mining and manufacturing industries has increased only from 10 percent to 15 percent. There are no factories in Bosa: The nearest are the beer, cheese, and textile factories in Macomer, twenty-seven kilometers away, which employ no more than fifty Bosans. None of the major "development poles" are within commuting distance, and even so they have never employed as many workers as was planned (Lelli 1975). Traditional crafts (cobbling, cooping, smithing, and tailoring) and semi-industrial activities (tanneries, canneries, olive and grain mills) are disappearing. The tertiary sector grew from 38 percent of the employed in 1951 to 67 percent in 1971. Most of the growth is in construction, tourism, and commerce, all of which are "precarious" in that they depend heavily on a prosperous economy for their own prosperity. In Bosa most of the tertiary sector is small in scale and "old-fashioned" in methods. Though exact figures do not exist, perhaps as many as three-quarters of the adult population receive government assistance of some sort (Brown 1979, 282). Overall, work in Bosa is a patchwork quilt of various short-term jobs supplemented by small but steady infusions of cash from government pensions and assistance checks. This has made possible a visible increase in consumption.

Bosans have more and more goods produced in factories in faraway places. They wear the latest Italian fashions and eat imported, frozen, and processed foods. They get national and international culture in their living rooms through television, radio, magazines, and newspapers. Bosans are living through social and economic transformations that have much in common with those of other peripheral Italian regions (Davis 1973, 1977; Schneider and Schneider 1976). This chapter describes the impact of those transformations on a particular sector of the Bosan people—those who were formerly primary producers— through a detailed study of changing relationships in the production, distribution, and consumption of bread.

BREAD IN SARDINIA

This chapter treats bread as a "total social fact" (Mauss 1967). Like all foods, bread is a nexus of economic, political, aesthetic, social, symbolic, and health concerns. As traditionally the most important food in the Sardinian diet, bread is a particularly sensitive indicator of change.[2] Bread has always been the *sine qua non* of food in Sardinia and all over Italy and Mediterranean Europe. Le Lannou estimates the daily diet of the Sardinian peasant in the 1930s as being 78 percent bread by weight—1200 grams of bread, 200 grams of cooked vegetables or legumes, 30 grams of cheese, and 100 grams of pasta (1941, 288). Other commentators on the Sardinian diet confirm this dominant role of bread over at least the last 150 years (Angioni 1976, 34; Bodio 1879, 200–206; Barbiellini-Amidei and Bandinu 1976, 82–86; Cannas 1975; Chessa 1906, 279–80; Delitala 1978, 101; La Marmora 1839, 243; Mathias 1983; Somogyi 1973). Although bread is still the most important food, its dietary significance has declined as other foods—especially meat, pasta, and cheese—have become more accessible (Counihan 1981, 178–226).

As the most important food, bread was central to the Sardinian economy for centuries. The Romans allegedly exported Sardinian grain (Bouchier 1917, 56). In recent times, durum wheat has been the island's principal crop, though total hectares planted has dropped noticeably since the beginning of the century (see table 2.1).

The wheat-bread cycle was pivotal to the Bosan and Sardinian subsistence economy. Peasant men devoted much effort to growing grain, and peasant women to milling, sifting, and baking it. The variety and beauty of the breads were astounding. There were three or four principal everyday types and tens of special, symbolic, and pictorial ones for holidays and rituals (see Cirese et al. 1977).

As the Sardinian staple food, bread was symbolic of life. Cambosu reports the peasant proverb: *"Chie hat pane mai non morit"*—"one who has bread never dies" (in Cirese et al. 1977, 40). In central Sardinia, security was *"pane in domu"*—"bread in the home" (Pinna 1971, 86). Minimal well-being was expressed in the words "at least we have bread"—*"pane nessi bi n'amus"*—and poverty as "they do not even have

TABLE 2.1
Hectares of Durum Wheat

Year	Hectares Planted in Wheat	Source	
1909	314,000	Le Lannou	1941, 293–96
1924	138,000	Le Lannou	1941, 293–96
1939	250,000	Le Lannou	1941, 293–96
1950	243,000	King	1975, 160
1970	112,700	King	1975, 160
1976	94,907	Regione	1978, appendix*

Production figures vary enormously from year to year, e.g. in 1912 production was 5.7 quintals/hectare; in 1911, 10 quintals/hectare; in 1970, 10.9 quintals/hectare; and in 1971,15.6 quintals/hectare.

bread"—"*non b'ana mancu pane*" (Barbiellini-Amidei and Bandinu 1976, 831). The outcome of the grain harvest was symbolic and determined the unfolding of life: "*Bellu laore annu vonu; laore mezzanu annu malu*"—"beautiful grain, good year; poor grain, bad year" (Barbiellini-Amidei and Bandinu 1976, 80).[3]

The symbolic centrality of bread in Bosan society emerges in a story told to me by an informant, Luisa Fois. In the first year of her marriage, she baked the traditional Easter breads out of her husband's wheat. One was a cross, representing Christ's crucifixion. This she gave to her husband to eat. But he said, "Don't you know that we have to eat the cross together, now that we are married. As we share our lives, so too must we share the cross, so that we bear life's burdens equally in the year ahead." Bread was a product of their union, and its shared consumption reaffirmed their interdependence. Let us now consider changes in bread production, distribution, and consumption in Bosa and through them assess the individualization of social relations in a situation of modernization without development.[4]

Bread Production

Up until the 1960s wheat was a major crop in Bosa. Peasants cultivated grain principally on marginal soils—on the hillsides surrounding the town and north towards Capo Marragiu. In 1929, there were 393 hectares devoted to cereal cultivation (Catasto Agrario 1929, 120); this had dwindled to 21 hectares in 1972 (ISTAT 1972).

Land ownership in Bosa has always been highly concentrated (see table 2.2). Since the terrain is mostly hilly and mountainous, the owners of large tracts of land have always used the open tracts called *tancas* mainly for grazing animals—sheep, goats, and some cattle and pigs. However, up until the 1960s, they also rented the land on long rotation

TABLE 2.2
Land Tenure in Bosa

1929

Size of holding in hectares	Number of Holdings	% of Total Number of Holdings	Total hectares	% of Total Hectares
0–3	342	64.9	445	3.9
3–10	127	24.1	654	5.6
10–20	12	2.3	160	1.4
20–50	3	0.6	86	0.7
over 50	43	8.1	10,230	88.4
TOTAL	**527**	**100.0**	**11,575**	**100.0**

Source: Catasto Agrario 1929

1972

Size of holding in hectares	Number of Holdings	% of Total Number of Holdings	Total hectares	% of Total Hectares
0–3	72	36.7	96	0.9
3–10	57	29.1	339	3.1
10–20	14	7.2	190	1.7
20–50	12	6.1	335	3.1
over 50	41	20.9	9,978	91.2
TOTAL	**196**	**100.0**	**10,938**	**100.0**

Source: ISTAT 1972

cycles (every ten years or so) to landless peasants for growing wheat. This periodic cultivation of wheat improved the soil for pasture and provided landlords with extra income in the form of rent. Peasants generally worked the land alone or with a father or son. But the harvest and threshing were big jobs that involved reciprocal cooperation with other men and women.

Men produced grain and brought it home; then it was women's responsibility. They took it to the mill. Once milled, they sifted the flour into four different consistencies: *su poddine, sa simula, su chifalzu,* and *su fulfere* which they used for different kinds of bread with different meanings and uses.[5] The women organized the collective labor of baking, calling together neighbors, relatives or *comari*[6] to help; this assistance was later reciprocated when those people did their own baking.

Women baked every ten to fourteen days. It was a long process, done entirely by hand. They used a sourdough leaven called *sa madriga* and made a stiff dough for the rounded figure-eight-shaped *palsiddas* and the flat, claw-shaped *ziccos,* and a sticky dough for the long, oval-shaped *covasas* with the characteristic hole in the middle.[7]

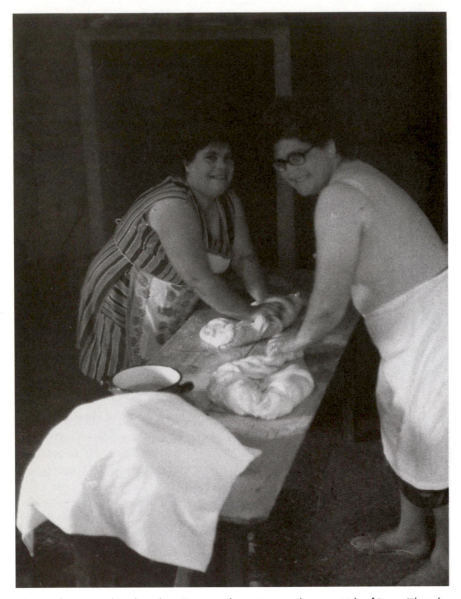

Nina and Teresa making bread at Nina's employers' country house outside of Bosa. (Photo by Carole M. Counihan.)

Women regularly worked together. In the work, they exchanged and intermingled their lives: their gossip, their skills, their pasts, their loves, and their losses. Barbiellini-Amidei and Bandinu say of central Sardinia, "The bread-makers are typical channels of social communication. . . . While they prepare the dough and bake the bread they make

Two kinds of bread baking in the wood oven: *palsiddas* in the background, and *ziccos* in the foreground. (Photo by Carole M. Counihan.)

an X-ray of the town. Secrets are revealed; the women judge and absolve or condemn" (1976, 83). By working together, Bosan women developed and acted out standards for "good bread," "good work," and a "good woman." Through the act of criticizing others (*fare la critica*) they collectively reaffirmed local norms and morality.

Informants told me that grain cultivation began to diminish in Bosa around 1960 and disappeared almost completely within six or seven years. This perplexing demise of a major crop becomes understandable in light of Italian agricultural policy and typifies modernization without development. The Italian government protected Italian grain from Unification in 1861 through the 1950s, by maintaining a price of about 60 percent higher than the world price for grain. In 1957 the government reduced the support prices for grain by L 100/quintal and in 1959 by L 500/quintal (Orlando et al. 1977, 26–27). At the same time, the government encouraged the mechanization and capitalization of agriculture by facilitating production and dissemination of tractors and fertilizer. In Sardinia the number of tractors increased from 993 in 1949 to over 7,500 in 1971 (Brown 1979, 302). Mechanization of agriculture stimulated industrial production in the north but reduced overall employment in agriculture by replacing workers with machines and causing increasing disparity in productivity between rich and poor zones (Orlando et al. 1977, 21–30). Furthermore, salaried wages were rising, making wage labor ever more attractive than subsistence farming and encouraging emigration from marginal areas of the south to industrial centers of the north (Di Giorgi and Moscati 1980; Graziani 1977). The result of these trends was that many marginal and hilly areas where production per effort and acre was relatively low were abandoned. Bosan lands and many others in Sardinia were among them (Counihan 1981, 64–80).

Specific events in Bosa exemplified these long-term socioeconomic transformations. The first public bakery opened in Bosa in 1912. At first business was slow because housewives all baked their own bread and it was a source of *bilgonza* (shame) to buy it. But then with fascism, the centralized grain collection (*ammasso di grano*), and rationing in the war, people began to follow the habit of going to the bakery. After the Second World War there seems to have been a short-lived revival of home baking, but the steady abandonment of wheat cultivation in the early 1960s dealt a final blow to the activity, which accompanied the demise of other home-processing activities like making tomato preserves, salting olives, and drying figs (Counihan 1981, 127–59).

People no longer had their own grain and thus had to buy it. If they were buying grain, it was easier to get used to the idea of buying bread. The grain mills in Bosa closed, forcing a woman to go nine kilometers away to Tresnuraghes to mill flour. That involved considerable trouble and some expense. Women wondered why they should bother when more and more of their neighbors and relatives were buying bread, and their own children were grumbling about stale bread. The shame of buying bread gradually disappeared, and Bosan women slowly stopped baking. Many have made the step irreversible by removing ovens, spurred on by the desire to enlarge and "modernize" their houses.

Today there is not one woman left in Bosa who still bakes bread for her own family.[8] Bosans rely on five local bakers and three from the nearby villages of Suni, Tinnura, and Montresta. The Bosan bakers produce from 80 to 500 kilograms per day and sell their bread in twenty-seven retail stores throughout the town. Bread making is the exclusive purview of male bakers and their salaried male assistants. It takes place on a larger scale, producing greater quantities with a wider dispersion than ever before. The culmination of this trend is the ironically named *"Pane della Nonna"*—"Grandmother's Bread"—a sort of Italian-style Wonder Bread made by northern industry and sold presliced in cellophane packages with preservatives to facilitate long life on supermarket shelves.

In the past, the "domestic mode of production" (Sahlins 1972, 41–99) characterized bread making in Bosa. Husband and wife did complementary tasks that insured the harvesting of wheat and the baking of bread. Of necessity, they cooperated with people outside the family in the harvest, threshing, and baking. Today, men and women still need each other for many things, but not to produce materially such a basic life necessity as bread. With a government pension or a salary, a man or woman can buy bread, obviating one form of dependence on each other. Furthermore, with the decline of subsistence production, Bosans have a less consistent need to rely on others outside the family. One of Pinna's informants expressed this change thus:

> In the old days, when we used to bake bread at home, we had to call on neighbors, and this was a form of dependence. Now that today we buy bread already made, this dependence has ended and we are all free in our own houses. And I am truly thankful for this progress, not so much for the sacrifice it cost to have to get out of bed at three in the morning to begin the job and to keep at it until four in the afternoon, but for the convenience of not having outsiders come into your house to help and go out of it to gossip about what they had seen, and even about what they had not seen. Now progress has brought the benefit that we all can be tranquil in our own houses. And this is a great comfort of the soul more than of the body (1971, 94).

This woman is expressing the trend of individualization: how she needs others less and is less subject to their moral scrutiny. She is culturally more autonomous because the incursion of new production methods has relieved her of her social dependence on others. Let us now look at how changes in distribution have contributed further to this trend.

Bread Distribution

Up until the Second World War, Bosa was a small but thriving center of maritime trade, exporting grain and other raw materials and importing consumer items. Today, Bosa is no longer a commercial center but is quite literally the end of the road. The town's failure to modernize its port, railroad, or road systems has rendered it commercially obsolete. Intrepid entrepreneurs bring consumer goods to Bosa by truck over the long and winding road from Macomer, but with the decline in local production the town has little to export. This situation is typical of modernization without development (Counihan 1981, 227–33).

There have also been changes in the market within Bosa. Shopping for food has become more important as subsistence production has declined. Women shop for bread and a few other small items daily in the small neighborhood stores that are centers of social relations. Increasingly, however, there is a trend away from reliance on these tiny, owner-operated neighborhood stores to bigger, self-service stores located in the center of town, staffed by salaried salesclerks, and owned by petty capitalists. Here women tend to buy greater quantities and hence to shop less often, decreasing their encounters with each other.

Because these stores attract clients from all over town, shoppers are less intimate with each other than in the neighborhood stores. In the self-service stores, shopper and merchant interact only at the end of the shopping process at the cash register. Since the cashiers are hired help, they have no power to grant temporary credit as owner-operators frequently do. These debts serve to maintain an enduring relationship between merchant and client. The increasing reliance on the new, large self-service stores has resulted in an erosion of the sociability of shopping, both among shoppers and between shopper and storekeeper (Counihan 1981, 242–66).

While market exchange has long governed commerce, a strict, incessant reciprocity has always been the basis of close and long-lasting social and economic relations in Bosa and all of Sardinia (Counihan 1981, 233–42). Every social interaction is mediated by the giving and receiving of food and drink. One has an obligation to accept, just as the Sardinian has an obligation to give. A Bosan woman said, "My mother always said that if you were eating and a person came to the door, you must always offer him some food. And if you were baking bread, and a person came to the door, you must always give him a piece of the freshly baked bread." Women sent gifts of fresh-baked bread to close relatives and friends. Cambosu (in Cirese et al. 1977, 40) remembers, "My sisters waited for the first light of day and vied with each other in every season to bring to our closest relatives and dearest friends a gift of our bread. It was one of the most enjoyed gifts, and they reciprocated it every time that they lit their ovens."

Today, with the decline in local primary production and the increasing reliance on the market, the incessant mutual giving and receiving of foods slows and becomes less crucial to survival. Thus one of the most important forces linking people together—reciprocal gifts—is fading away, and with it goes people's interdependence. More and more they acquire goods through economic exchanges in the formal market rather than through gifts which reaffirm relationships. Hence the changing distribution patterns accompanying modernization contribute further to the individualization seen occurring in production.

Bread Consumption

Study of the mode of consumption reveals human relationships and basic values in a group. Commensalism demonstrates fundamental social units and reinforces important relationships. Meals are a central arena for the family in Italy, one of the domains through which domestic ties attain their strength (Belmonte 1979; Pitkin 1985). In rural Sardinia in the past there was an ironclad ethic and practice of consumption: Daily consumption took place within the family and was parsimonious; festive consumption took place within society at large and was prodigal (Barbiellini-Amidei and Bandinu 1976, 139; Gallini 1971). The rhythmic oscillation between these two different modes supported and mediated the individual's connection to the two most important social units—family and community.

Bosan meals involved consumption of a relative's labor: one's father, brother, or son in the wheat; one's mother, sister, or daughter in the loaf. Consumption of bread reaffirmed the complementarity of men and women and the nuclear family social structure, the basis of society and locus of individual identity (Barbiellini-Amidei and Bandinu 1976, 80–84). Consumption of bakery bread involves not this reaffirmation of Bosan society but rather participation in the broader world economy in which relationships are beyond Bosans' ability to retouch them.

The fundamental interdependence of consumption and the family and its current erosion are revealed in the case of a youth who died of hunger while I was living in Bosa, such an extraordinary event that it made the front page of the regional Sardinian newspaper: "On the death certificate the doctor wrote 'cardiocirculatory collapse,' two words to veil a disturbing tragedy with a 23-year-old victim. I.C. died, more simply, of hunger. . . . Out front [of his house] only a few curious onlookers and neighbors: 'He died like a dog, no one realized it.' Did he live alone? 'Yes, alone. His mother had been in a nursing home for years. He didn't have anyone else. . . . Alone, in that cave of a house, he lived worse than a dog'" (L'Informatore del Lunedì, 1979). I.C. did not die of poverty as so many did in the past; he had a government pension. Rather he died because the sustaining web of family and community had broken. Emigration and the decline of the domestic mode of production have made possible the existence of people like I.C., people who are totally alone.

Analysis of the evolution of redistributive feasts in Sardinia illustrates an erosion of the community solidarity that was once necessary for survival in the subsistence economy. In the past the collective *festa* (feast day) was the only legitimate locus of excessive and conspicuous consumption. "Exaggerated consumption was an exceptional act—festive and grandiose—to be carried out at an exceptional time and place" (Gallini 1971, 11). As in many noncapitalist societies, excess consumption in the *festa* served to bring the community together; temporarily to obliterate social and economic differences; and to satiate hunger collectively, madly, and equally, at least for this one day (Mauss 1967; Turner 1969).

To a great extent, Bosan *feste* have lost this role. I observed it only in the Feast of Saint Anthony, January 17, the start of the Carnival period. People donated bread to the saint, and the priest blessed it at

Thirteen sheep carcasses hanging outside the cooking huts at the Church of St. Mark in the countryside near Tresnuraghes (Sardinia) on Saint Mark's feast day, March 25, 1979. These sheep were offered to the saint by local shepherds in thanks for favors received or desired and were about to be boiled with onions, garlic, and potatoes and offered to the populace. (Photo by Carole M. Counihan.)

People eating the communal meal at the Feast of St. Mark near Tresnuraghes (Sardinia). They are eating the bread and mutton offered by villagers and shepherds and blessed by the priest at a special Mass. (Photo by Carole M. Counihan.)

the morning Mass. Members of the saint's confraternity distributed it to the two hundred or so faithful. People took it home to eat with family and neighbors, for it was supposed to ward off stomachaches. Although this feast day contained some elements of a collective, redistributive feast, it was a minor, poorly attended event, peripheral to most people's lives.

The Feast of Saint Mark on March 25 in Tresnuraghes, a village nine kilometers from Bosa, was a much more significant feast of communal redistribution. Local shepherd families in this predominantly pastoral community offered sheep and oversaw cooking them in a gesture of thanks to Providence. Other families offered bread as thanksgiving or for favors desired. Hundreds of people, mostly Tresnuraghesi, but with a significant number of Bosans and outsiders, ate and drank to satiation.

The Feast of St. Mark is typical of the traditional Sardinian *festa*, a theater of excess consumption that serves to solidify the social community (Angioni 1974, 232–79; Gallini 1971). That *feste* of this sort persist today only in the less modernized areas of Sardinia (in Tresnuraghes but not in Bosa, for example) is an indication that their demise accompanies modernization. Tresnuraghesi expressed concern about the fate of the Feast of Saint Mark, their most important *festa*. The growing presence of outsiders who came not to participate in strengthening social community but only to acquire free food threatened the meaning of the ritual and strained the economic ability of the community.

The ethic of consumption of the modern world market to which Bosa and Sardinia increasingly belong is very different from the one that traditionally animated Sardinian collective *feste*. In the past, "opulent consumption . . . was never an act to be carried out in private because this would have transformed it into secret guilt" (Gallini 1971, 10). Today, opulent consumption increases and becomes a private, stratifying, and individualizing act rather than a public, altruistic, and communalizing one. It becomes a mode of separating and differentiating people rather than bringing them together. People compete for prestige by buying and displaying high-fashion clothes, color televisions, and all sorts of consumer goods. In the past, having more than others was dangerous, for it could draw the evil eye and misfortune (Gallini 1973, 1981), but today it is a legitimate source of prestige (Barbiellini-Amidei and Bandinu 1976, 139–45).

Not only is the meaning of consumption in general changing, but the specific messages conveyed in foods change as well. Think of the two Easter breads (see figures 2.1 and 2.2) and the different world views they reflect. The traditional one (figure 2.1), though clearly evolved itself, was modeled by hand by a middle-aged woman in Tresnuraghes.

A traditional Easter bread made by an older woman at home in the village of Tresnuraghes, near Bosa. Note the points recalling breasts or birds, and the cross covering the egg, a traditional symbol of Easter and fertility. (Photo by Carole M. Counihan.)

A modern Easter bread made in a bakery in Bosa. Note the alteration in symbolic language with letters replacing images except for the egg that persists. (Photo by Carole M. Counihan.)

It reflects meaning in shape; it is an artwork. The egg and the points that recall birds in flight speak of fertility, sexuality, and procreation—basic themes in Easter and its pagan precursors. The new bread was made by machine and sold by Pinna's bakery. It has no meaningful shape: It is round to encircle the egg, all that is left of the traditional iconography. It conveys its message in the letters "BP" which stand for "*Buona Pasqua*" or "Happy Easter." Letters rather than forms express meaning. Letters are symbols of civilization and, Lévi-Strauss suggests (1975, 299), of hierarchy. The "reading" of the letter-message necessitates formal education, something many Bosans, especially the poor and the elderly, have not had. Thus the BP bread represents and strengthens social hierarchy, differentiation, and separation. The more traditional bread, on the other hand, contains a message whose "reading" necessitates participation in the local community and its symbolic language. Thus, in contrast to the new bread, its production and consumption represent and strengthen social communalism.

CONCLUSION

Anthropology's particular contribution to social science is to examine social phenomena holistically and to reveal the personal and qualitative side of large-scale economic and political processes studied more abstractly and quantitatively by other disciplines. This chapter has attempted to fulfill anthropology's mandate by studying the nature of modernization and its effects on social relationships in rural Sardinia by using bread as a lens of analysis. Focusing on the production, distribution, and consumption of this most important food enables simultaneous examination of material changes in people's lives and their symbolic and social repercussions. Thus the chapter demonstrates how the study of food habits can be an effective channel to attaining the holism central to anthropology.

Study of contemporary socioeconomic changes in Bosa contributes to development studies by offering data from a backward region within an industrial nation. Bosa reveals the dynamics of internal underdevelopment. Furthermore, data on Sardinia are scarce in the literature and can increase our understanding of recent change in the Mediterranean region. Data from Bosa balance the strong concentration in Sardinian studies on small, mountainous, pastoral villages of the interior.

The findings presented here give support to the thesis of economic anthropology that the capitalist mode of production and exchange leads to an atomization of social relations. In subsistence wheat and bread production, men and women depend on each other for assistance and are unable to make a living without mutual exchange of labor and products. Social interdependence declines with the concentration of wheat production on capital-intensive farms and of bread production in a few bakeries operating with wage laborers to make profits. Bread acquisition takes place through increasingly impersonal money exchange. The continuous giving and receiving of bread and other foods so important to tying people together and ensuring their survival in the past fades away with the demise of subsistence production. Daily bread consumption used to be an affirmation of male and female complementarity and the integrity of the family unit. Although bread is still essential to meals, it has lost this particular symbolic meaning. Thus this study demonstrates that one effect of modernization without development is increasing autonomy of actions and identity.

This chapter offers the reader the opportunity to assess the impact of individualization on Bosan people's lives. Pinna's central Sardinian informant offered one hint in her relief at the freedom gained through her productive independence, a freedom from grueling gossip. But one is tempted to ask another question: How does independence affect the human need for others? Anthropology is based on the belief that humans are social beings. What happens to humanity if humans become increasingly separate and lose overriding communal ties? Finally, what does individualization signify in a class society? Bosans are gaining economic independence from each other, but they remain dependent on the state and the economic elite for pensions and jobs. Perhaps their independence would be more rewarding if it were accompanied by real control over the production, distribution, and consumption of their survival necessities. For, as they say, "one who has bread never dies."

3

Food, Power, and Female Identity in Contemporary Florence[1]

INTRODUCTION

This chapter examines how the vast changes in Italian society since World War II have affected the identity and power of urban women. Modern Italy has witnessed an exodus from the countryside and an increase in urban living. There has been a concomitant decline in subsistence peasant farming and small-scale artisanry and a rise of capitalist economic activity relying on wage labor in industry, commerce, construction, and tourism. The standard of living has risen, marked by increasing wealth and consumerism. Material well-being has extended across the population through the rise of the welfare state with vast sums of money pumped into free national health care, retirement and disability pensions, unemployment compensation, and civil service (Sgritta 1983). These economic processes have brought about social and cultural changes in men's and women's personal lives—in their values, goals, sex roles, self-definition, and relationships to each other (Balbo 1976).

Urban Italian women, like many others in the urban industrial West, are undergoing a transition in their status and power relative to men. They are challenging the dominanace of men over women inherent in the traditional division of labor where men control the public, political, and wage-labor spheres and women are in charge of the domestic spheres of reproduction and nurturance. Today women are increasingly participating in wage work and gaining access to money so important to status and self-definition in modern consumerist Italy (Barile and Zanuso 1980; Saraceno 1984). At the same time they are gradually exerting political influence and altering the organization of society to facilitate male and female equality (Veauvy 1983; Saraceno

43

1984). Yet women are still subordinate in the public political and economic spheres. Although official data are blind to much of women's employment due to its semilegal status (Balbo 1976, 66; Barile and Zanuso 1980), statistics show that women suffer significantly higher unemployment than men—17.1 percent versus 6.8 percent (ISTAT 1985, 228). In addition, women earn less than men (Saraceno 1984, 15) and wield far less political power (Anzalone 1982). Women at the same time suffer a strong and debilitating identity conflict because of the unresolved contradiction between their public and domestic roles. They consider both roles essential to their self-esteem and self-fulfillment today, and yet they cannot materially perform both roles effectively. Hence they suffer frustration and self-doubt. I will describe here their changing economic and social position by focusing on alterations in their relationship to food-provisioning and on their own words that express the resulting identity conflict.

I analyze the position of women from the point of view of power because in stratified societies positions of dominance and subordination affect every aspect of life chances—physical health, mental health, life expectancy, marital happiness, wealth, political influence, criminal justice, and so on (Eitzen 1985). A central concern in contemporary anthropology is to explain the widespread asymmetry of power between men and women (Atkinson 1982; Hrdy 1981; Rosaldo 1974; Sacks 1979; Sanday 1981). While most anthropologists acknowledge that in no societies do women dominate men, there is considerable debate over the different powers wielded by men and women, their extent, the conditions under which they flourish or change, and their impact on the quality of social life. Furthermore, in modern industrial democracies like Italy there is growing agitation that women be guaranteed social equality with men (Chiavola Birnbaum 1986). There is concern over whether recent changes in Italian society—like the rise of the wage labor economy, the increased tutelage by the state of traditionally domestic concerns like health and child care, and changes in residence and family structure—have improved the position of women.

THE FLORENTINE WOMEN

My data came from fifteen Florentine women of one extended family whom I knew well for over a decade when I conducted directed life-history interviews with them during the summers of 1982 and 1984 (see figure 3.1). My informants have lived through the Italian socioeconomic changes described earlier. I will describe their experiences and present their own interpretation of the meaning and effect of those experiences, thus enriching our understanding of how statistical trends are played out in people's daily lives. Then I will draw conclusions

FIGURE 3.1

Life Synopsis of Informants in 1984

Name	Age	Residence	Situation
Marta	22	Florence	temporarily employed in ceramics factory, engaged (married March 1986)
Cinzia	26	Scandicci (Florence)	Sales clerk in COOP supermarket, recently married to dental technician (had baby 1986)
Vanna	50	Florence	married housewife, runs household with her parents, chronically ill husband and son in public housing in Florence, garment worker before marriage
Bruna	76	Florence	married, living with married daughter, retired, moved from countryside to Florence at middle age and with husband had flower shop near Ponte Vecchio (died 1985)
Loretta	48	Empoli (Florence)	garment worker, married, lives with husband and two children in town 35 kms from Florence
Paola	20	Empoli (Florence)	secretary in plastics firm, engaged, lives with parents and brother
Gloria	17	U.S.A.	high school student, lives with parents and sister in Boston suburb
Sandy	14	U.S.A.	junior high school student, lives with parents and sister in Boston suburg
Gigliola	39	U.S.A.	married to Italian-American and emigrated to U.S. at age 21, U.S. citizen, just received M.A. in international relations, formerly high school teacher
Elda	66	Florence	housewife, recently widowed, worked in family bakery in Florence until age 46
Tina	64	Florence	housewife, lives with retired husband, worked in family bakery in Florence before marriage
Sandra	41	Monte Oriolo (Florence)	housewife, lives with factory owner husband and two daughters, worked as gym teacher before marriage
Elena	14	Monto Oriolo	student in middle school in Florence suburb
Olivia	12	Monte Oriolo	student in private middle school in Florence
Maria Luisa	61	Florence	retired clerk for city of Florence, recently married for first time at age 57 (died 1986)

⌐ = sisters   ⌐ = mothers & daughters

(Florence) means in the province of Florence

about the general significance of changes in Florentine women's identity and power.

I selected my informants through personal ties. They vary in age, occupation, residence, and family composition.[2] Older informants were born into peasant and artisan families, some in the countryside around Florence. They moved to the city in later years and participated in wage-labor jobs in industry, commerce, and civil service. All have achieved a much higher level of material well-being than they knew as girls. Women of the younger generation grew up in urban areas and had more education than their parents; they aspire to paid jobs and suffer the disappointments of Italy's high unemployment rate, especially for youth in search of their first jobs (Balbo 1976). Many informants today benefit from the welfare state; some live in public housing, have had civil-service jobs, or have earned disability and retirement pensions or maternity leave. I believe that my informants are representative of modern urban middle-class Italian women, both in the characteristics and ideas they share, and in the range of diversity among them. The lives of the older women differ significantly from those of their daughters and granddaughters; the changes and their reflections on them are a commentary on the alterations in Italian society.

WOMEN, FOOD, AND POWER

In all kinds of societies—foraging bands, horticultural tribes, peasant villages, and industrial cities—women have always had primary responsibility for preparing food and giving it to others (D'Andrade 1974, 18). Particularly in preindustrial societies, women contribute heavily to producing, processing, and distributing food as well. The predominant role of women in feeding is a cultural universal, a major component of female identity, and an important source of female connections to and influence over others. Hence, although there are other components of female identity and other sources of their authority, the power of women has often derived from the power of food.

I am concerned here with two kinds of power. The first, coercion, is attained through control of might and essential resources that can be denied to others. This is the power of provincial Italian prefects who can raise the price of bread and of the U.S. government that sent food to the Nicaraguan Contras but denied it to Chileans after Allende's election (Burbach and Flynn 1980, 70). The second form of power is influence. It accrues not through force and the ability to deny but through giving, through the obligations created by giving, and through the influence wielded in the act of giving. This is the power Mauss described in his masterpiece *The Gift* (1967). It is the power of the tribal big man who distributes enormous piles of yams at feasts and "leads because the people wish to be led;" it is also the power of women who feed, who satisfy hunger, who are viscerally needed, and who influence others through manipulation of the symbolic language of food.

True coercion is typical of class societies where resources are concentrated in the hands of the few, who are usually male. The power of the gift, on the other hand, predominates in egalitarian societies where women's relatively high status comes from their full participation in the giving that creates obligations and from their control of a particularly powerful channel, food (see Brown 1975). Interestingly, although control of food can be the strongest weapon of coercion, for women it is not. In no culture is it acceptable for women to deny food to their families, whereas it is acceptable for politicians—mostly male—to deny food to entire populations for political ends (Lappé and Collins 1978). Like women in stratified societies, individuals and groups in tribal societies do not permit groups to starve others as a path to power; rather they achieve power by shaming other groups with their magnanimity (Young 1971). Food is a special substance that follows exceptionally strong rules of sharing and generosity (Sahlins 1972, 215–19). It would be unthinkable for Italian women to starve husbands and children to force them to do certain things. Rather, individuals in tribal societies and women in stratified societies have the culturally sanctioned ability to manipulate the giving of food and thus to attain influence through means other than coercion. Women in stratified, market-oriented, agro-industrial societies like Italy and the United States are often defined as subordinate to men because, although they control feeding, as a group they lack the coercive ability to withhold grain shipments or control corn futures. Gender equality involves, then, an effort by women to gain public political and economic power, and with it the ability not just to influence, but to coerce as well.

Control of alimentation is a source of power because food is a very special substance. It satisfies the most basic, compelling, continuous, and agonizing human need: hunger. The terror of hunger has been well documented by anthropologists, historians, psychologists, and sociologists. The people of Kalauna call it "the worst disease" (Young 1986) and enact rituals to curb appetite so food will rot in abundance rather than lack when needed. The voluntarily self-starved victims of anorexia nervosa see hunger as a "dictator" and manifest an obsession with food similar to the behavior of starving World War II prisoners (Bruch 1978, 8). Cultures across the globe enact rituals to ward off hunger by propitiating fertility and limiting appetites (Holmberg 1969, 240–41; Malinowski 1961, 169; Young 1986). Over and over again people in the grip of hunger have broken normal rules of social organization as witnessed in the anomie of the famine-struck Ik (Turnbull 1972) and the popular food riots epidemic in history. The screams of the hungry infant appear to express both terror and pain; they are passionate and disturbing, designed through millennia of evolution to bring mother and food immediately. The lactating mother has the power to feed and calm her infant, and this is the power of life itself.

Because food is such a gripping need day in and day out, it takes on additional social and symbolic significance. It is a powerful channel for communication and a means to establish connection, create obligations, and exert influence. Sardinians and many other peoples give food to the dead in return for peaceful coexistence in separate spheres (Counihan 1981, 276–79). The Maori return a portion of hunted birds to the forest spirits to extract future abundance (Sahlins 1972, 158). Florentines, Sardinians, and many other peoples welcome strangers with food and drink, thereby obligating amity in return (Counihan 1981, 292; Mauss 1967). Women everywhere, like my Florentine informants, feed their husbands and children in return for love, favors, good behavior, and the power that comes from being needed.

Because food is so essential and so frequently used to affirm connection, it takes on rich symbolic meaning. In addition, the particular characteristics of food give it semantic wealth, something noted famously by Lévi-Strauss (1966, 1969), Mary Douglas (1966, 1974), Roland Barthes (1975), and others. In transforming food from raw nature to edible product, humans convey messages by manipulating food combinations, cooking mode, color, texture, taste, and form (Verdier 1969), as the unleavened bread, bitter herbs, eggs, and wine in the Passover meal convey "the miraculous deliverance of the Jews from bondage in Egypt" (Feeley-Harnik 1981, 124). The symbolic power of food enables prohibitions and taboos to signify social boundaries (Douglas 1974), religious integrity (Douglas 1966), status (Bennett et al. 1942, 655), and gender differences (Meigs 1985). Feeding can symbolize fosterage, adoption, and family (Mead 1935; Young 1971, 40). Voraciousness symbolizes the untamed or untamable animality struggling against social control that parents enforce by teaching table manners (Freud 1946). Food refusal connotes rejection of social mores and control as exemplified in anorexia nervosa, in political hunger strikes, and in obstinate children everywhere (Bruch 1973).

Women's daily control of food preparation and presentation gives them much influence. While men dominate ceremonial and special-occasion food offerings in many societies—as male priests consecrate the host and offer it to communicants, as fathers orchestrate the Seder meal, and as male chefs abound in haute cuisine—day after day the predominant agent of food provisioning is female. Caroline Bynum (1986) has shown how medieval female saints, often in a lay context, used food to express their piety, convert others, work miracles, and challenge institutionalized male clerical authority. Giving food to a great extent defines the nature and extent of female power.

It is a power largely exercised over family members and only occasionally beyond to members of the wider society. Giving food connects women to close relatives through an extremely intense emotional channel; women become identified with the food they offer. Anna Freud (1946) has discussed the psychological significance of the feeding relationship between mother and child. A common theme in the enormous literature on eating disorders is how a girl's voluntary self-starvation is a reflection of her ambivalent relationship with her mother.[3]

Scholars of Italy (for example, Belmonte 1979; Parsons 1969; Saunders 1981; Silverman 1975) have described the importance of mothers and the influence they gain through nurturance. Belmonte defines the poor Neapolitan family as "mother-centered" and argues that the mother "is at the center because she controls and distributes the twin sources of human vitality, food and love" (1979, 89). Donald Pitkin has written about southern Italians: "First from breast and then from fireplace and stove has come an often meager but increasing flow of food . . . , a constant reminder that it is the mother alone who gratifies the most primitive need. Oral dependency is but one aspect of a much larger configuration, but its primacy in survival and psychic well-being ensures power to she who satisfies it, for in being fed both husband and children are subordinate to her" (1985, 214).

The mother determines when, what, and how much family members will eat. She controls the social mores of the table, which are a microcosm of behaviors and values deemed right and just by society at large. She controls the symbolic language of food, determining what her dishes and meals will say about herself, her family, and the world (Quaggiotto 1987). Through her role in food provisioning, a woman can administer a significant portion of the budget, particularly in Italy where an average of over one-third of family income goes for food (L'industria alimentare 1978, 5–9). Although the anthropological literature on Italy regularly describes women's food production and provisioning activities, no studies focus directly on food habits to reveal the full extent of women's position, power, and identity, nor do they examine the conflict between women's domestic and public roles in the urban setting.[4]

I document in detail here my informants' descriptions of the significance of food in their self-concept and relationships. It is I, not they, who conclude that feeding brings them influence, for I believe that this fact is so fundamental that it goes unrecognized by them. They cling to their food provisioning as part of their very selves, but at the same time they seek jobs and salaries that grant the power of economic autonomy and an additional component of identity, that of remunerated worker in the public world.

TRADITIONAL FLORENTINE FEMALE IDENTITY AND POWER

The Florentine woman is born into a world that defines the constituents of femininity as family, nurturance, and altruism. Through providing food, Florentine women sustain life in others and give their own lives meaning. Perhaps the quintessential form of nurturing for these women is breast-feeding, for in this act the child is absolutely dependent on nurturance from the mother's own body. One of my informants, fifty-year-old Vanna, said that while nursing, it seemed as if she was "giving life again" to her children. Another informant, sixty-six-year-old Elda, said "It seemed such a beautiful thing to me that I never would have stopped because in that moment my baby belonged completely to me. In that moment she was really all mine. And I reflected, I said to myself, 'Look, the baby is growing because I'm giving her my milk, because I'm giving her life, I'm giving her nourishment.' And it seemed such a beautiful thing that I never would have stopped."

All the women approved of breast-feeding in general, and the younger ones intended to practice it when they had children. All my informants felt that a woman should breast-feed if she could, and they sharply criticized women who decided not to breast-feed so as to preserve their figures.[5] They implied that a woman should sacrifice herself—her looks, her physical well-being, her time, or her convenience—for the benefit of nurturing her child.

Preparing food has always been a principal way in which Florentine women have related to others and defined themselves. As my informant forty-one-year-old Sandra said, "I'm a housewife. If I don't know how to cook, what's left?" A Florentine woman's skill as a good cook is acclaimed and appreciated by family and friends. Vanna said how much she enjoyed "the satisfaction of seeing that you make something that the others like, something that turns out well." Elda explained that before her husband died and her daughter left for America, "Cooking was the greatest satisfaction that I had, because I loved to invent new dishes, to rework all the recipes of the things I knew how to make, and to make new things. I found satisfaction for myself and for the family. Because I saw how much they appreciated me and all that I did."

Dedication to home and family has always been a fundamental part of Florentine womanhood. Thirty-nine-year-old Gigliola, a Florentine woman who emigrated to the United States at age twenty-two, described the Italian woman thus, "I think that all told the Italian woman wants to *sistemarsi*—to get herself settled. She wants to have a house to take care of and to have a husband and children, even while having certain freedoms. The Italian woman is dedicated to her family and without personal ambition to reach an important position." This picture was corroborated by the statements and experiences of my older informants, as well as by other sociological studies (Areni, Manetti, and Tanucci 1982; Pagliari 1982).

Like Barile and Zanuso's subjects (1980), all of my older female informants ran the households in which they lived. Their duties were diverse and many. Most importantly, they bore, gave birth to, nurtured, and raised children. As the primary socializers, women developed strong emotional ties with and profound influence over their offspring largely through feeding. They gained a personal sense of worth that was confirmed by the value Italian society places on children. In addition to raising children, women shopped, cooked, and cleaned up after meals. They dusted, vacuumed, washed windows, mopped floors, swept, and straightened up the house. They picked up, washed, ironed, folded, and put away the family laundry. They mediated between diverse family members, smoothing over quarrels, finding compromises, and making peace. They administered part of the household budget, and sometimes all of it, as Vanna and Elda did. The latter said that her husband brought her his paycheck at the end of the month and that she administered the whole thing herself. Overseers and administrators of the home, Florentine women have rarely been the primary producers.

My informants shared the employment patterns discovered by Barile and Zanuso in their research on two thousand women in the Lombardy region (1980). Subjects worked at low-paying jobs, interrupted employment for marriage and child-rearing, and often worked at home or in the unofficial "black economy" without rights to pensions and unemployment compensation. All of my female informants worked before marriage at wage-earning jobs. All of the older women except sixty-six-year-old Elda quit their jobs at marriage; she continued, but worked in her parents' bakery attached to her home so she was able to watch over her baby daughter. Since Elda's parents never paid her wages or contributed in her name to a retirement fund, her work was like domestic labor, clearly oriented toward helping her family rather than toward attaining economic independence for herself. Fifty-year-old Vanna and her sister, forty-eight-year-old Loretta, did piece work at home after marriage, and Loretta returned to full-time factory work when her children were grown. Gigliola worked full-time as a tour guide in Italy but quit when she married and left for the United States. She attended college at nights while her daughters were young and began teaching high school only after her children entered school. Sixty-one-year-old Maria Luisa was the only woman who worked full-time for her entire adult life—at a civil-service job for the city of Florence—but she didn't marry until she was fifty-seven and retired soon thereafter. For married women born before 1950, work was seen as an economic necessity and a contribution to the family budget, not as a personal necessity or something essential to their identity as women (see also Balbo 1976).

Florentine women's identity has traditionally been based not on satisfaction of their own needs, but on altruism and self-sacrifice (see Pitkin 1985, 7). The older women believe that they should struggle to prevent pain for others, even at the cost of absorbing it themselves. So Vanna for years withheld from her husband Bruno the news that he had cancer, bearing the burden of constantly cheering him up, caring for him physically, and hiding her anxiety from him to spare him additional pain. She also said that having children involved "many, many responsibilities. There are sacrifices. I do without a dress for myself, I do without eating a steak for myself, so as to be able to do something for my children." Gigliola, not long after her mother was widowed, defined the Italian woman's identity as being completely other-directed: "The woman who doesn't have anything to do for another person finds herself dead and lost because she has nothing to do for another person. And for herself she does nothing. For her whole life she does things for her husband."

Yet while not without sacrifice, the life of the traditional woman who married and bore children also had rewards. The women felt secure in the knowledge of what their role was and in the certainty that they could fulfill it. They gained psychological affirmation and influence from the neediness and devotion of their dependent children and husband. Through caretaking and socialization, they had power over how their children felt, thought, and acted. In giving their families food, they gave them mores, values, and worldview.

CONTEMPORARY CONFLICT

In contrast to the older women, the young women I interviewed in the early 1980s were living in a different world and were subject to different expectations from society and from themselves. Paola, Marta, and Cinzia, all in their twenties, were no longer content to be cloistered in their homes with a life of altruistic devotion to family. They wanted and needed to work at paid jobs outside the home. They gained satisfaction from working—from the independence, the money, the social contacts, and the personal gratification. Twenty-year-old Paola, a secretary in a small plastics firm, expressed clearly her pleasure and fulfillment at having a job. She also enjoyed having her own income and not having to ask her parents for money, and she was pleased to be able to save so that some day she and her fiancé could buy a house. "Without two salaries today," she said, "you just can't make it." Twenty-two-year-old Marta, sporadically employed in factory work and looking for a permanent job, said, "A woman has to realize herself through work and family, but not only through her family, also with her husband."

Twenty-six-year-old Cinzia, a clerk in a supermarket and married without children, expressed poignantly her desire to work: "A woman has to have her independence, her own activity. " She continued:

> I work in part for economic satisfaction, in part also because I can't stand to stay home. I tried staying at home; it's depressing, believe me. It's enough to cause a nervous breakdown. It's depressing for a young person to stay at home. What can you do, you always have to ask others for money. I work for my independence, and also to round out our economic situation because, you know, expenses are many today. And I also do it because it gives me more satisfaction. That is, work is the only recompense that there is to give you satisfaction; without it, you'd shoot yourself.

Yet she also expressed bitterness at having a job she found hardly rewarding, with long hours and poor pay. Trained as a nursery school teacher, she was frustrated because she could not find employment in her field, doing a job she loved. She chafed against the boredom of ringing up prices and stocking shelves all day, but would rather do that than be without work (see Dalla Costa and Schenkel 1983).

The younger women clearly expressed their desire for equality with men in both public and private spheres, wanting more than the traditional complementarity of the sexes where women were socially, politically, and economically subordinate to men.[6] Sandra, at age forty, manifested the conflict in evolving expectations. In describing the husband she would like for her teenage daughters, she said, "not a man who commands, but a man who converses with his wife, asks her advice, and makes decisions together with her. A woman should be independent and should speak as an equal with a man, and also she should be considered equal as well." Although in one breath she said she was content to be exclusively a housewife, in the next she expressed her regret at not having been able, due to her parents' objections, to follow her desired career in biology. She also stated that she hated having to ask her husband for money: "Doing this means I have to demean myself, and I don't like it. So often I do without asking. I make do with what I have." For her daughters she wanted a different model of woman: "a woman who has a certain intelligence, including a mental independence, and also culture, so that she can live tranquilly and work tranquilly without having to subordinate herself to her family. I'd really like my daughters to be women who work."

Yet the women who were struggling to make it in the public world of work—to reconcile home, jobs, and family—were bitter that their desired equality did not exist. Paola said, "Men just won't lower themselves to do certain things. People talk about equality and other things, but in my opinion, we have not even achieved a tiny bit." Cinzia, overburdened by long hours at work and the demands of running a household with no help from her husband, a dental technician, lamented that men no longer help even in ways they used to, like moving heavy boxes at work. Nor do they help at home: "Women wanted equality between the sexes and they have lost out. Because, listen, equality of the sexes just does not exist. What is equality of the sexes? We see it at home, the men sitting around doing nothing as if they have too much else to do."

Working women like Cinzia, Marta, and Paola were torn by the demands of work and home. It was worst for Cinzia, because she was also married. Paola and Marta were still living at home with their parents, so they did not have responsibility for running an entire household. None of the women had children, but they all desired to have them eventually, in spite of the fact that they believed having children would only increase the strains on them. Even without children, though, they suffered the conflicts of trying to do it all. They lamented openly the fact that their fiancés and brothers did nothing at home and hence were much freer—both materially and psychologically—than they. They complained that the men did not see the dirt or the mess and that they just were not taught to pick things up. The young women resented this psychological freedom of men from domestic duties and even recognized the role of women in perpetuating male nonchalance, yet they could not escape their own domestic obsession. The identity of the Florentine women depended on taking good care of the house; they and others judged them badly if they were slack in these chores. As Cinzia said, "If the bed is unmade at 9 P.M., be sure that it isn't a man who will notice it. The woman notices it, like my mother, or my husband's mother. They criticize it to you; it's you who look bad. Not him. That's why it bothers me, understand? And also, I sincerely don't like having the bed unmade, and after all, it's nothing—it only takes five minutes."

Here twenty-six-year-old Cinzia expressed the dilemma. As a woman, she had an image of herself as the perfect housewife. Although she knew it was impossible to be that and a working woman too, she could not free herself of the ideal she had grown up believing in. The same was true of thirty-nine-year-old Gigliola, in spite of her twenty years' residence in the United States, where definitions of women were more open. "It's really I myself who have to overcome this tradition that I have behind me," she said," trying to reconcile the role of mother, wife, and woman who wants to live a life." Even when a woman managed to gain some assistance from her husband in the home, she was not without ambivalence. Forty-eight-year-old Loretta had a grueling full-time job sewing pieces together in a factory, and her husband was retired. He shopped for food and cooked their meals but never washed dishes or did any of the other household chores. She was glad for the help, but at the same time, she said, "You feel a little excluded, you know, not doing the shopping and coming home and making dinner. It's only for convenience that he does it. But for other reasons, I'd feel better doing it. Going shopping, doing it all yourself, you feel like more of a woman."

Feeling like women also involved ensuring that their men acted like men, and that women and men had separate, complementary competencies rather than overlapping ones. Hence women themselves actively perpetuated male domestic incompetence, both in their husbands and in their sons, to solidify their own importance and indispensability. Sixty-six-year-old Elda explained how she would not let her husband help her bring wash in from her terrace in a rainstorm once, because "the neighbors could have seen him from the other windows," and she thought that "it would look bad to have him doing that thing." She made a telling statement when she said, "So as you can understand, the bias against men doing these chores begins with women as well."

Younger women lamented male domestic incompetence more vociferously than their elders, but they too recognized the role of women in perpetuating that incompetence. Twenty-year-old Paola lamented, "My brother doesn't lift a finger. He's worse than the majority of men. He's been badly raised, perhaps by my mother and me who are always picking up after him. Mom is always ready, always behind him doing the smallest tasks that he could easily do himself." Twenty-six-year-old Cinzia, who worked full-time and tried to run a household, most explicitly of all my informants recognized her difficult situation but also appeared most ambivalent. Speaking of her husband, she said,

> He works all day. He arrives home. Honestly, what am I going to say to him, "Help me fry a minute steak?" No, if I were cooking great meals, I would say, "Give me a hand," but to ask someone to help you make a minute steak, well it seems absurd. It's approaching the absurd. So I don't ask him to help me fry the steak. And then I'm the type who nobody satisfies the way I satisfy myself in doing the household chores. In fact, one time he washed the dishes, and afterwards I went to check on what he did, and he said, "That's it; I won't wash dishes for you any more." Because, he said, "There's no way to satisfy you." I'm very precise and he knows it. And he really did a good job. That is, knowing me, he tried to do his best, but he is just more imprecise by nature. You understand, it's also habit for men. They have been raised in a certain way.

The complicity of women in isolating men from domestic chores was clear in Cinzia's remarks, yet so was her frustration. She clung to the chores herself because doing them well was important to her sense of self, and yet she could not do them really well because she just did not have time.

Thus contemporary Florentine women were caught in a bind. They wanted to hold jobs and earn money, yet they felt incomplete and incompetent unless they were also perfect housewives, *brave massaie*. Yet once married, it was just not possible to carry out both responsibilities well, especially given the perfectionism of Italian house-cleaning standards and eating habits, with a large, multicourse meal at midday and an almost equally large one in the evening.

In fact, young women in contemporary Florence were far less competent in food provisioning and had far less control over the foods they ate than their mothers. Cinzia's mother and Paola's paternal grandmother (and later her father) prepared all meals for their families. The girls were totally freed of food-provisioning duties, something that was only possible due to the middle-class status of their own and many other Italian families during the Italian "economic miracle" of the 1960s and 1970s (Balbo 1976, 66). Cinzia and Paola continued their studies past middle school to achieve vocational diplomas—Paola as a business secretary, Cinzia as a nursery school teacher. Right after graduating they began to work. Hence neither has spent time around the home or received any training in shopping and cooking. Paola said that she does not know one cut of meat from another and would be helpless if she had to go shopping. "I am the desperation of my father," she said, when I asked her if she knew how to cook. "If I were home alone, I would cook, but if I had to put myself to cooking out of pure desire, I'd never do it." And Cinzia said, "I learned little about cooking in my mother's house, because when she was cooking, I didn't like to watch her; she was willing to teach me but I just wasn't interested. Anyways, I said I'd always have time to learn."

But that time slipped away, and Cinzia admitted that she did not even know how to make a *pomarola* sauce—the most basic tomato sauce for pasta and stews (see page 247 for recipe). "If my mother doesn't give me some, I buy it ready-made. It's too much work to make sauce for two people. It's easier to eat pasta with cream and ham." Here she indicated not only her lack of cooking knowledge, but her lack of time and the changes in diet that occurred as a result—pasta with cream and ham is an entirely new dish in the Tuscan food repertory (cf. Codacci 1981 and Costantini 1976).

Both Paola and Cinzia felt that they should know how to cook; both admitted that it was their responsibility and knew they could not expect their husbands to do it. Yet they just could not fit cooking into their lives. They were caught in a conflict to which, as Paola said, it would be "difficult to find a solution." Furthermore, the industrial food economy had taken over many of the food-processing chores that traditionally belonged to women, reducing the time necessary to put meals on the table but simultaneously limiting women's control over food content and meaning (Counihan 1981; L'industria alimentare 1978). Prepared and processed foods were increasingly available in *supermercati* as well as in neighborhood stores. People occasionally ate frozen and canned foods and dinners, like lasagne, fish sticks (*bastoncini di pesce*), and vegetable turnovers (*sofficini*). "Fast foods" were increasingly prevalent in urban centers. Lunch breaks were shrinking to an hour from the traditional two or three hours. People lacked time to go home to cook complex meals and thus ate in *pizzerie, spaghetterie, rosticcerie* "snack bars," and self-service cafeterias, as well as in more traditional *ristoranti* and *trattorie*.

Thus, although most people still ate most of their meals cooked at home by close female relatives, eating was increasingly becoming part of the money economy. It was less under the strict control of women and thus of declining importance in constituting female identity. A roast chicken bought from the corner *rosticceria*, a pizza at the neighborhood *pizzeria*, or cannelloni prepared by the multinational Kraft corporation were neither shaped by women nor representative of their creativity. Women were not in charge of the symbolic content or meaning of food. Foods increasingly represented not the values of home, family, and women, but the values of consumerism.

Women clearly felt ambivalence and conflict about their declining role in food provisioning. They wanted to control their family's foods, but did not have time because they also wanted to work. Cooking was still essential to femininity, but working women could not achieve the standards of their mothers. They ended up dissatisfied and at war with themselves, insecure about this part of their femininity. They suffered identity conflict and lacked the security of their mothers, who were more able to fulfill the roles they had internalized as necessary for themselves (Pitkin 1985, 15). Yet on the other hand, the definitive entry of modern Florentine women into the workplace introduced them to an economic power their mothers never had.

Often, their new role expectations brought young Florentine women into potential conflict with their mothers. For example, daughters appeared unwilling to share the total altruism of their mothers. As twenty-six-year-old Cinzia said, "It's just not right that life is like this, of sacrifice, always working. You can't do anything, because you don't have time to permit yourself to enjoy that thing or eat the other thing." Simultaneously their mothers' lives called into question their own choices. Fifty-year-old Vanna thought it wonderful that her daughter Cinzia worked full-time, and she willingly prepared meals daily for Cinzia and her husband; she still pointed out to her daughter, however, the unmade bed or the piles of unironed laundry. Cinzia felt her mother's disapproval at the same time as she was proud to be able to give her mother groceries and occasionally money, something made possible by the fact that she worked. Although the money in this case was part of a reciprocal exchange, use of money in this way was still rare among Florentines. They regularly exchanged gifts but rarely used money in exchanges other than market transactions, recognizing that it belonged to a separate sphere. Similarly, while Florentine women were increasingly likely to buy processed foods for themselves or their families, they considered these inappropriate for guests, reflecting their awareness that these processed foods were stripped of personal value and meaning. Most Florentine girls remained near to their mothers all their lives and identified closely with them. Yet the inevitable identity conflict young girls suffered due to their different choices perhaps led to psychological stress on them similar to what has been observed in American girls who reject their mothers' choices and opt for different lives and self-images (Chodorow 1974).

At the same time, contemporary working Florentine mothers lost input into the socialization of their own children. The full-time housewife had enormous influence over her offspring, for she was with them constantly. She exercised her influence largely through food, and often she encouraged them with the words *"Mangia che l'ha fatto mamma"*—"Eat, for Mother made it." Italian mothers regularly weighed their infants before and after nursing to make sure they had eaten enough, something U.S. mothers rarely did. Silverman reported this practice in rural Tuscany in 1961 and said that "most mothers take inordinate pride in weight gains" (1975, 188). The ingestion of food is in my opinion a metaphor and vehicle for the ingestion of parental—particularly maternal—culture. But food produced by multinational corporations much less directly embodies parental values than food produced in the home.

Florentine children were supposed to accept their parents' habits, opinions, values, and power along with their food. Working women who give up much of their food-provisioning responsibilities lose this influence. Their children are largely raised by others—sometimes by day-care centers, often by grandmothers—eating others' food and internalizing others' values. To be sure, in the Tuscan extended families of the past, mothers sometimes shared child rearing with other adults, but all belonged to one family and household where the mothers' influence predominated (Silverman 1975; Pitkin 1985, 10–13). But today in urban Florence the other adults raising children generally belong to other nuclear families and live far away (due to neolocality and the difficulty of finding housing). Thus the mothers who work outside the home have less influence on their children's lives, and the children are less dependent on them.

Cinzia expressed the dismay of working women by referring to her sister-in-law, whose only child spent weekdays from 7 A.M. to 7 P.M. with his grandmother. When Cinzia asked if she was going to have another child, the sister-in-law responded, *"Chi me lo fa fare?"*—"Why in the world would I do it?" She felt it made no sense to have another child only to leave him with her mother all day. Commenting on the professionalization of child care through the expansion of day-care centers in Italy, Saraceno said that mothers have "lost their monopoly not only on responsibility but also on control and power in defining and satisfying their children's needs" (1984, 18–19). This loss attacked the Italian mother's sense of self, for she believed that her children should be dependent on her and that she should do everything for them.

CONCLUSION

Florentine women responded to changes in Italian society and economy by entering the workforce, yet they were still subordinate there to men in pay, access to jobs, and status. Their very position as workers, however, brought them some status, potential equality with men, and the ability to earn and dispose of their own money—things of increasing importance to their sense of self and their independence.

However, their new role, despite its possibility of economic power, brought them conflict and a loss of their traditional influence. They were at odds, either explicitly or implicitly, with their mothers over the different ideal of female behavior that they personified. They lost some control and socializing power over their children. Their inability to fulfill both traditional and new role expectations caused them to suffer frustration and self-dissatisfaction amounting to psychological confusion and insecurity.

The difficult position of women can only change if society changes. Alterations in the organization of meals and standards of cleanliness would allow women more slack in the performance of these duties. Greater expectations for male participation in domestic chores would relieve women of having to bear the exclusive burden in this domain. Yet among my informants, there was little evidence that these things were happening or that either men or women were working to make them happen. Young women did not seem to be raising their sons in ways that were substantially different from how their mothers raised their brothers. Although my young informants decried the lack of domestic help they attained from brothers and husbands, they did not seem psychologically prepared to ask for more from their own sons, though this remains to be seen.

Italians could agitate politically for more public assistance to reduce the burden on women. During the 1960s and 1970s there was progress in this regard—universal mandatory paid maternity leave, for example—but the government economic crisis of the late 1970s led to halts and cutbacks (Sgritta 1983; Saraceno 1984). Day-care centers have proliferated, though as Saraceno (1984) noted, the staff was preponderantly female, reflecting Italian society's attribution of nurturing activities to women. Women could renounce wage work and devote themselves entirely to the home, but the strength of the feminist movement and the increasingly consumerist orientation of Italian society mandate against the likelihood of this happening. In the meantime, Florentine women struggle in what is not an easy situation and continue to rely on the inner resources that have sustained them for generations.

Florentine women and many others like them in cities around the globe are making gradual and incomplete inroads into the spheres of political and economic power traditionally controlled by men. Because of the demands of salaried work, however, women are contributing increasingly less to the care and feeding of relatives and children. Thus they are losing an important source of their traditional prestige and influence and are joining a world where coercion predominates as a means of getting people to act in desired ways at the expense of the gentler means of influence and obligation. Women are losing the manipulative power of food, and perhaps the world is losing it as well.

4

Food, Sex, and Reproduction

Penetration of Gender Boundaries[1]

INTRODUCTION

Beliefs about men's and women's roles in eating, copulation, and reproduction reveal deep-seated ideas about men's and women's identities
and relationships. Because these activities all involve male and female
interconnection and passage of body boundaries, they symbolically
represent not only gender roles and relations, but also beliefs about
individual autonomy, self-definition, and self-control. This essay will
contrast views about the body and its alimentary and sexual functions
prevalent in Western, stratified, industrial societies with those of some
tribal societies in the Amazon and New Guinea to point out how
Western notions are inextricably tied to beliefs about male dominance
and female subordination.

In the nonstratified tribal societies of New Guniea and the Amazon
that I examine here, men and women are linked politically, economically, and socially in complementary opposition. They perceive their
bodies as permeable and subject to both salutory and harmful influences of the opposite sex through food and copulation. This reciprocal
permeability contributes to an uneasy opposition and equilibrium
between the sexes where men both recognize and struggle against
women's important roles in providing food and babies, even as they
try to control these activities through economic, symbolic, and social
means.

But in the patriarchal, stratified United States, men and women
hold the views that their bodies are not reciprocally permeable and that
women's bodies are more vulnerable than men's. These views contribute to and stand for the hierarchical relationship between men and
women, symbolically and physically expressed in the Western cult of
thinness. This cult is most mercilessly directed at and espoused by

women. It involves the negation or "reducing" of the self through abstinence from food and reaches its extreme form in the life-threatening
disorder of anorexia nervosa. Anorexic women refuse bodily penetration through food and often sex and voluntarily starve themselves,
sometimes to death, in an effort to achieve autonomy, control, and
power.[2] That Western women strive for power and identity through
closing off the body and denying their own physicality and penetrabil-
ity is a clear statement that their bodies are source and symbol of their
subordination (Jacobus, Keller, and Shuttleworth 1990).

I will clarify these arguments in this chapter by discussing the significance of body boundaries and the meaning of eating, intercourse, and
birth for men and women. I will compare cultural conceptions prevalent in the United States with those of some tribal societies in New
Guinea and the Amazon on which there are good ethnographic data
available.[3] For New Guinea, I will principally cite the work of Anna
Meigs (1984) on the Hua, Gilbert Herdt (1987) on the Sambia, and
Miriam Kahn (1986) on the Wamira; for the Amazon, I will refer
mainly to the work of Thomas Gregor (1985) on the Mehinaku and
Yolanda and Robert Murphy (1985) on the Mundurucú. The cross-cultural data underscore some salient features of Western belief that connect gender inequality with cultural attitudes about eating and
reproduction, especially as they involve the penetration and vulnerability of the female body.

FOOD, SEX, REPRODUCTION, AND BODY BOUNDARIES

I focus on the body in this chapter because it can represent both the
social order and the self (Douglas 1966, 115–22). The boundaries of the
body can symbolize the separateness of the self from others and from
the external world. As Freud noted (1962, 57), the recognition of
boundaries between child and mother is the first step in self-differenti-
ation and maturation of the infant. The body's margins can stand for
the wholeness of the self and its potential for influence, nurturance, or
harm. Penetration of the body through eating or intercourse, while
essential to life and growth, can also involve challenges to personal
integrity (Kahn 1986, 61–62). Study of cultural notions about male and
female bodies and their boundaries—with particular attention to the
role of food, sex and birth in crossing those boundaries—can reveal
much about a society's beliefs about men's and women's relationships,
autonomy, and vulnerability.

In many cultures there are associations between eating, intercourse,
and reproduction.[4] These activities share certain biopsychological
attributes that endow them with metaphorical and symbolic identity—

particularly their contributions to life and growth, their passing through body boundaries, and their mingling of discrete individuals. In many cultures these activities involve and demonstrate clear gender distinctions. Moreover, for women, food and reproduction are particularly emblematic activities, universally associated with femaleness.

Food and sex are analogous instinctive needs (Freud 1962, 1), and there is a lifelong connection between oral pleasure and sexual pleasure (Freud 1962, 43). Food and sex are metaphorically overlapping. Gifts of food may represent offers of sex, and sex may be described through food images. Eating together connotes intimacy, often sexual intimacy or kinship (Freud 1918, 175; Siskind 1973, 9). Both eating and copulation produce social merging.

Precisely because eating and intercourse involve intimacy, they can be dangerous when carried out with the wrong person or under the wrong conditions. Hence food and sex are surrounded with rules and taboos that both regulate their use and reinforce beliefs basic to the social order, most notably beliefs associated with gender (Meigs 1985). Food and sex both have associated etiquette about their appropriate times, places, and persons; often people with whom one can eat are those with whom one can have sex and vice versa (Tambiah 1969). Maleness and femaleness in all cultures are defined through specific foods and the rules governing their consumption (Meigs 1984; Brumberg 1988; Frese 1989).

In general the association between food and sex is deeper, more extensive, and more intimate for women than it is for men: In all cultures, women's primary responsibilities involve food provisioning and the bearing and rearing of children (D'Andrade 1974; Moore 1988). Women *are* food to the fetus and infant, and the breasts can be sources of both sexual pleasure and food. Although women's feeding activities are undertaken with widely ranging amounts of autonomy, prestige, and control, they are nonetheless universally linked to womanhood, even in our own culture where many individual women neither cook nor have children. As Mead noted, for women but not for men both food and sex involve a posture of inception: "The girl finds that the reinterpretation of impregnation and conception and birth fits easily into her early experience with the intake of food" (1967, 143). This means that when women feel personally and socially devalued and vulnerable, as they may in highly gender-stratified Western societies, alimentary and sexual acts may be analogously threatening to their body boundaries and sense of identity. However, in societies with more equality between the sexes, the passing of food and sexual substances across the body may be dangerous and/or empowering to both sexes.

GENDER, SEX, AND REPRODUCTION:
COMPLEMENTARITY AND BOUNDARIES

Conceptions of bodily interpenetrability in tribal societies are associated with political, economic, social, and ideological balance between
the genders. Tribal societies are characterized by sexual separation into
"two worlds—one male and one female—each consisting of a system of
meanings and a program for behavior. . . . Sexual inequality is irrelevant in societies where the two worlds are balanced. Sexual inequality
becomes relevant when one world expands and the other fades away"
(Sanday 1981, 109–10). This is the case for stratified Western societies
where the male world has taken ideological, economic, and political
priority and the female world has "faded away" in value and significance. This is a situation ripe for male dominance, which is associated
with devaluation of female activities of nurturing and reproduction;
one-way bodily permeability; and female self-abnegation through
refusal of food, sexuality, and reproductive potential. Let me argue
these points by examining practices and beliefs surrounding male and
female roles in food provisioning and sex in the United States and in
tribal cultures of New Guinea and the Amazon.

The Economic and Political Sphere

In tribal societies, there is a clear division of labor by sex whereby both
men's and women's activites are essential (D'Andrade 1974). Men and
women work for the most part separately and autonomously, contributing different and essential goods to the family and group. In the
Mehinaku, for example, men fish, hunt, clear gardens, make arrows
and baskets, and occasionally care for their own children. They work in
subsistence activities approximately three and one-half hours per day.
Women garden, process manioc (which is an extremely time-consum-
ing and laborious activity), carry firewood and water, care for children,
make hammocks, and spin cotton. Their subsistence activities take
seven to nine hours each day (Gregor 1985, 24). According to Gregor,
men and women accept each other's different skills, strengths, and abilities. They recognize and respect women's long hours and the importance of their contribution to subsistence, and they acknowledge that
men's superior strength and fierceness is crucial for hunting and fishing. Access to society's full range of foods and services depends on a
marital partnership and on the giving and receiving between men and
women (see also Pollock 1985).

Among tribal societies, male political dominance is evidenced in
their control of public rituals, myth, warfare, and decisions affecting
the group. However, in both the Amazon and in New Guinea, there is
evidence that although the men are firmly convinced of their domi-

nance, they recognize its fragility. Many tribes of the Amazon and New Guinea (Meigs 1984:45) have myths that describe how women held power in ancient times but had it seized from them by men, through men's control of hunting, through physical and sexual violence, or through women's lack of crucial knowledge (see, e.g., Bamberger 1974; Murphy and Murphy 1985, 114–18; Gregor 1985, 112–13; Meigs 1984, 45). These myths imply that male dominance is not an inevitable fact of nature, but rather is a result of the structure of society and thus can be changed.

In Western industrial societies we find a different situation in politics and economics, one where complementarity between the sexes is not nearly so pronounced. In economic activity, there is a situation of dominance and subordination where males hold the most prestigious, high-paying, and interesting jobs. Female work, although essential to both the family and the economy, is trivialized through low or no pay. Food provisioning, still principally the domain of women, is not highly valued and in many families is subject to the monetary control and decision-making power of men, thereby reproducing female subservience (Charles and Kerr 1988; DeVault 1991). The sexes are separated in work, but they are separated vertically, into high and low, whereas in tribal societies their separation is horizontal and based on unity and respective autonomy.

In Western politics, we also witness a clear situation of dominance and subordination that is upheld by an absolutist ideology of male biological superiority and female biological unsuitability for power (Murphy and Murphy 1985, 116; Bleier 1984; Fausto-Sterling 1985). Although the Amazonian myth is part of the Greco-Roman tradition, our contemporary ideology lacks any beliefs that women might once have held power and thus might hold it once again.

I believe that the sexually complementary political and economic situation of tribal societies is associated with a mutuality in influence marked by beliefs about interpenetrable body boundaries and that the dominance-subordination relations of men and women in U.S. politics and economy accompany a belief in one-way bodily influences. I will illustrate these claims by considering beliefs and practices associated with sex, birth, and nurturance and their connection to conceptions of men and women and their relationships.

Sex and Reproduction

Gregor (1985, 3) makes the debatable claim that a cultural universal of sexual practice is the greater desire for and interest in copulation on the part of men in general over women in general. This, he suggests, is accompanied by widespread cultural practices that define men as the intiators in sex. This is generally the case in the U.S., New Guinean, and Amazonian cultures under scrutiny. However, there is much variation and complexity of sexual behavior related to beliefs about who does what to whom in sexual relations. In the United States we would perhaps agree with Verdier's generalization that in spite of all kinds of personal variations, cultural expectations define men as active in sex, and women as passive (1969). We tend to view "man as sexual consumer, woman as consumed object" (Ferguson 1989, 118). Women have sex done to them, receive semen, and get pregnant, while men do sex, ejacualate semen, and impregnate. The male processes are active and superior, the female passive and inferior (Martin 1989).

In many tribal societies, however, especially in New Guinea, there is a clear sense that not only do women receive semen through male penetration in sex, but that women penetrate men with powerful doses of masculinity-threatening female essence. Hence, in New Guinea, we observe a variety of strategies to reduce male contamination in sex, including infrequent heterosexual sex, preference for homosexual intercourse (practiced by at least thirty societies in the Pacific and the Amazon [Herdt 1987, 201]), and consumption of foods to replenish the male essence lost in ejaculation and to counteract the pollution from females. The Hua, for example, eat sugarcane to replenish semen (Meigs 1984, 79), while the Sambia eat the white sap of a certain tree (Herdt 1987, 164). The fear of contamination by female substances appears to be related to men's fragile gender identity and their fear of being swallowed up by the woman in intercourse, back into the womb from which they issued and back to a state of dependence and symbiosis that is the negation of adult masculinity (Gregor 1985, 182–83; Herdt 1987; Murphy and Murphy 1985). As Gregor says of the Mehinaku, "What was so highly prized in early childhood as warmth and closeness is feared in adulthood as a crushing attack. The path back to maternal symbiosis is closed; the memories of union with the mother are tinged with fearful meaning. Temptations of sexuality arouse fears of a destroying and negating parent, a mother who smothers and crushes her son's efforts to be a man" (1985, 183).

U.S. men may also fear contamination by women, but in adulthood it does not appear to be explicitly linked to contagion from female foods and sexual substances. Children sometimes fear getting "cooties" from the touch of a member of the opposite sex, but in adults this fear of physical pollution is absent, replaced by symbolic forms. For example, men may fear spending too much time with women or in feminine activities, as this might threaten their masculinity. Fear of being a sissy is deep-seated and probably reflects concerns similar to those of the Mehinaku about the fragility of male gender identity (Chodorow 1974).

However, although distaste for menstrual blood is widespread (Delaney, Lipton, and Toth 1988), in the United States men do not seem to fear that the incorporation of female foods or sexual excretions will dilute their masculinity. In Western culture male bodies are relatively impermeable; female bodies are vulnerable, particularly to rape.[5]

Ideas about male and female roles in reproduction in tribal societies, like those about copulation, reveal much more complementarity than in the United States. This is perhaps related to the fact that reproduction is so important and so obvious in tribal societies, whereas in the United States, although valued in rhetoric, it is relatively devalued, invisible, and trivialized by cultural practice (Martin 1989; Mead 1967, 87; Rich 1986). The low value on reproduction in Western society is related to the fact that in advanced industrial societies, labor is a relatively undesired commodity, infant mortality is relatively low, and children are extremely expensive; in labor-intensive tribal horticultural economies, in contrast, children and reproduction are valued because of children's labor contribution and high infant mortality. The relatively low U.S. birth rate, the lack of publically funded day care, the miserable pay standards for child-care workers, and the cultural value on monetary compensation as the measure of value all contribute to and demonstrate our cultural devaluation of bearing and raising children, which both results from and contributes to the subordinate position of women (Pollitt 1990).

In the United States, scientific knowledge establishes the equality of male and female roles in conception and in the genetic makeup of the fetus. However, men's social role largely ends at conception. Responsibility for the health of the fetus belongs totally to the mother. There have even been court cases directed at women who fail to fulfill what patriarchal law defines as "proper" sexual and nutritional behavior—at women, for example, who have sex when subject to miscarriage, or who drink or take drugs (Bordo 1993; Pollitt 1990). There is no notion of a continuous, ongoing paternal role in nourishing the fetus through specific feeding, copulating, or nurturing activities as there is in so many tribal societies like the New Guinea Arapesh (Mead 1963). In fact, Pollitt (1990) notes that husbands who take drugs or drink with their pregnant wives are immune from legal sanctions, while their wives can be prosecuted.

In tribal societies there exist a variety of ideas about the roles of men and women in conception and gestation, but often the male role is defined as predominant and/or essential throughout the pregnancy. Even the Trobriand Islanders, who deny any paternal role in conception, recognize the importance of continued injections of male semen to the gestation of the fetus (Malinowski 1927). The Mundurucú

(Murphy and Murphy 1985, 128) and Mehinaku share the belief that "the infant is formed through repeated acts of intercourse that accumulate enough semen to form the baby. . . . The baby is almost entirely a male product" (Gregor 1985, 89). As one of Gregor's male informants said, "We are our former food, our father's semen" (1985, 90). Interestingly, the Mehinaku recognize women's specific role in reproduction through their belief that men are able to make semen only through the consumption of food produced by females (principally manioc), which is then returned to the female body through intercourse: Women give men food to make semen that men return to women to make the fetus. Clearly, both male and female roles are complementary and essential throughout gestation, not just in the act of conception (1985, 91). Similarly for the Sambia, "The male and female parts in reproduction are clearly defined" (Herdt 1987, 76). Male semen enters the womb and eventually forms fetal skin and bone tissue, whereas the mother's blood eventually becomes the fetus's circulatory blood (see also Mead 1963, 31; Meigs 1984, 51–52; Kahn 1986).

In the United States the total responsibility of women for gestation and birth is countered by men's appropriation of the female reproductive experience through the patriarchal medical and scientific establishment. Many feminists have argued that male doctors use anesthetics, the flat-on-the-back birthing position, stirrups, fetal monitors, and cesarean sections to control birth and to reduce women's power over their reproductive experience, a power they have only recently begun to seize back against much medical resistance (Boston Women's Health Book Collective 1984; Davis-Floyd 1992; Martin 1989; Oakley 1980, 1984; Rich 1986; Rothman 1982, 1989; Treichler 1990). Again we seen a nonreciprocal gender system: It is women's responsibility to control gestation but it is men's job to control women and their births (Pollitt 1990). Adrienne Rich argues that across all class, race, and ethnic groups, men's control of women's reproduction—including contraception, abortion, fertility, sterilization, and birth—is "essential to the patriarchal system" (1986, 34).

In some tribal societies, however, a different theory and practice of birth has evolved, one that involves both men and women. In fact, fathers of newborn children may be subject to even stronger postpartum taboos than mothers (Mead 1963, 35). Among the Mehinaku, for example, new fathers are enjoined both from having sexual relations and from eating certain foods; illness of the child is attributed to paternal infringement of either of these taboos (Gregor 1985, 74, 194–95).

Often in tribal societies men express symbolic emulation and envy of the female power of birth through rituals that establish male participation in reproduction. One such ritual is the couvade. Quite common in

South America, it involves a father's imitation "of some of the behavior of his wife at the time of childbirth," including her birth pains, postpartum seclusion, food restrictions, and sex taboos (Gregor 1985, 194). The couvade has long been thought to be evidence of men's envy and imitation of women's reproductive activities due to "high female saliency in the lives of young boys ... producing conflicts in males' sex identity" (Munroe and Munroe 1989, 730; see also Bettelheim 1962; Munroe, Munroe, and Whiting 1973). A more recent theory of the couvade, however, suggests that it is associated with "father-salience" and is most likely to occur in societies where men's role in child rearing is greatest (Broude 1988, 1989). Furthermore, "couvade-like practices are devices for minimizing sex differences in societies where sex roles are relatively flexible and female power and status are high" (Broude 1988, 910; Zelman 1977). The couvade may serve to establish fathers' role in their children's lives and to balance male-female parental roles. According to Gregor, "The most striking feature of Mehinaku couvade symbolism ... is the feminine nature of a father's connection to his offspring" (1985, 195). Again we witness the complementary and interrelated roles of men and women in reproduction in some tribal societies where the sexes are relatively equal.

Another ritualistic behavior that demonstrates male emulation of female reproductive powers is what Delaney, Lupton, and Toth call the *saignade*, ritual bleeding in emulation of menstruation (1988, 261–66). Although menstrual blood is almost universally feared, it is also believed to carry great power and in some cultures to be a source of women's superior health and rapid growth (Meigs 1984). Hence, men often simulate menstruation in themselves or in boys undergoing initiation by ritual bloodletting. Gregor states the beliefs of the Mehinaku thus: "For the Mehinaku, menstruation is the most anxiety-charged of the physiological characteristics of women. Caused by deadly fauna living in the vagina, menstrual blood is associated with wounds, castration, poison, disease, stunted growth, and enfeeblement. Yet there are a number of occasions in which the men symbolically menstruate, the most significant of which is the ritual of ear piercing" (Gregor 1985, 186).

For the Sambia of Highland New Guinea, "blood is identified ... with the vitality and longevity of women and their femaleness" (Herdt 1987, 76). To grant men similar health and longevity, Sambia adult males perform a brutal and painful ritual of nose-bleeding on young boys during their initiation ceremony. "The ritual bleeding amounts to a forcible penetration of the boy's body boundaries" in a highly symbolic way, for the nose is a strong component of Sambian self-image, beauty, and masculinity (Herdt 1987, 139). Not only is nose-bleeding

an emulation of menstruation, but it also serves to free men of contamination from their wives' menstrual blood and is performed on a
monthly basis after marriage (Herdt 1987, 164–65). Nose-bleeding
serves symbolically to eradicate femininity, represented as blood, from
boys. "Nose-bleeding violates one's body boundaries in order for the
whole self to be reclaimed as exclusively male by the ritual cult" (Herdt
1987, 185). In this ritual, then, we see several components relevant to
our argument: the permeability of male body boundaries to female
influences, men's fear of those influences, and men's emulation of
female processes to rid themselves of female contamination. Sambians
symbolically make similar male and female bloodletting and thus
demonstrate men's and women's interpenetrability, complementarity,
and symmetry.

An even more explicit example of male emulation of female reproductive power is shown in cultures where men believe they can become
pregnant, give birth to, and/or nurture palpable cultural "children."
Kahn reports that Wamiran men grow taro as "the ritual creation of
their own 'children'" and thus demonstrate their "appropriation and
imitation of female powers of reproduction" (1986, 90–91). Meigs
claims that "Hua males believe that they can become pregnant" but are
unable to give birth and will die from a ruptured abdomen unless their
condition is counteracted (1984, 46, 52). Meigs also notes, interestingly,
that Hua believe that male pregnancy has three causes, all associated
with contamination by female substances: Men get pregnant from "eating a food that has been touched or stepped over by a menstruating
woman or a woman newly married into the community" (52); from
eating possum, "the counterpart of women" (53); and from sorcery
involving ingestion of food soaked in menstrual blood (52–53). Male
substances produce constructive female pregnancy, and female substances produce destructive male pregnancy.

A final example of male participation in reproduction in tribal societies are secret male initiation rituals that express the belief that
"women, it is true, make human beings, but only men can make men"
(Mead 1967, 103). These rituals occur among the Sambia, the Hua, the
Mehinaku, and the Mundurucú as well as in a host of other Amazonian
and New Guinean societies.[6] They involve the separation of boys from
their mothers, their seclusion, their subjection to harrowing physical
and mental stress, their introduction to secret rituals and lore, and
their transformation into men (Herdt 1987, 101–69). Often, the process
of transformation involves rituals structured around food and sex: the
ingestion and avoidance of certain foods; abstention from intercourse;
and purging the body of female sexual substances, such as through the
nose-bleeding of the Sambia and the ear-piercing of the Mehinaku.

In New Guinea, male initiation sometimes involves the ingestion of male semen or substances representing it. Herdt has explicitly documented this practice for the Sambia, who believe that the long-term ingestion of semen by young boys through homosexual fellatio of older youths is absolutely essential to their physical and psychological development as men (1987; see also Kelly 1976). Such ritual beliefs clearly indicate the complementarity of men and women in making human beings; while women give birth to children and socialize daughters, men make men and do so through explicit manipulations of their permeable bodies. Although men in the United States perhaps also believe that "only men can make men," their role in child rearing is generally so minimal and exceptional that in practice it is up to women to make both men and women. Complex identity issues are implicated that I will now address.

GENDER IDENTITY AND BOUNDARIES

Researchers like Chodorow (1974, 1978), Dinnerstein (1977), Gilligan (1981), and Rubin (1983) have suggested that boys and girls undergo different psychological and personality development due to the fact that women are the primary parent during infancy. Boys have to break with their first figure of identification to become men, and hence they construct rigid boundaries to the self through severing themselves from the mother and from feminine influences. They tend to be independent and fearful of both intimacy and women (Gilligan 1981; Rubin 1983). "The attainment of masculine gender identity ... involves the repression and devaluation of femininity on both psychological and cultural levels" (Chodorow 1974, 51).

But girls have an enduring close relation to and identification with the primary love object, the mother, and hence have strong gender identity, but "flexible ego boundaries" (Chodorow 1974, 57). While they have little trouble with their sense of self as woman, they have difficulty knowing where the self begins and ends; this dilemma is exacerbated when the girl herself becomes a mother and is bonded to her child first in utero and later through breast-feeding. Furthermore, "a mother is more likely to identify with a daughter than with a son, to experience her daughter (or parts of her daughter's life) as herself" (Chodorow 1974, 47) which means that the daughter has "particular problems about differentiation from [the] mother" (Chodorow 1974, 59).

While for boys, then, the attainment of a secure sense of masculinity is difficult, for girls the most problematic issue in maturation is separating from the mother and establishing the firm ego boundaries that constitute a clear sense of independence and of their own identity as separate from that of mother and children. In Western society there is a premium on developing this independence; women's self-definition in relational terms has been a cause and justification for their subordination (Gilligan 1981). Interestingly, women's struggle to establish a firm and separate sense of self is complicated by the fact that their "biosexual experiences (menstruation, coitus, pregnancy, childbirth, lactation) all involve some challenges to the boundaries of ... body ego" (Chodorow 1974, 59). These experiences of bodily penetration, like eating, can constitute threats to the psychological integrity of the self. This may be particularly difficult for the Western woman whose "tenuous sense of individuation and of the firmness of her ego boundaries increases the likelihood that experiences challenging these boundaries will be difficult for her and conflictive" (Chodorow 1974, 60).

There is evidence, however, that men's bodily—and by extension ego—boundaries are more penetrable in the tribal societies under consideration than is described for Western men. This, I suggest, makes them more susceptible to female influences and less able to separate from women in a stance of simple domination. Furthermore, the very permeability of women's bodies is a source not only of vulnerability, but also of mystery and power.

Because of boys' early identification with the mother, all cultures face the challenge of promoting boys' identification with men, principally their fathers or father figures. It appears that in the New Guinean and Amazonian tribal societies under consideration men are available to boys and take an active role in their socialization. They provide explicit channels through myth and ritual to express male hostility to, difference from, and superiority to women, but all within a context of interconnection to women, and with underlying notions of male vulnerability; all this is manifest in the symbolic language of sexual and alimentary interpenetrability. In the United States, the channels to boys' male identification are less formalized and fathers are more distant, hence there seems to be a more thorough separation from and dominance over women, that is manifest in the permeability of women and the impermeability of men.

In tribal societies, as we have already noted, men believe that women are subordinate but powerful and men are dominant but vulnerable. In fact, Gregor, Herdt, Kahn, Meigs, and the Murphys all conclude that the identity of the males in the Amazonian and New Guinean societies they studied is fragile, whereas women—although perhaps imbued with cultural notions of their own pollution or inferiority—have a psychological confidence in their identity and power as women. Kahn suggests that because in Wamira "women are natural creators of society" whereas "men create society symbolically ...," women's reproductive identities and statuses are more substantive and tangible, and thus less vulnerable, than those of men, which rest precariously on extrinsic powers and factors.... Secure in the knowledge of their naturally endowed reproductive powers, women, unlike men, do not need to shout out their abilities in symbolic ways. What appears as passivity, can be interpreted as confidence" (1986, 124).

Herdt concludes of the Sambia of New Guinea that "at rock bottom men regard femaleness as more powerful than maleness" (1987, 193). Men envy women's power and emulate it through their secret ritual identity, which "must be kept hidden to keep women politically inferior, and it must be carefully controlled in oneself to keep being fierce.... The men imitate [women's] *natural* creativity through their *cultural* creations.... Male mythology thus hints that women have more real power in everyday life than the men say" (1987, 193–94).

Meigs (1984) believes that Hua males hold an "attitude of reproductive impotence and sexual inferiority" (31) and that much of their ritual life involves a "quest by politically dominant males for access to and control of the physiological powers belonging to their political subordinates" that is, women (136).

Murphy and Murphy say of the Mundurucú, "The status of the Mundurucú woman is quite high when compared with women in other societies. What she lacks in public prestige and respect is more than balanced by autonomy and collective strength" (1986, 251). "Mundurucú men are, in a way, the overlords of the women, but it is a suzerainty born of overcompensation for weakness and fear" (256). Gregor, too, finds in the Mehinaku men weakness and insecurity about their identity which, he believes, are not restricted to them alone. "Between us and the Mehinaku there remains the common bond of masculine gender with all of its uncertainty and ambivalence" (1985, 210).

Gregor suggests that the fragility of masculinity in the United States is similar to that of men in tribal societies and is demonstrated by exclusionary men's clubs and fraternal organizations; anxiety over menstruation; and hostility toward women evinced through violence, rape and sexual joking (1985, 200–10). Yet I am arguing that our culture defines men's bodies, and hence their persons, as much less vulnerable and permeable than women's, and that this is part of a more extreme situation of gender dominance and subordination in our culture than in those of the tribal societies we have been examining. I argue, following Chodorow (1974, 60), that for U.S. women the permeability of their bodies represents their weak sense of automony and power, and that as a result the acts of eating, copulation, or birth—which cross the physical barriers of the body—can constitute terrifying threats to the psychological integrity of the self.

Western women's pursuit of extreme thinness and their refusal to eat can be seen as a reaction to their perceived bodily vulnerability and permeable boundaries, for these acts involve closing off the self not only to food, but usually to sex and birth as well. Women's obsession with severe food restriction and thinness is a phenomenon associated with Western-style bourgeois capitalist society (Bordo 1993; Brumberg 1988; Chernin 1981; Schwartz 1986). While thinness and sparse eating are valued in some tribal societies (Young 1986), never to my knowledge do tribal peoples voluntarily starve themselves in the midst of plenty solely to achieve a thin body (see chapter 6, Messer 1989). To U.S. women, a slim body they fast to attain symbolizes not only "qualities—detachment, self-containment, self-mastery, control—that are highly valued in our culture," but also "freedom from a reproductive destiny and a construction of femininity seen as constraining and suffocating" (Bordo 1990, 105).

Many U.S. women choose food as a channel for self-expression both because its restriction is a central cultural obsession and because it may be the only thing women feel they fully control and can manage without threatening the power structure (see chapters 5 and 6; Brumberg 1988; Orbach 1978). Abstinence from food has been valued in the ideology of Western culture for at least eight centuries (Bell 1985; Brumberg 1988; Bynum 1986). It shows self-control, dominance of mind over body, and regulation of the permeable boundaries that stand for the threatened self; it produces a desired state of thinness that is associated with perfection; and it gives a sense of accomplishment (Bruch 1978; Brumberg 1988).

Women's feelings of threat from outside forces, their attempts to close their body to food and sex, and their denial of female sexuality and reproduction reach an extreme in anorexia nervosa, "voluntary self-starvation in pursuit of excessive thinness" (Bruch 1978, ix). Anorexics are women with a particularly weak sense of self, autonomy, effectiveness, or power—in effect, their ego boundaries are so permeable as to be almost nonexistent (Bruch 1973, 1978; Brumberg 1988; Palazzoli 1971). Refusal to eat signifies rejecting the passage of any object, contact, or relationship across the margins of the self; it is a desperate attempt to close the boundaries to the ego and complete the self. The Freudians Waller, Kaufman, and Deutsch (1940) have suggested that anorexics' food refusal represents a fear of oral impregnation. Although this does not appear to be literally true in most cases, it is suggestive. We can interpret women's food refusal more broadly as a "fear ... of being invaded by the object" (Palazzoli 1971, 205), as a refusal of outside forces impinging on, penetrating, and threatening the self.

For many anorexics, menstruation ceases, womanly curves disappear, and men and sex are despised. Rejection of food parallels and is associated with rejection of sex and fertility. Thoma demonstrates this rejection by citing the reaction of a patient of his who had observed a boy and girl eating from the same piece of bread: "The patient regarded this act as an intimate and disgusting form of intercourse. In her associations, she centered upon receptivity, and the chain of her thoughts was as follows: 'Bottle—child—disgust, if I think of it—injections—the idea that there is something flowing into me, into my mouth or into the vagina, is maddening—integer, integra, integrum occurs to me—untouchable—males cannot be touched as females—a man is untouched—he does not have to bear a child—a man is what he is—he need not receive and he need not give'" (1977, 444–45).

Anorexics express in extreme form issues common to many women in Western society (Bordo 1993; Brumberg 1988; Gordon 1988, 1990). They deny receptivity, connection, and reproduction; they negate fundamental attributes of their female selves while striving to achieve some value in the eyes of their culture. Sadly, though, they often end up annihilating themselves completely in death. They evince a bind common to all women in patriarchal societies whose permeable ego boundaries become a threat to their integrity and identity.

Perhaps we can learn from the Mayan women studied by Lois Paul for whom the permeable body boundary "implies not only vulnerability to dangers but a sense of union with transcendent powers that are the sources of life as well as death" (1974, 299). In other words, we need to establish a world where the reciprocal interpenetrability of men and women is recognized and linked with our interdependence, as it is in tribal societies. We need to work for political, economic, social, and sexual complementarity and union between men and women. We need to establish a world where women's permeability to food, sex, and birth is not a threat to their autonomy and integrity, but a manifestation of their uniqueness and power.

5

What Does It Mean to Be Fat, Thin, and Female?

A Review Essay[1]

Boskind-White, Marlene, and William C. White. 1983. *Bulimarexia: The Binge/Purge Cycle.* New York: Norton.

Bruch, Hilde. 1978. *The Golden Cage: The Enigma of Anorexia Nervosa.* New York: Vintage.

Chernin, Kim. 1981. *The Obsession: Reflections on the Tyranny of Slenderness.* New York: Harper & Row.

Millman, Marcia. 1980. *Such a Pretty Face: Being Fat in America.* New York: Norton.

Orbach, Susie. 1978. *Fat Is a Feminist Issue: The Anti-Diet Guide to Permanent Weight Loss.* New York: Paddington.

The five books under review address what it means for women to be fat and thin in contemporary North America. They discuss in its extreme forms women's obsession with food: the compulsive eating of obesity,[2] the self-starvation of anorexia nervosa, and the oscillating binging and purging of bulimarexia. All of these books are about women and with the exception of one co-author, all are written by women. They are all feminist in that they link women's obsession with eating to broader social, political, and economic forces affecting women in twentieth-century North America. They concur that the problematic relationship between women and food is invariably linked to women's difficulty in being women—to their feelings of powerlessness and sexual ambivalence—although they stress different forces in accounting for that difficulty. Forces they propose include the contradictory expectations of families for girls; the objectification of women and the degradation of their sexuality; the institutionalized cultural, political, and economic powerlessness of women; and the cultural slighting of female experience and female values. An excessive concern with food is a product of and response to these important factors in American women's lives.

THE BOOKS

All five volumes provide social-psychological analyses of women's obsession with fat. They are compellingly and vibrantly written, easy to read and fascinating. The authors present their insights in a clear and organized manner and support them with extensive quotations from female subjects. The books express a humanistic sensitivity to women tormented by obsessive thoughts of food, starvation or gorging; and caught in a vicious cycle of guilt, self-loathing, and despair. At the same time, the books are convincing; their data and arguments speak strongly.

Chernin's book ranges the most broadly of the five. Her insights come from her own vanquished food fixation; from observations of contemporary fashion and advertising; and from Western philosophy, literature, mythology, and psychology. She argues that the "tyranny of slenderness" is a product of the mind/body dichotomy fundamental to Western culture in which men hold power and are identified with the exalted mind, and women serve men and are likened to the denigrated body. Her feminism is as strong as her exuberant argument that women's obsession with fat is "an effort to control or eliminate the passionate aspects of the self in order to gain the approval and prerogatives of masculine culture" (187) and that this effort explains "all those particular sensations of emptiness, of longing and craving, of dread and despair" (187) shared by compulsive eaters and starving anorexics.

While Chernin discusses both fat and thin, Millman and Orbach deal principally with overweight women, though all six authors view obesity and skeletal anorexia as two versions of the same obsession. Millman is a sociologist. Her data come principally from interviews with fat women and from participant observation at helping organizations for fat people: the National Association to Aid Fat Americans (NAAFA, now renamed the National Association to Advance Fat Awareness), Overeaters Anonymous, and a summer diet camp for children. Her book is richly sprinkled with her informants' words, which give poignancy to the argument that obesity is a sadly misdirected personal response to the grievous difficulty of being a woman in our society.

Orbach, Boskind-White, and White are therapists. Their approaches are similar although Orbach deals with overeaters and the Whites with bulimarexics, compulsive eaters who gorge and then purge by self-induced vomiting, laxatives, diuretics, and violent exercise. Both use group therapy and attempt to help their patients deal with the problems of womanhood by building a positive female identity. Orbach takes a strongly feminist approach. She bases her inquiry and therapy on the question, "What is it about the social position of women that leads them to respond to it by getting fat?" (19). Boskind-White and White take a similar approach to binging and purging. They contest traditional explanations of the obsession which blame it on the mother. Orbach goes further by showing links between the paradoxical position of a socially oppressed mother raising a daughter into inevitable oppression, the problematic character of femininity and the mother-daughter relationship, and eating disorders. Both books abound in observations of and by patients, and both contain concrete suggestions about specific group-therapy techniques that have been successful in helping women overcome their obsession.

Bruch is a physician and psychotherapist who has been working with eating disorders for forty years. *The Golden Cage* is a moving discussion of anorexia nervosa based on close reference to the troubled girls Bruch has treated. Anorexia nervosa is a voluntary starvation that most often afflicts adolescent females from privileged backgrounds; like bulimarexia, it seems to have been increasing at an alarming rate in the last fifteen to twenty years (viii). Bruch is the least overtly feminist of the authors under review, yet her findings contain an implicit indictment of U.S. society. Her patients are characterized by an undeveloped sense of self, overcompliance, and a fixation with being thin as the sole way to exert control over the world around them. Bruch locates the cause of this pathetic condition not in the victim but in forces around her, principally in familial and cultural expectations that women be unreasonably compliant and thin.

These books are not diet books, though all aim to help women achieve a more tranquil relationship to their bodies that may result in weight loss (see also Boskind-Lodahl 1976; and Orbach 1982). Nor are these books biophysiological investigations of food disorders; discussion of the hormonal and metabolic conditions of weight are in fact conspicuously lacking. Although all the books refer to aspects of the social, political, and economic context in explaining the meanings of fat and thin, they do not explicitly consider political economy: the ways in which the evolution of North American capitalism has produced this particular form of mental slavery. Finally, though relying heavily on informants' words, these books are not directly biographical.[3]

All five books take issue with traditional interpretations in several ways. First, they take eating disorders seriously, something that many physicians and psychologists have failed to do (Broughton 1978;

Chernin 1981, 1). The authors all understand how the simple command to diet or to eat, characteristic of many treatments, fails to
address the underlying causes and identity confusion. Bruch specifically cautions against behavior modification therapy, which merely
reinforces the sense of helplessness basic to the anorexic's problem
(107); Millman points out the futility of standard diet strategies
(89–90), which have an estimated 90 to 95 percent recidivism rate
(Beller 1977, 264). In their compassion for their subjects, the authors
do not emphasize the dangers of obesity—which are exaggerated by
the media, medical plans, doctors, and insurance companies (Millman
1980, 87–88)—but concentrate instead on the physiological burdens of
constant weight fluctuations, fasting, and amphetamine consumption
(see Broughton 1978), the stressful nervous effects of maintaining an
excessively low body weight, and the isolating self-centeredness of the
obsession. Boskind-White and White contest the regnant explanation
of bulimarexia as a symptom of rejection of the traditional female role
and posit that on the contrary it seems to be a consequence of an excessive adherence to that role. Ambivalence about that role is recognized
by all the authors as part of the obsession. Orbach rejects the Freudian
diagnosis of obesity as "an obsessive-compulsive symptom related to
separation-individuation, narcissism, and insufficient ego-develop-
ment" (17). Her objections characterize the approach of the five books.
They reject explanations of eating disorders as individual character
failures. Eating disorders, rather, express conflicts in the social process
of becoming an American woman.

CHARACTERISTICS OF THE OBSESSION

Four principal themes emerge from the books as explanations of eating
disorders: confusion over sexual identity and sexuality; struggle with
issues of power, control, and release; solitude and deceit; and family
strife. Before examining these themes in detail, however, it is important
to note differences among the three eating disorders. Obesity is defined
as a body weight statistically determined as being from 10 to 25 percent over "normal" body weight. An estimated 40 percent of American
women may be obese (Beller 1977, 6–9), and many more women "feel
fat" (see Dyrenforth, Wooley, and Wooley 1980). Fat people belong to
all walks of life, though there are proportionately more among the poor
than among the rich (Millman 1980, p. 89).[4] They are victims of vehe-
ment and irrational disgust, denigration, and discrimination (Millman
1980, 90; Beller 1977, 9; Dyrenforth, Wooley, and Wooley 1980). Anorexia nervosa is voluntary starvation; as Bruch emphasizes, the physiological effects of starvation are crucial to the distorted perceptions of
self and reality that make anorexia hard to treat. Anorexics tend to be

white adolescent girls from socially and economically advantaged families (Bruch 1978, chap. 2). The same is true for bulimarexics, but they include older women of more varied backgrounds as well (Boskind-White and White 1983, chap. 3). They tend to be thin but not starving and may go through long periods of eating normally before erupting into a cycle of binging and purging. Chronic bulimarexics may go through the cycle from once a week to as many as eighteen times per day, consuming from 1,000 to 20,000 calories per binge (Boskind-White and White 1983, 45). Boskind-White and White feel that bulimarexics are "more tenacious," more independent, and less needy of "showing" their pain than anorexics are (34). Yet the female subjects of these books—whether obese, starving, or compulsively gorging and vomiting—share an extreme obsession with food; the characteristics of this obsession, the authors suggest, strike a chord in all women.

Sexuality and Sexual Identity

"It is often this critical question of how women can define and manage their own sexuality that is being grappled with in the fat/thin dilemma" (Orbach 1978, 73). Bulimarexics, anorexics, and the obese "typically loathe their bodies" (Boskind-White and White 1983, 115). This hatred of the body often comes with adolescence, when the slim, androgynous body begins to change. One anorexic said, "I have a deep fear of having a womanly body, round and fully developed" (Bruch 1978, 85). Such fear often accompanies antipathy to menstruation about which one anorexic girl said, "It's like a conviction for a crime I never committed. I vow to prove my innocence somehow and release myself from this punishment" (Liu 1979, 34). Later, when Liu drops to 95 pounds and her periods consequently stop, as they always do for anorexics (Bruch 1978, 65), she rejoices: "I don't suppose the reprieve will last forever, but for the moment it delights me. And the more weight I lose, the flatter I become. It's wonderful, like crawling back into the body of a child" (Liu 1979, 41). While anorexics retreat from female sexuality by becoming childlike and asexual, overweight women accomplish the same end by becoming fat. They become sexually neuter by violating cultural standards of ideal femininity (Millman 1980, chap. 6; Orbach 1978, 60).

Becky Thompson calls attention to the relationship between eating problems and sexual abuse (1994). She reports that "many studies confirm that beween one-third and two-thirds of women who have eating problems have been sexually abused," but cautions that "having an eating problem does not necessarily mean a woman has been sexually abused" (1994, 47). Childhood sexual abuse can distort a woman's psychological and physical sense of self. Food can provide a refuge from sexual abuse by giving comfort, numbness, and pleasure, as well as by enabling a woman to attain a body size that will free her from sexual exploitation. "The effectiveness of eating problems as coping devices lies in their versatility—in their ability to soothe the mind and the body simultaneously" (1994, 95).

The women described in the books under review not only hate their bodies and fear their womanly shapes but are obsessively concerned with their size and weight. The thin constantly weigh themselves and assess their shape in mirrors; the fat retreat from looking but cannot escape their thoughts. Their common concern involves establishing unrealistic standards for themselves and holding a distorted perception of their own and other's bodies (Bruch 1978, 81): "Thin is never thin enough" (Boskind-White and White 1983, 29).

Characteristic of women's troubled relationship to their bodies is a conscious opposition of mind and body that becomes a sense of being split in two (Boskind-White and White 1983, 33) or of being disembodied (Chernin 1981, 55; Millman 1980, chap. 9). Susan Bordo (1993) has afffirmed that mind-body dualism—the splitting of mind and body and the linking of men with the exalted mind and women with the denigrated body—is at the heart of both patriarchal power and of women's particular problems with food. Fat women refuse to look at or even acknowledge their bodies, so great is their loathing and shame for their expansiveness. One of Millman's informants said, "I feel so terrible about the way I look that I cut off connection with my body. I operate from the neck up. I do not look in mirrors" (1980, 195). Anorexics "speak of feeling divided, as being a split person or two people" and, significantly, "when they define this separate aspect, this different person seems always to be a male" (Bruch 1978, 58).

Dieting becomes an attempt to eliminate or render invisible that part of the self represented by the body (Orbach 1978, 169). A woman's attempt to escape hunger is "a terrible struggle against her sensual nature" (Chernin 1981, 10), a struggle destined to failure because all human beings have physiological needs that cannot be denied. According to Chernin, women's antipathy toward their own sensuality reflects Western culture's repression of appetite, which may be particularly strong within the Puritan tradition. The obese, anorexics, and bulimarexics all display an irrational terror of hunger that is often accompanied by an inability to allow, recognize, or satisfy the physiological stirrings of appetite (Bruch 1978, 42–43; Orbach 1978, 108). They may also feel disgust and fear toward sexual contact (Bruch 1978, 73) and a great insecurity about their own sexuality. There may be an unsatisfied longing for sexual intimacy as well (Chernin 1981, chap. 4; Millman 1980, chap. 6; Orbach 1978, 60). "Sexuality is a great wasteland of unfulfilled pleasures, confusion, guilt, fear, and disgust" (Boskind-White and White 1983, 113).

Obsession with food serves as an escape: "It distracted me from problems like the future, my parents' marriage, men, and all the other questions over which I had absolutely no control" (Liu 1979, 109). Obesity serves as a buffer between a woman and men. Being fat makes her unattractive, asexual, and remote, and she can avoid sex entirely (Millman 1980, 172). Though being excessively thin begins as an attempt to satisfy the cultural ideal of "slim is beautiful," it also isolates women from sexual encounters. The excessive pursuit of weight loss results in androgyny: a boyish body without breasts or menstruation, the overt and insistent symbols of femininity (Bruch 1978, 64–65; Orbach 1978, 169). Liu says, "Maybe, I mused, if I lost enough weight, men would start to ignore me. Sometimes I felt it would be worth it to bind my breasts and veil my face" (1979, 87).

These five books address the question of why women have such a troubled relationship to sexuality. After all, sexual pleasure can be wonderful, and women's sexuality is linked to their generative power. Yet, the books suggest, in North America female sexuality is not venerated but rather is degraded and objectified. In fashion and the media, women are repeatedly presented with idealized, objectified, and sexualized images of themselves. Pornography—degrading sexual violence—is directed at women with the most splendidly voluptuous female bodies (Chernin 1981, 133), while patriarchal U.S. media and advertising idealize as beautiful a standard of thinness that for most adult women is inaccessible. An attractive woman with a normally curvacious body is subject to leers, whistles, come-ons, and vulgar comments from men. She may feel assessed first as a physical object, only second as a human subject (Liu 1979). Some women attempt to flee from the objectification and degradation of their sexuality by becoming asexual through excessive thinness or fatness (Thompson 1994, 54).

Chernin is the only author to propose an overt explanation for the denigration of female sexuality and plumpness in our society. She links it to the mind/body split basic to Western ideology that "may well characterize patriarchal culture altogether" (56, see also Bordo 1993). The body and its passions are set apart from the mind and identified with oppressed groups—women and also African-Americans (Chernin 129). The history of slavery institutionalized the complete objectification of African-American men's and women's bodies by defining them as solely bodies (Thompson 1994, 17). White men's power over oppressed groups is an assertion of their control over those passionate, sensual, instinctual, and explosive tendencies that represent all in life that is threatening. In addition, Chernin suggests, men fear and envy women's sexuality and fertility. They cope with their own feelings of sexual inadequacy and jealousy of women's procreative ability by devaluing sex and procreation. This devaluation serves as an ideological buffer to male power—a power that is wielded in the economy, in politics, and in culture. In women's problematic relationship to food we also see their struggle to deal with their lack of power.

Power, Control, and Release

All five books under discussion share the perspective of popular feminism that the denigration of women's physicality parallels the cultural subordination of their values and ways of being, which extends even to the muting of their voices (Gilligan 1983). "Men both act for them and describe their experience" (Orbach 1978, 71). The books suggest that the growth of the feminist movement and rise in the numbers of working women have increased the contradictions of the female role. Women have not surrendered their traditional expectations of being wives and mothers, but they have added new goals of productive work and independent public identity (Brumberg 1988; Howe 1977). They are educated to be passive and compliant but find these postures unsuited to success in the workplace. They want to be producers but find society casting them in the role of consumers and loading that role with more conflicts: Eat junk foods but don't get fat; wear sexy clothes but be a faithful wife. The tensions in living out these conflicts, according to the five books, can become unbearable, especially for women lacking a strong sense of self. Some respond through compulsively restricted or excessive eating.

Anorexics and bulimarexics are particularly notable for their overcompliance. The former are typically "good girls" who have always done what they were supposed to do (Bruch 1978, chap. 3; Liu 1979, 39). Bulimarexics are often extremely subservient to men (Boskind-White and White 1983, 20). Anorexic, bulimarexic, and overweight women all have a difficult time asserting themselves, going against societal or familial programs, and choosing their own paths. Food becomes the one sure way they can exert control in the world: "When the rest of my life is going out of control I always say to myself, there's one thing I can control, what I put in my mouth" (Millman 1980, 161). Some women exercise this control by eating and becoming fat. Physical bulk can be a source of power, giving women stature and removing them from the category of frail, helpless females (Orbach 1978, chap. 2). For many women, however, control consists of denying themselves food. For example, the anorexic Betty explained that "losing weight was giving her power, that each pound lost was like a treasure that added to her power" (Bruch 1978, 5). Starving becomes a channel to achievement. As Aimee Liu said, "In this one respect, I'm the best" (1979, 40).

But while food may be a domain for control, it can be a channel for losing control, for attaining release and repose: "The inside of a binge is deep and dark; it is a descent into a world in which every restriction you have placed on yourself is cut loose. The forbidden is obtainable. Nothing matters—not friends, not family, not lovers. Nothing matters but food. Lifting, chewing, swallowing—mechanical frenzied acts, one following the other until a physical limit, usually nausea, is reached. Then comes the sought after numbness, the daze, the indifference to emotional pain. Like a good drug, food knocks out sensation" (Roth 1982, 15–16).

Compulsive eaters describe over and over again the oblivion and ecstasy they achieve while binging. "Some people describe binging not only as taking place outside of rational consciousness, but like getting drunk, as being an activity that actually *produces* a state of unconsciousness" (Millman, 1980, 141). One girl described anorexia this way: "It is as if you were slowly poisoned, something like being under the chronic influence of something like alcohol or dope" (Bruch 1978, 15). Eating can also be a substitute for sexual release and a way of trying to fill emotional hunger (Chernin 1981, 11). "I'm taking care of everyone else, and food takes care of me" (quoted in Millman 1980, 109).

Furthermore, the six authors point out, women are trained to be nonaggressive, pacifying, and self-sacrificing. They are conditioned not to express strong emotions (Orbach 1978, 52). So if they feel angry about gender or race discrimination, their husbands' failure to help around the house, or about abuse, they may react by turning their anger against themselves: eating, eating, eating, or starving, starving, starving. As Thompson says, "Eating problems begin as survival strategies—as sensible acts of self-preservation—in response to myriad injustices including racism, sexism, homophobia, classism, the stress of acculturation, and emotional, phyiscal, and sexual abuse" (1994, 2). The food fixation, however, blots out other battles and may impede the struggles for social justice necessary to reduce the atrocities suffered by women. Many women, in fact, put off living fully until after they have resolved their struggle with food. Characteristic of women obsessed with food is this postponement, accompanied by a transformation fantasy: "Once I am thin, everything will change" (see Atwood 1976, 47; Boskind-White, and White 1983, 158; Millman 1980, chap. 10; Orbach 1978, 132–33). Women are socialized to believe that their problems come from being too fat. Being thin then becomes a panacea, a totally absorbing quest, a pathetically reductionist channel for attaining control in a world where women suffer institutionalized powerlessness.

Solitude, Withdrawal, Deceit, Competition

One of the strongest characteristics of the food obsession that emerges in the five books is its individualism. Women gorge, purge, or starve in secret. Their attitudes toward their obsession—whether the pride of the anorexic or the guilt of the compulsive eater—serve to isolate them further. Like anorexics, all these women become "completely self-absorbed.... Food thoughts crowd out their ability to think about anything else" (Bruch 1978, 79). They practice their rituals—of gorging, vomiting, scrutinizing their bodies in the mirror, or fanatically exercising—alone. The need to hide their weird behavior from others and to lie about their eating habits leads to increasing withdrawal. Deceit becomes fundamental to their lifestyle and leads in turn to increasing self-hatred, despair, and withdrawal. The solitude of these tormented women can only exacerbate what the books suggest is one of the main underlying causes of their obsession: their poorly developed sense of self. One might ponder whether the social atomization characteristic of the United States facilitates the secrecy and increases the isolation of these women, further hindering exit from their compulsion.

The solitude of women with eating disorders is often characterized by competition with and mistrust of others, particularly other women. Anorexics take pride in being superior to—that is, thinner than—other girls (Bruch 1978, 18). Liu is reluctant to tell her friends the secret of her extreme weight loss lest they weaken her triumph by becoming thinner than she. "Bulimarexic women are constantly comparing their bodies—and their lives in general—to those of other women—and almost always unfavorably, with further loss of self-esteem" (Boskind-White and White 1983, 38).

Orbach explicitly argues that the difficulty women in the United States have in dealing with competition permeates their struggle with food, and data from the other books support her thesis (1978, 49–51). While men are socialized to achieve and are trained in techniques of success, competition in women, particularly with men, is seen as unfeminine. Female socialization emphasizes cooperation; women who strive for competitive achievement may find themselves on foreign and threatening terrain (Gilligan 1983, 42; Orbach 1978, 49–51). Getting fat may be a way of coping with difficult feelings about competition by hiding the feelings behind the wall of fat, by using the body as an excuse for failure, and by providing in compulsive eating an outlet for uncomfortable competitive feelings (Orbach 1978, 51).

Again, however, the authors expose the futility of the struggle. In a society that institutionalizes competition in every aspect of life—for grades, for jobs, for shape—at the same time as it denies women the ability to compete and still be feminine, it is no wonder that women opt out of the competition, internalize it, or limit it to the trivial domain of body weight. Women's isolated, competitive individualism in their struggle with food, the books suggest, is an internalization of the competitive values and practices fundamental to Western society.

Because our society tends to define all problems as individual ones and to suggest that they can be overcome by personal effort aimed at raising oneself above others, individual rage is focused not against society but against the self; this permits the continuance of a status quo built on the systematic oppression of women.

Family Strife

The five books contend that anorexia, bulimarexia, and obesity respond not only to the social conditions of womanhood but also to familial organization. Food is a central, readily available battleground for issues of "autonomy, control and love" in the growing girl's relationship with her parents (Millman 1980, 72). Some girls overeat to rebel against parents. The heroine of Atwood's *Lady Oracle* (1976) stuffs herself like "a beluga whale" (78) as a way of waging war against her mother and demanding autonomy. Thompson (1994) uses interview case histories with eighteen women of diverse race, class, and sexual preference who suffered long-term eating problems to suggest that many women use food to escape from horrific family problems, including sexual, physical and emotional abuse and intrafamilial as well as societal racism. Most of her informants used compulsive eating to cope with family problems and found that food acted like a drug to soothe both emotional and physical pain.

Other women use self-starvation as a way of coping with family problems. Anorexics have a history of being "perfect" daughters, and their starvation is a way of expressing their feelings of powerlessness and their anger at their parents for depriving them of the right to live their own lives (Bruch 1978, 38). Refusal to eat is an act of defiance (Bruch 1978, 38). Triumphant self-denial may provide a girl with a concrete outlet for achievement in a world in which she feels inconsequential. Starvation may allow the anorexic to return to a childlike dependence on her parents to feed her and thus free her from the burden of their expectations. Bruch's patient who described herself as "a sparrow in a golden cage" (24) captures this feeling, and Liu's words describe the situation typical of many anorexics and bulimarexics: "Mine was a childhood frosted with affluence, filled with adventure, and sprinkled generously with loving care. Throughout the early years I led a cupcake existence, wrapped in my parents' unspoken promises that they had me destined for the best of all possible worlds" (1979, 1).

These high expectations and privileged family conditions make all the more painful the girls' encounter with the difficulties of female achievement in "the real world." Girls may encounter the different possibilities open to their brothers (Boskind-White and White 1983, chap. 4) and the lack of societal approval of their mothers' achievements. Indeed, these mothers are often women who gave up personal aspirations and careers to devote themselves to their families (Bruch 1978, 28). They may simultaneously be seething with resentment, living life again by pushing their daughters to go farther than they did, proving by their own limits the difficulty of female achievement, and attempting to validate their own lives by limiting their daughters (Orbach 1978, 26–32). Daughters may be angry at mothers for their dominance and overinvolvement, for their subservience to their husbands, and for their failure to achieve (Boskind-White and White 1983, 67; Liu 1979). Daughters may be angry at their fathers for being cold, domineering, and distant (Boskind-White and White 1983, 172–74) or for being sexually threatening (Millman 1980, 173–74). Overeating and self-starvation are ways of asserting control, demanding attention, and expressing anger. They are ultimately self-destructive ways, however, which do nothing to alter the social conditions that produce distant and idealized father-daughter relations and conflict-ridden mother-daughter relations. As Orbach says, "As long as patriarchal culture demands that women bring up their daughters to accept an inferior social position, the mother's job will be fraught with tension and confusion which are often made manifest in the way mothers and daughters interact over the subject of food" (1978, 113).

WHY NOW?

Reported cases of anorexia and bulimarexia have increased alarmingly in the last twenty to thirty years (Bruch 1978, viii), and concern with obesity also appears to be rising (Chernin 1981, chap. 9). Several reasons are suggested by the five books under review.

First, in the culture of North American commodity capitalism, food is plentiful and consumption is pushed. In the context of abundance and rampant consumption, self-denial through voluntary starvation is a powerful symbolic act (Bruch 1978, 9; Chernin 1981, 103). But societal affluence also means that women can allow themselves the luxury of overeating, or of binging and vomiting a week's worth of groceries in a day (Boskind-White and White 1983, 48). The growing prevalence of junk foods means women can overeat yet never satisfy the body's craving for adequate nutrition. As John Keats (1976, 12) said, "Some Americans are now starving to death even as they gain weight."

The U.S. food industry contributes to the problem (see Aronson 1980; Hacker 1980; Hess and Hess 1977; Hightower 1975). Like all capitalist endeavors, it must grow to remain viable. With a relatively stable population, advertising must create markets for new foods. Once women have converted these foods into fat, they are exhorted to buy diet foods to shed the fat. The economy depends on manipulating consumers to buy as much as possible, and one way is to project simultaneously the urge to eat and the need to diet. As Bordo says, eating disorders reflect "the tantalizing (and mystifying) ideal of a perfectly managed and regulated self, within a consumer culture which has made the actual management of hunger and desire intensely problematic" (1992, 68).

Current standards of fashion and beauty contribute to women's obsession with food by projecting a particularly thin ideal. Chernin notes that standards for female beauty have fluctuated over the years in the United States and have demanded the greatest thinness at times when women have demanded greatest rights. She points out that as feminism's projection of strong women has increased, so have child pornography and incest (108–9), and she ventures: "In this age of feminist assertion, men are drawn to women of childish body and mind because there is something less disturbing about the vulnerability and helplessness of a small child—and something truly disturbing about the body and mind of a mature woman" (110; see also Bordo 1993, 207). The media contribute by promoting a thin ideal that is almost impossible to attain and whose attainment will result in the literal physical weakness of undernourishment for most women (see Kaufman 1980). This ideal increases the distance between a woman and herself, exacerbating her conflicts and making it harder for her to be at one with herself—hence the obsession.

Feminism has also raised women's expectations about their potential lives. But real opportunities have not kept pace, increasing the disparity between hopes and reality (Bruch 1978, ix; Brumberg 1988; Chernin 1981, chap. 9). Furthermore, feminism has demanded an end to all double standards, including sexual ones. In conjunction with the freer sexual mores that have permeated Western culture, this demand has led to increasing pressure on girls to have sexual relations ever earlier. Greater sexual freedom may be an important cause of the greater frequency of anorexia nervosa and in bulimarexia by augmenting the adolescent's anxiety about her transition to womanhood (Bruch 1978, ix; Boskind-White and White 1983, 90).

ALTERNATIVES TO THE OBSESSION

We have noted the common characteristics of obesity, anorexia nervosa, and bulimarexia. The five books under review point out that these self-destructive and unproductive disorders are often responses to the cultural problems of womanhood.

Being excessively fat or thin does challenge stereotypes of femininity through their negation but leaves victims with only negation. Such responses offer neither a new positive self-image nor an empowering analysis of why our society's female stereotype is damaging and oppressive (Millman 1980, chap. 5). They do not attack what Bruch implies and the other authors state is the basis of the obsession: the subordinate position of women in society. Victims of bulimarexia, anorexia, and obesity are caught in a vicious cycle of guilt and despair. The women punish themselves over and over again: They eat, starve, or binge and purge to escape their shame and desperation; they end up hating themselves more than before; and again they plunge into their excesses, to forget or punish themselves further. In the process they ruin their health, weaken their bodies, and render themselves socially ineffectual as obese nonpersons or as "invisible" anorexics (Orbach 1978, 146). All their energies are focused on food; all their hope is pinned on the expected miracle of transformation that will occur when they defeat their obsession.

All five books propose an alternative to eating or starving. The alternative is based essentially on developing a strong, positive sense of female identity. It involves teaching women to make their personal problems part of a broader social analysis.[5] Here the books prescribe techniques common to popular feminist pedagogy: intellectual liberation through discussion of oppression, and self-help and support groups. With anorexics, Bruch insists that the first step is to counter the severe psychophysiological effects of starvation by raising body weight, even if hospitalization is necessary. Then therapy should aim at penetrating the web of dishonesty, self-deception, and overcompliance characteristic of anorexics; this will enable them to develop "a valid self-concept and the capacity for self-directed action" (1978, 130). Orbach and Boskind-White and White suggest that their patients cease tormenting themselves about why they eat compulsively and ask what their behavior *does* for them, so that they can come up with other ways of doing the same things and reduce their total reliance on food as panacea. Food obsession is not the entire problem, but it is the channel through which deeper psychosocial problems are worked out. Hence they propose healing strategies that focus on uncovering and dealing with the problems below the surface (see Bruch 1988).

All of the authors believe in the benefits for women of recognizing that others share the obsession and of linking the obsession to women's oppression. Boskind-White and White and Orbach practice group therapy, which aims to help women out of their loneliness, make their problems less shameful and easier to bear, provide perspective, and strengthen their weak self-image. It also teaches women to be assertive and to use their mouths to express anger rather than to eat (Orbach 1978, 58). All the authors imply that women need to learn that they have a right to eat and that contrary to what society tells them, their identity consists of more than how they look.

Some African American women appear able successfully to challenge the cultural mores that objectify women's bodies and deny their right to eat. Several recent studies indicate that many African

American women are able to define alternative, flexible, and progressive ways of thinking about the female body even though they continually contend with media messages that define beauty as white and skinny.[6] Among African Americans, a woman's ample body can represent beauty, power, and victory over racism and poverty (Hughes 1997). In poor, inner-city black communities, a fat body can symbolize freedom from drugs and self-respect (Freedman 1990a). Consumption of soul food demonstrates success at keeping African American memory and traditions alive (Beoku-Betts 1995; Harris 1994; Shange 1998).

A major recent study found important differences between African American and white adolescent females in body image and weight concerns (Parker et al. 1995). Overall 70 percent of black girls were *satisfied* or *very satisfied* with their weight whereas in sharp contrast, 90 percent of white girls were *unsatisfied*. Researchers found that black teens were more flexible and less absolutist in their definitions of beauty than white teens. Black girls saw beauty as deriving from "having the right kind of attitude" rather than the right body. They linked beauty to dress, style, and movement, emphasizing that beauty was within the reach of any woman who had pride in herself and her culture. Many black teens reported receiving compliments on their looks from their girlfriends and mothers, who contributed to their ability to feel good about whatever body they had. Parker et al.'s study shows that many young black women are ignoring the "tyranny of slenderness," defining themselves as subjects, and valuing their personhood rather than their objectified bodies.

More research is needed on how and why black women are able to challenge patriarchal, white supremacist definitions of beauty. Can their experience provide helpful clues for white women who wish to challenge the cult of thinness? Two key facts emerge as important from Parker et al.'s study: the support black women receive from other women and the value their culture places on the contribution of women to family and society—through cooking as well as through other forms of productive work. These facts indicate that to challenge bodily oppression all women will have to work together to affirm diverse definitions of female beauty and productive value.

FURTHER QUESTIONS

Several questions come to mind as one ponders the data and explanations these books offer about excessively fat and thin women. If these excesses are responses to the problematic character of being a woman, why do men also suffer from eating disorders? About one-tenth of Bruch's anorexic patients are male (1978, viii), and "seriously overweight" men seem to be nearly as common as women (Beller 1977, 6). The books give no figures on bulimarexic men; they seem to be few or nonexistent, though they may just be sociologically invisible. Of the five books, only Millman's explicitly considers male eating disorders, in an appendix entitled "Fat Men, a Different Story." Because her interviews with men involved a smaller, older, and more restricted group than her female sample, she is cautious, but she finds that the male experience of being fat is vastly different from the female. Men think less about being fat; they are less prone to connect it with psychological, personal, or emotional problems; they fight social disdain rather than internalizing it; and they really do not think obesity affects their relationships, careers, or masculinity. In short, they live relatively easily with their fat.[7] Millman (1980, 244) suggests, however, "As we are all increasingly socialized to be consumers rather than producers, men as well as women will be evaluated increasingly in terms of how they measure up to media images of attractiveness rather than their achievements in work. Thus men's experiences with weight will increasingly resemble those of women." Perhaps men who suffer from eating disorders have found themselves through particular familial and social situations in positions of extreme powerlessness, overcompliance, and poor self-image. If the concentration of economic and political power produces more dependent and insecure men, there may well be an increase in men suffering from eating disorders.

If the food obsession is connected closely with a girl's troubled transition to womanhood, why do preadolescent children experience it as well? Cam Reed was a compulsive eater for as long as she can remember; her autobiography begins with recollections of ecstasy over the arrival of the ice-cream truck (Broughton 1978). The heroine of *Lady Oracle* (Atwood 1976, 43) recounts that in her earliest baby pictures, "I was never looking at the camera; instead I was trying to get something into my mouth." Some children, both boys and girls, appear to have a tendency from the very beginning to eat a lot, and/or to gain weight easily (Beller 1977, chap. 2; Bruch 1973). Thompson's work on the link between eating problems and abuse, especially child sexual abuse, may explain why some children develop compulsive eating at an early age and may force us to think further about differences between women with anorexia nervosa and those with compulsive eating disorder (1994).

There are biological forces that affect desires for food, weight gain, and the abilities to recognize and satisfy hunger normally. None of our five books considers them, but Beller (1977) does at length and suggests that biology and evolution have played an important role in both shaping a given individual's relation to food and in facilitating weight gain in women. Although social and psychological factors may be extremely important in contributing to eating disorders, some people may become excessively fat because of how their bodies work.

Biological, genetic, and endocrinological studies can make important contributions to this question, and failure to consider them weakens the books under review.

If very young children exhibit noticeably different yearnings for food, one wonders not only about the influence of individual and sexual biology but also about the role of feeding patterns in early infancy (Bruch 1973). Elena Gianini Belotti (1975), for example, reports that in one study, Italian mothers breast-fed their sons more often, longer, and more attentively than their daughters (cited in Orbach 1978, 18). Is such differential feeding by gender widespread? How might it affect women's obsession with food and thinness? Cross-cultural data suggest that feeding practices can have a lifelong effect on a child's personality and relationship to food (Du Bois 1941, 1960; Mead 1935; D. Shack 1969; W. Shack 1971). More studies are needed to determine to what extent early childhood feeding in the United States is responsible for the obsession with food and its particular form.

Are there women who are fat and happy in the United States? The books describe a host of overweight women who are miserable. The authors imply that a successful struggle with the social and psychological constraints on becoming female will result in tranquility with self and usually a loss of weight. But are there women at ease with themselves and their social positions who are fat because they eat a lot and with pleasure? There are fat women in other cultures, Italy for example (chapter 10), who accept weight gain as part of the inevitable and normal process of maturation. Fat Samoan women seem to be content with their size and, significantly, suffer none of the hypertension associated with obesity in the United States (Mackenzie in Chernin 1981, 32). Is a certain amount of fat biologically "normal"? Is our society so full of conflicts as to render a happy, healthy, sociable fat woman an impossibility?

Cross-cultural comparisons can offer insights (see chapter 6). We learn that in many cultures, and among ethnic groups in the United States as well, plump or fat women are preferred over thin ones due to associations of fat with fertility, well-being, nurturance, and affluence (Becker 1995; Beller 1977; Brink 1995; Chernin 1981; Emmons 1992; Massara 1989; Parker et al. 1995; Pollock 1995; Sobo 1994; Styles 1980). Further cross-cultural investigations can test the feminist explanation for the food obsession in the United States by investigating the relationships among the societal valuation of women, their autonomy, their attitudes toward their bodies, and their body sizes. In particular, data from societies without the political and economic stratification that characterizes our own can offer perspective on how women's obsession with food is a product of female powerlessness in the United States.

6

An Anthropological View of Western Women's Prodigious Fasting

A Review Essay[1]

Bell, Rudolph M. 1985. *Holy Anorexia*. Epilogue by William N. Davis. Chicago: University of Chicago Press.

Brumberg, Joan Jacobs. 1988. *Fasting Girls: The Emergence of Anorexia Nervosa as a Modern Disease*. Cambridge: Harvard University Press.

Bynum, Caroline Walker. 1987. *Holy Feast and Holy Fast: The Religious Significance of Food to Medieval Women*. Berkeley: University of California Press.

In prodigious fasting, sometimes to death, Western women have expressed an extraordinary relationship to food for almost eight centuries. This essay attempts to explain such behavior by weaving together the fine-grained and fascinating historical data presented in the three books under review and viewing them from the cross-cultural and holistic perspectives fundamental to anthropology. I aim to show that Western female fasting differs radically from other kinds of fasting observed by anthropologists across the globe and that it involves a highly symbolic alteration of women's universal relationship to food. I argue that it is best understood as a multidetermined behavior, an interplay of ideological, economic, political, and social factors. Although Western culture has changed greatly over the eight centuries that women have refused food, certain forces persist, making radical fasting a significant statement. These forces include the identification of women with food, a dualistic and absolutist Judeo-Christian ideology, a patriarchal political and economic structure, and a family organization that limits female autonomy and potential.

The three books under review provide complementary data and interpretation that together illuminate the puzzle of fasting women. Rudolph Bell contributes a psychoanalytical approach and rich, in-depth case material on several Italian holy women who between A.D. 1200 and the present practiced extreme fasting. Where sources are available, he focuses on the saints' family lives, on childhood and breast-feeding experiences, and on evidence of the women's oral fixation. His illumination of the holy anorexics' individual psychology and family experiences provides an essential part of the explanation of why women fast.

Caroline Walker Bynum uses a "functionalist and a phenomenological" approach to focus on the cultural and symbolic dimensions of fasting (6). She aims "to show the manifold meanings of food and its pervasiveness in religious symbolism" for medieval women (5). Although she discusses hagiographers' descriptions of her subjects, she pays particular attention to the words of the saints themselves, convinced that they reveal the richness and complexity of the fasting, eucharistic devotion, food miracles, food donations, and miraculous bodily emissions central to the religious expression of medieval female saints. Her book is richly documented with the saints' poetic, erotic, ecstatic, and symbolic statements about union with God through food and fasting. It makes a crucial contribution to the interpretation of their behavior and enables us to examine the role of ideology over time as a meaningful context for fasting.

Joan Jacobs Brumberg's book has the broadest historical and explanatory focus as she sets out to explain "the emergence of anorexia nervosa as a modern disease" by considering changes in female fasting and responses to it from the Middle Ages to the present. She uses rich primary source material from medical journals, newspapers, and unpublished case records on the "miraculous fasting maidens" of the sixteenth and seventeenth centuries, the "fasting girls" of the eighteenth century, and especially the anorexics of the nineteenth century. Brumberg concentrates on how anorexia lost its primarily spiritual dimension and became, during the Victorian era, firmly established as a disease. She shows how "love and work in the bourgeois family" (126) incited nineteenth-century adolescent girls to refuse food, and she adeptly documents how female fasting in the present day is related to beliefs about thinness and perfection, to the subordinate position of women in society, and to family relations. She advocates a multicausal model that considers anorexia nervosa an "addiction to starvation" triggered and supported by biological, psychological, and cultural factors.[2]

ANTHROPOLOGY: HOLISTIC AND COMPARATIVE

A holistic concept of culture is central to anthropological method and interpretation. Culture, to quote the venerable Edward Tylor (1958, 1), "is that complex whole which includes knowledge, belief, art, morals, law, custom, and any other capabilities and habits acquired by man as a member of society." Anthropologists believe that any cultural artifact— whether object, behavior, symbol, or thought—must always be viewed as a product of a biological, psychological, and social human being and explained as part of a whole cultural system consisting of economy, political organization, social structure, and ideology. These components, separated for analytical simplicity, are nested like Russian dolls. A fundamental belief of anthropology is the functional unity of cultural systems (see, e.g., Geertz 1973; Wolf 1974; Peacock 1986).

An anthropological explanation of Western women's fasting begins, then, with the assumption that fasting is a piece in a cultural mosaic— an extraordinary piece but one that fits, nonetheless.[3] It can be understood only in relation to the rest of a cultural picture that includes production, distribution, consumption, resource control and allocation, power structures, public decision making, family organization, marriage patterns, child rearing, and belief systems, especially as these are manifest through the culture's foodways (see, e.g., Richards 1939; Kahn 1986).

The cross-cultural approach, fundamental to anthropological epistemology, can also contribute to understanding the prodigious fasting of women from the Middle Ages to the present in Europe and North America. It enables us to know how unusual or common such behavior is worldwide and to examine the conditions that incite or deter extreme fasting. The comparative view enables us to see the common threads in the diversity of Western female fasting and its radical differences from the ways in which women in non-Western cultures relate to food.

THE GIFT AND ITS REFUSAL

Food refusal, I argue, is a meaningful statement in all cultures and signifies denial of relationship. In his classic study *The Gift*, Marcel Mauss showed how culture is a system of functional unity where exchange plays a key role in linking people together, maintaining the peace, and affirming beliefs (1967).[4] He argues that gifts are one of a number of "*total* social phenomena. In ... them, all kinds of institutions find simultaneous expression: religious, legal, moral, and economic" (1). The gift involves a tripartite obligation: to give, to receive, and to repay. Refusal to give or receive is a vast insult that severs relationships. Refusal to repay signifies inability to do so and loss of face. Giving to others is the basis of power, for recipients are beholden to donors.

Mauss considers all kinds of giving and receiving, but many of his examples involve gifts of food, which are primary among primitive cultures and important in all societies. Marshall Sahlins underscores the particularly strong pressures in social groups toward food sharing and its power to determine sociability:

> Food is life-giving, urgent, ordinarily symbolic of hearth and home, if not of mother. By comparison with other stuff, food is more readily, or more necessarily, shared. . . . Food dealings are a delicate barometer, a ritual statement as it were, of social relations, and food is thus employed instrumentally as a starting, a sustaining, or a destroying mechanism of sociability. . . . Food offered in a generalized way, notably as hospitality, is good relations. . . . Food not offered on the suitable occasion or not taken is bad relations. . . . In these principles of instrumental food exchange there seems little variation between peoples. (1972, 215–16)

Groups as diverse as the hunting-gathering Bushmen of southern Africa (Lee 1979, 1984; Marshall 1976; Shostak 1981; Thomas 1959), the Sharanahua Indians of the Peruvian Amazon (Siskind 1973), and rural Sardinians (Counihan 1981) make food sharing the definition of relation. Commensalism—the sharing of food—establishes communion and connection in all cultures. Self-denial of food and refusal to eat with others represent a severe rupture of connection. Although the three authors differ on how similar they think female fasting is over time, and Bynum is right that specific meanings for food come from and vary across cultures (206), the ethnographic data suggest that on the most general level food refusal universally signifies rupture of connection and that this meaning is expressed by prodigious female fasters.

WOMEN AND FOOD

The ethnographic data suggest another universal of relevance to holy and modern anorexia: the deep connection between women and food. Food is a particularly important concern and symbol for females in all cultures. Women have universal responsibility for food preparation and consumption (D'Andrade 1974), and in many cultures for production and distribution as well (see, e.g., Lee 1979). They are defined as nurturers and carry out this role principally through feeding. In addition, women themselves become food for their children during pregnancy and lactation, intensifying their identification with food and its relevance as symbol. In many cultures, as among ancient and modern Aztecs in Mexico (Taggart 1983), women are associated with the fertility of the earth and its bounteous food.

Western women also use food as symbol of self, but the prodigious fasters base their identification with food on negation and obsession. Most fasters throughout Western history have been female. Although men also fasted in the Middle Ages, Bynum (chap. 3) makes clear they did so with neither the prevalence nor the rigor of women who persistently "used bread, blood, hunger and eating as their dominant images for union with God and neighbor" (93). As Brumberg notes, throughout the seventeenth, eighteenth, and nineteenth centuries, those who abstained from food relentlessly and totally were "miraculous fasting maidens" (49) and "fasting girls" (chap. 3); "there were, in fact, no 'fasting boys'" (99). Only rarely did men practice extreme fasting, and then they did so to prove a specific point, like the eclectic physician Henry S. Tanner, who rented Clarendon Hall in New York and fasted for forty days to show it could be done (89–90). Today, most researchers estimate that about nine out of every ten anorexics are women and conclude that the disorder is a female one, suffered by some men who share certain aspects of the feminine experience (Lawrence 1984, 13).

Obsession characterizes the identification of female fasters with food throughout Western history. For example, of the medieval saint Colomba da Rieti (b. 1497) her friends said, "[We] never saw her taste bread, or fish, or eggs, or cheese or anything similar, nor any other food except that on some evenings she would taste a piece of fruit, sort of licking it to draw out the juice, and she drank water . . . sometimes she would sip a bit of chick-pea soup remaining in the nuns' bowls or suck on (but not eat) leftover salad leaves. . . . This she did to punish her senses because the food had spoiled and was covered with flies" (quoted in Bell, 156).

Other medieval holy women had tortured dreams full of food temptations, used imagery of food as God and God as food, and had an ecstatic relationship with the Eucharist. Although we lack data on the thoughts and feelings toward food of the fasting girls of the seventeenth, eighteenth, and nineteenth centuries (Brumberg, 165), Colomba prefigures modern anorexics who are endlessly preoccupied with food. As Aimee Liu says in her autobiographical account of anorexia nervosa, "Food. That's the scourge. I can't get away from it. If I don't eat I gloat, but think constantly of what I'm missing. If I do eat, I damn myself, and over and over again count up all that I regret eating. But the thing that's truly unforgivable is the way it blinds me to the rest of life" (1979, 153–54). Some anorexics enact secret rituals with food, like chewing every bite one hundred times (Levenkron 1978). Others focus completely on one tidbit, like Hilde Bruch's patient Tania, who "would eat one tiny M & M candy very slowly, just nibbling on it, and told herself that she could feel her stomach getting full" (1978, 91).

From the thirteenth century to the present, food has provided an important channel for female self-expression, although its specific meanings vary. Medieval women, Bynum tells us, were culturally defined as nurturers (277) and found a source of holiness in seeing themselves as food, for they identified with Christ who becomes food in the Mass to redeem humanity. Their own ability to breast-feed paralleled their association of "the breasts of Mary with eucharistic feeding of the soul" (271). In the Victorian era, bourgeois women used elaborate food preparation and consumption as a symbol of their social position and of the love they offered their families (Brumberg, chap. 5). Modern women, particularly those with anorexia nervosa, make food and its denial in pursuit of extreme thinness the central focus of their identity, "an important analogue of the self" (Brumberg, 260).

There are major differences in what food has meant for women in different historical periods, differences that parallel the overall secularization noted by both Bell (170–77) and Brumberg (passim) and reflect the radically different attitudes toward life and nature noted by Bynum (300). Modern women seek mastery of their bodies to achieve perfection through thinness; medieval women sought transcendence of their bodies to achieve holiness through asceticism; Victorian women sought a sublime and delicate femininity through denial of bodily needs. What all these meanings have in common is negation: of the body, of female physicality, and in extreme cases of life itself.

Medieval female saints made food a central vehicle of their quest for piety. Bynum interprets their behavior thus: "Women fast—and hunger becomes an image for excruciating, never-satiated love of God. Women feed—and their bodies become an image of suffering poured out for others. Women eat—and whether they devour the filth of sick bodies or the blood and flesh of the Eucharist, the foods are Christ's suffering and Christ's humanity, with which one must join before approaching triumph, glory or divinity" (186).

Their extraordinary behaviors included not only fasting—called holy anorexia or anorexia mirabilis—but, as Bynum emphasizes, a host of other food-centered activities (93, chaps. 4 and 5, and passim). Medieval holy women cured the sick with oil or milk flowing from their bodies, before or after death. Some multiplied food in miracles, emulating Christ's miracle of the loaves and fishes. Many gave food away to the poor, often against the wishes of their fathers or husbands. Some chewed and spit out food or vomited meals they were forced to consume, like today's bulimics or bulimarexics (Boskind-White and White 1983; Cauwels 1983; Striegel-Moore, Silberstein, and Rodin 1986). Other holy fasters ate only the Eucharist, saw visions in the Eucharist, tasted the Host as inebriating or sweet, and could supposedly tell the consecrated from the unconsecrated Host by vomiting the latter. Some—like Saint Veronica (Bell, 76–77), Catherine of Siena (Bynum,

172, Bell, 25), Catherine of Genoa (Bynum, 182), and Angela da Foligno (Bell, 108)—ate filth as sacrifice and self-abnegation, consuming pus, scabs, lice, leprous water, rotten and bad food, cat vomit, insects, worms, and spiders. Many of their actions involved distortions of women's usual relationship to food: They bestowed their effluvia not as physical substance to their infants but as spiritual nourishment to the poor; they did not incorporate food but vomited it; they ate not food but its opposite—filth or spirit.

Modern anorexics also have a distorted relationship to eating; they strive not for holiness, however, but for thinness and self-control through food denial (Bruch 1978, xi).[5] Anorexic girls feel great pride in their cachexia and suffer a severely disturbed body image. They cannot see their own emaciation and continually feel fat even as they starve to death. They undergo loss of over 25 percent of body weight, and many related health effects of starvation. They are obsessed with food and their bodies; devote themselves fanatically to dieting and exercise; and, like their medieval counterparts, convince themselves that hunger is pleasurable and valuable (Bruch 1973, 1978). Modern anorexics do not ordinarily seek religious transcendence and union with God through fasting, though many report the experience makes them feel clean, pure, and good (Bruch 1978, 18).[6] Liu exemplifies this: "Dieting, as far as I was concerned, was like a contest between good (abstinence) and evil (indulgence). If I followed through with the game, I'd purify myself. As long as I continued to eat in my wanton manner, I was tainted" (1979, 109). Food is transformed from physical sustenance into a vehicle for morality.

Modern anorexics, like the medieval ones before them, have a distorted relationship to food. Rather than focus primarily on nurturing others, they concentrate on denying self. Food no longer serves primarily to connect them to others but rather to enable them to transcend their mundane and earthly selves in the quest for piety or perfection.

FASTING IN CROSS-CULTURAL PERSPECTIVE

"Holy anorexics," "fasting girls," and modern anorexics share further characteristics that appear in clear relief when contrasted to fasting by other non-Western, nonstratified peoples (Powdermaker 1960). Such differences provide a key to understanding Western women and the meaning of their food use. In all cultures, food is an important symbol; however, the meanings attributed to food and the ways in which food is manipulated to convey messages vary widely across cultures.[7] Mary Douglas asserts that "the human body is always treated as an image of society" and that the passage of food in and out of the body can stand for social boundaries and their transgression (1973, 70). Most important for our concerns here is her claim that "bodily control is an expression of social control" (1973, 70). Western women's strong concern to control their food intake is a metaphor for their efforts to control their own bodies and destinies in a culture that makes self-control a moral imperative. This, however, reveals prevalent Western concerns and is not a cultural universal.

Many non-Western peoples practice fasting,[8] but rarely with the totality or relentlessness of Western fasting women (Katona-Apte 1975, 317–21; Messer 1989). "Abstinence is followed by indulgence" (Goody 1982, 78), and feasts regularly interrupt periods of reduced consumption, as in the harvest festivals that follow the annual lean times among the Gonja of northern Ghana. Muslims, for example, break the daily fast during Ramadan each night with hearty eating (Messina 1988). Anorexia nervosa and mirabilis are, by contrast, endless.

In tribal societies fasting is ordinarily collective and ritualized. A social group or the whole of a society will avoid certain foods; their fasting will follow traditional forms, be endowed with specific meanings, and be sanctioned by society. The LoDagaa of northern Ghana, chronicled in Goody's 1982 work, hold an annual Bagre ceremony where a series of food prohibitions is laid on initiands and then gradually lifted over a period of several weeks (chap. 3). The "cancellation of the prohibitions takes the form of a public demonstration" (81) where initiated boys eat foods previously forbidden. Their temporary and partial fasting is followed by a public feast and is imbued with significance through collective celebration. Both feasting and fasting—through the abilities to control appetite, defer consumption, and share food—affirm humanity and sociability. By contrast, the Western fasting we are considering is solitary, sometimes secretive, and not publicly ritualized.

Fasts by non-Western peoples most commonly "demand an alternative diet rather than total denial" (Goody 1982, 117). The Kalaunans of Goodenough Island eat "hard, dry foods . . . to fill the belly and satisfy the appetite for long periods" rather than "soft, pulpy food" (Young 1986, 117). The Trobriand Islanders perform *vilamalya* magic to make their cultivated food last a long time by making them "inclined to eat wild fruit of the bush" (Malinowski 1922, 169). Boys undergoing initiation among the Hua of New Guinea are enjoined from eating certain foods associated with females because these are believed dangerous, but they are simultaneously encouraged to eat a host of foods believed to fortify and protect them (Meigs 1984, chap. 2). Even in medieval Western Christendom, the norm was limited fasts on Fridays, holy days, and during Lent, when meat and rich foods were spurned but simple foods such as bread, fish, water, and greens were allowed (Bynum, 40). In fact, as Bynum (47) and Bell (118ff.) note, total fasting was condemned by the Church, and many of the holy anorexics faced staunch opposition from church authorities—opposition they steadily circumvented with claims they were unable to counter God's will by eating.

In spite of ecclesiastical, medical, and social opposition, Western women have fasted to death since at least the thirteenth century. Whereas in tribal cultures people never (to my knowledge) die of voluntary starvation, an estimated 15 to 19 percent of severe anorexics die (Brumberg, 13; Gordon 1988). Brumberg documents case after case of seventeenth, eighteenth, and nineteenth-century girls who died from their refusal to eat. Many of the holy fasters explicitly wished for death, among them Margaret of Cortona, who said to her confessor after he urged her to eat, "Dear Father, I have no intention of making a peace pact between my body and my soul, and neither do I intend to hold back. Therefore allow me to tame my body by not altering my diet; I will not stop for the rest of my life until there is no life left" (quoted in Bell, 101).

Western women's fasting is antisocial, endless, total, and deadly; it is unlike what people in most other societies practice. Perhaps certain cultures in history share characteristics that explain why a significant number of women have fasted to death. I consider here the causal significance of ideology, patriarchal and stratified political and economic structure, and family organization. These factors are partially described in the books under review, which give some data on historical differences; systematic consideration of their interrelation and similarity over time can illuminate Western women's food refusal.

IDEOLOGY

Absolutism and the Quest for Perfection

Western women's fasting has manifestly different goals in different historical periods. These differences are related to the overall process of secularization (Bell, 170–77; Brumberg, passim) and to significant differences in culture. Yet even as the West has become manifestly less religious, certain ideological tenets have persisted because they are deeply ingrained in Western culture. The Judeo-Christian ideology—unlike that of many other societies—is both dualistic and absolutist, based on

> a dichotomy of absolute goodness and evil, absolute strength and weakness, absolute truth and absolute untruth. . . . The Judeo-Christian orientation contrasts sin and virtue, grace and non-grace, fall and redemption in order to comprehend the role of the divine in sustaining goodness, virtue and so on. Within the general schema of Judeo-Christian thought it is necessary to have diametrically opposed contrasts, and within the lives of individuals a person judges the virtuousness of his present life, achieved through the grace of God, with his sinful past. (Pandian 1985, 50)

During the Middle Ages, Pandian notes, Western culture lost the "conceptual package of the vast range of human possibility and self identity" that had been presented in Greek mythology, with its array of gods—jealous, wise, silly, angry, composed, weak, powerful, and so on (1985, 51). What remained was perfection simply and radically contrasted with perdition.

Medieval women strove for holiness through fasting, Victorian girls sought the wasting and weakness associated with social and spiritual superiority, and modern women strive for thinness—all aspects of perfection in the value system of their culture. William Davis suggests that "both [thinness and holiness] represent ideal states of being in the cultural milieus under consideration" (1985, 181–82). Brumberg says that "anorexia nervosa appears to be a secular addiction to a new kind of perfectionism, one that links personal salvation to the achievement of an external body configuration, rather than an internal spiritual state" (7). Thus women persistently seek to attain an absolute standard of perfection through fasting but alter the definition of perfection as their societies become increasingly secularized.

The persistence of the absolutist ideology over time is implicated in the obsessive way in which Western women fast. Food refusal must be total; anything less fails to achieve the desired state of perfection. Although many medieval saints, like Catherine of Siena (Bell, chap. 2; Bynum, 169) and Margaret of Cortona (Bell, 101), were ordered by their confessors and religious superiors to take food, they refused in the belief that total fasting was essential to their holiness and union with God. Brumberg documents many cases of women in the seventeenth, eighteenth, and nineteenth centuries, like Ann Moore (60) and Sarah Jacob (64ff.), who either pretended to or did refuse all food, for the impression of total fasting was integral to their self-concept and impact on others. Modern anorexics tenaciously adhere to a rigid diet and feel that any transgression undermines their quest for achievement. As Aimee Liu says, "I'm becoming famous around school for my display of self-discipline. . . . In this one respect, I'm the best, but if I let it go, all is lost, so I cling to my diet tenaciously" (1979, 40). But total fasting is too painful and difficult for most women, and so many—whether perennial dieters or severe bulimics—oscillate dangerously back and forth between fasting and binging, overeating and purging, consumed with guilt over their failure to fast or diet perfectly.

Mind-Body Dualism and Denigration of the Female

Another persistent foundation of Western ideology that is unlike that of many non-Western tribal peoples is the dichotomy of mind and body (Pandian 1985). The literature under review on medieval, Victorian, and contemporary female fasters makes clear that central issues for such women are beliefs in the separateness of mind and body and the moral value in dominance of body by mind (see aso Bordo 1993; Chernin 1981). Brumberg (77ff.) tells us, for example, that the fourteen-year fast of the "Brooklyn Enigma," Mollie Fancher, was seen by her spiritualist followers as evidence of "the duality of the mind and the body" (87).

This duality has been integral to Western morality from at least the time of the ancient Greeks (Bell, 118–19). The two chief ways of enacting mind's control of the body are fasting and chastity. Bynum (2) argues that for medieval people, "to repress eating and hunger was to control the body in a discipline far more basic than any achieved by shedding the less frequent and essential gratifications of sex or money." For Victorians, sexuality was tightly controlled and "appetite was regarded as a barometer of sexuality" (Brumberg, 175); hence denial of appetite stood for suppression of sexuality. In modern society, control of food intake has assumed paramount importance in the demonstration of morality. Sexual control may have become relatively unimportant, but limitation of eating in the midst of affluence, constant availability of food, and advertising's relentless promotion of consumption is both difficult and highly revered (Brumberg, Afterword; Mackenzie 1976; Schwartz 1986).

In the Western dualistic tradition, women are identified with nature and the sensual body that must be controlled, and men are associated with culture and the mind that controls (Bynum, 282; Chernin 1981), as in the story of Adam, the doubting mind, tempted by Eve, the wanton flesh (see Chernin 1987). Women who seek value and worth in the definitional terms of Western culture must dominate their appetites by their wills, thus affirming their spirituality, discipline, and morality. In a culture that postulates dominance of mind over sense and associates women with the body and its appetite, the burden of control falls particularly strongly on women.

Because of women's depiction in the dichotomous worldview, their quest for perfection necessitates dominance of the body through control of food consumption and endurance of hunger. Bynum and Bell describe over and over again how medieval women tortured themselves by trying to repress their hunger in an effort to become holy. Pain and suffering were equated with pleasure and love (Bell, 60), and hunger stood for "hungering for God" (Bynum, 152). The thirteenth-century Flemish mystic Hadewijch, for example, wrote beautiful mystical poems expressing her belief that "hunger ... is incorporation with Christ's suffering humanity, which is our path to his divinity. The more we hunger with Christ, the more we are filled" (Bynum, 160). Brumberg shows how Victorian women found appetite vulgar, unfeminine, unspiritual, and immoral (chap. 7). Food was associated with lower-class status, work and drudgery, gluttony, and physical ugliness; appetite was associated with sexuality and a lack of self-restraint (178–79). Abstention from food signified social refinement, delicacy, daintiness, and morality—those characteristics most admired by Victorian women. Similarly, anorexics, like Aimee Liu, define their self-worth in terms of the self-discipline they muster to limit consumption (1979, 40).

While affirming the importance of mind-body dualism as a meaningful context for holy women's fasting, Bynum claims that medieval women were not merely expressing an internalized cultural misogyny based on masochism or dualism (208). Rather, unlike modern anorexics, they were seizing power and making a positive statement with their fasting. She argues, in fact, that the Middle Ages contained a lesson for moderns:

> Medieval people saw food and body as sources of life, repositories of sensation. Thus food and body signified generativity and suffering. Food which must be destroyed in order to give life, and body, which must be torn in order to give birth, became synonymous; in identifying themselves with both, women managed to give meaning to a physical, human existence in which suffering was unavoidable. . . . In contrast, modern people see food and body as resources to be controlled. Thus food and body signify that which threatens human mastery. . . . Body and food are thus symbols of the failure of our efforts to control ourselves. (300)

Bynum underscores an important difference in medieval and modern attitudes toward suffering. In the Middle Ages, women reveled in bodily agony, which they saw as redemptive; although the body could be a source of evil, its suffering could also bring salvation. Victorian women viewed suffering with some reverence, as a path to bodily delicacy (Brumberg, chap. 5). Modern women attempt to negate the body and its pain, which represent failure of the mind's ability to control the senses. In spite of this difference, fasting women share both a belief in the body as a potential source of evil and a fear of their own susceptibility to temptation. Although Lois Paul (1974) reports a similar belief for Mayan Indian women (heavily influenced by Christianity) and many cultures define the female body as polluting (Douglas 1966; Meigs 1984; Delaney, Lupton, and Toth 1988), I know of no culture where women attempt to purify their bodies with the total and inexorable food refusal that characterizes holy, Victorian, and modern anorexics.

Denial of Female Sexuality and Reproduction

Across time a shared characteristic of Western women who fast excessively is the denial of their reproductive potential and their sexuality. This, I believe, stems from the ambivalent attitude of Judeo-Christian

peoples toward the body, simultaneously source of life and of temptation. All starving women, including medieval (Bynum, 138, 148, 214,
217), Victorian (Brumberg, 132), and modern (Bruch 1973, 275)
fasters, stop menstruating and their feminine curves disappear. A starving person loses all sexual desire (Firth 1959; Holmberg 1969; Turnbull
1972; Winnick 1979). As Margaret Mead noted (1967, 144), for women
both eating and sexual intercourse involve inception; cessation of eating can stand for denial of all inception, including the sexual. Appetite
and the sexual instinct, the mouth and the vagina, are symbolically
connected (Freud 1962, 1); closing the mouth to food stands for closing
the vagina to sex.

Fear of, disgust with, and refusal of sexual connection are common
themes in the worldviews of anorexics and medieval saints and are
linked to their food refusal. Although explicit discussions of sex are
rare among late nineteenth-century anorexics, there is evidence that
"confused or unfulfilled expectation in the domain of courtship was a
common precipitating agent in the mental disorders of adolescent
girls" (Brumberg, 134–35). Numerous studies of contemporary women
with eating disorders report their hostility toward sexual contact with
men (Orbach 1978; Millman 1980, 188–89; Chernin 1981; Bruch 1973,
275–80). Aimee Liu, for example, says, "God, how I hated men! They
made my skin crawl. Worse, they made me despise myself, my body,
my sex. They were bastards, it was true, but mine was the flesh that
teased them. Ugh, what an abominable business. There had to be a way
out, to become androgynous" (1979, 101). And so she stopped eating,
delighted in the disappearance of menses and breasts, and wished to
crawl "back into the body of a child" (41). Her attitude is similar to that
of the fourteenth-century Dominican nun Francesca Bussa, who
refused food as part of her total horror of sex:

> The consummation of the marriage, when she was but thirteen, had an
> immediate and traumatic effect on the girl; no sooner had the wedding
> celebration ended, than without warning she suddenly lost all her
> strength, became paralyzed and dumb, and she was totally unable to
> eat.... By the age of seventeen or eighteen Francesca had reduced her
> food intake to only one meal each day, and this one spartan in the
> extreme: no fish, eggs, chicken, or anything sweet or delicate, only bitter
> legumes and beans not even flavored with oil.... She slept only two
> hours each day, and even during these times she told of being tortured by
> dreams of men who carried giant cooked onions (a food she detested and
> that always nauseated her) and smeared them over her face and stuffed
> them in her mouth. (Bell, 136–38)

The absolutism, dualism, and diffidence toward female sexuality
characteristic of Judeo-Christian ideology provide a context for women
who evince strong ambivalence toward their sensual appetites. They

deny them but are tormented by thoughts of food or by sexual demons. They attempt to quench their desires, but constant self-denial only exacerbates them. Negation of bodily appetite unites Western fasting women and provides a path to individual autonomy and achievement where few other such paths exist.

PATRIARCHY AND FEMALE SUBORDINATION

The holistic and comparative perspective can illuminate how Western women's fasting relates to their historically evolving subordinate social and economic position, which limits channels to their self-expression. Bell, Bynum, and Brumberg all raise and treat in different ways the question of whether women's prodigious fasting is a response to and struggle against patriarchy.[9] To a certain extent they, like many contemporary scholars of anorexia nervosa, believe it is. Although they present important insights related to this question, not one offers an explicit definition of patriarchy and a clear exposition of how women's fasting protests against it.

From an anthropological perspective, a patriarchy is a society where women are politically, economically, socially, and ideologically devalued and disadvantaged, where they lack control of economic resources and power, and where they are deemed morally and physically inferior to men. Systematic analysis of the fasting women's specific place in a system of class and gender inequality is lacking in the three books; however, they do give some information.

Some of the holy fasters were from urban, well-off families (Bynum, 18). Modern anorexics are predominantly of upper-middle-class, white families or of upwardly mobile, lower-middle-class families (Bruch 1978; Lawrence 1984), with an incidence of around one case per hundred thousand Americans and somewhere between one and twenty severe cases per hundred female college and high school students (Brumberg, 13). Anorexia nervosa and bulimia are relatively rare among black girls in the United States and Western Europe (Brumberg, 280, n. 14; Emmons 1992; Hsu 1987; Parker et al. 1995). It has been suggested that black women achieve noticeably more respect and status than white women within the family and community and that control of food exchanges is an important source of their power (Stack 1974; Styles 1980). A number of Brumberg's nineteenth-century examples were middle class, like Mollie Fancher, of a "moderately circumstanced, respectable, intelligent and well connected family" (*Brooklyn Daily Eagle*, June 7, 1866, quoted in Brumberg, 79). Others, however, were of more humble origin (47): Ann Moore was the daughter of a laborer (56), and Sarah Jacob was one of seven children of crofters in rural Wales (64). In fact, Brumberg says, "late nineteenth-century fasting girls were generally not the daughters of the urban, educated, or secularly minded bourgeoisie" (91). Rather, they were the last relics of "an older female religious culture" (100). More data on the fasters are needed to test Pamela Quaggiotto's (1987) suggestion that perhaps women chose to fast to reaffirm themselves as actors, a role denied them when their labor became superfluous. Western society has changed enormously from the Middle Ages to the present, of course, but over time some women have had a particularly powerless, secondary, and mute position when compared to women in nonhierarchical, non-Western societies.

Anthropologists (e.g., Brown 1975; Lee 1979; Murphy and Murphy 1985; Shostak 1981; Weiner 1988) have documented case after case of nonstratified societies where women have much influence through their control over resources and their important role in food production, distribution, preparation, and consumption. Women among the Iroquois, for example, possessed considerable power because they produced the most important foods—corn, beans, and squashes, the "three sisters"—and because they controlled distribution, which was a main channel for creating obligations in others (Brown 1975). Iroquois women also held the stores of food (a main source of wealth) and used that control to influence political decisions.

But unlike their tribal sisters, many of the Western women who have practiced prodigious fasting do not control important economic resources, work actively in production, or manage distribution; they administer only food preparation and consumption, largely within the home. Although Bell (e.g., 88) and particularly Bynum (chap. 7) mention how medieval women circumvented male authority by distributing food to the poor, this was not their legitimate purview; the act incited opprobrium from fathers, husbands, and religious authorities. Control of consumption is Western women's principal channel for expression of identity, influence, and will. Refusal of food produced and given by others is, as we discussed above in reference to Mauss, a refusal to be beholden. Fasting is one of the few legitimate ways for women to exert control without overtly challenging male power. This is perhaps why they are obsessed with food and fasting in a way non-Western women, who have other channels for influence, are not.

FAMILY, FASTING, AUTONOMY, AND RELATIONSHIPS

Patriarchal Western society not only restricts women's economic and political opportunities but also defines their role within the family as nurturer and food provider, a role compatible with the use of food as voice. Although most women in Western society have been relatively powerless, only a few have chosen prodigious fasting. These are women who, because of specific family experiences, may have had particularly severe psychological difficulties with autonomy, intimacy, and eating.

Researchers of contemporary anorexia nervosa have suggested that anorexia is related to specific family dynamics (e.g., Bruch 1973, 1978; Lawrence 1984; Minuchin, Rosman, and Baker 1978). In particular, eating disorders arise in families where parents are concerned with perfection and are overinvolved with, overidentified with, and overprotective of their children, restricting their independence and autonomy. Furthermore, eating disorders are likely to arise in families where parents confuse food with love and fail to respond appropriately to children's needs, interfering with their ability to recognize hunger and satiety and to use food appropriately (Bruch 1973, chap. 4). Some parents are themselves overly concerned about the relationship between food, the body, and self-worth. They see food consumption primarily as the path to moral rectitude. How such family patterns are implicated in modern eating disorders is well established, but the paucity of data on the family relationships of medieval and Victorian fasters make it harder to tell whether similar patterns existed in past cases of female fasters.

Food refusal is denial of relation, and fasting to death is the ultimate rupture of human connection. Difficulty with intimacy and relationship is a clear theme in all Western female fasting, which is self-absorbed and narcissistic. Medieval holy women turned inward to search for God in themselves; as Catherine of Genoa wrote, "My *ME* is God" (Bynum, 277). Modern anorexics become totally self-involved; as Aimee Liu writes, "The mirrors, this one and another large wall mirror over the sink in the bathroom, play an important part in my life now. For hours I hold court through them with myself" (1979, 75). Medieval, Victorian, and modern fasters have solitary lives and few friends; in fact, adherence to the fast and the ascetic routine involve hours of reclusion each day, leaving little time for relations with others.

In his epilogue to Bell's book, William Davis offers an interesting hypothesis to explain the inward-facing stance of fasting women. He refers to Carol Gilligan's (1981) findings that female identity is based on relationships and suggests that the prodigious fasters have a particularly strong need for superhuman connection. The holy faster sought and established a direct union with God, unmediated by male authority. "She wanted above all to be deeply connected to just herself, independent of the needs that would inevitably bring her into a hierarchic, submissive, and 'possessed' relationship with men" (184). Modern anorexics "ignore affiliation and focus instead upon acquiring power" (185); they find themselves totally bereft of the sense of identity that women achieve through relationships. Less clear is the difficulty of middle-class Victorian girls with relationships; perhaps the fact that their "options for self-expressions outside the family were limited by parental concern and social convention" (Brumberg, 188) made their relationships similarly limited.

The family is the most immediate breeding ground of the girl's refusal to eat, and it is the domain most radically upset by her fasting. Brumberg aptly describes the nineteenth-century girl's refusal of the food so fundamental to middle-class nurturance as "a striking disfunction in the bourgeois family system" (134). Many researchers have considered the role of family dynamics, particularly the mother-daughter relationship, in causing contemporary anorexia nervosa. Feminists such as Susie Orbach (1978, 1982) and Kim Chernin (1981, 1985, 1987) have suggested that the mother-daughter relationship is extremely problematic in a patriarchal society where daughters identify with their mothers but cannot respect them because of their subordinate position. Mothers want their daughters to excel but inhibit their development because it would emphasize the mothers' own lack of achievement. Girls respond by seeking autonomy and excellence through a channel that strikes mothers literally in the gut but does not challenge their life choices.

Brumberg's discussion of "love and food in the bourgeois family" in the Victorian era (chap. 5) shows how family conflicts can result in anorexia nervosa. In this social milieu food was of central importance; daughters underwent prolonged dependence; and the family, particularly the relationship between mother and daughter, was oppressive. The nineteenth-century girl was the symbol and vehicle of maternal social striving; her food consumption reflected love, social status, and proper etiquette. The Victorian girl suffocated by familial possessiveness and aspirations found a perfect form of rebellion in food refusal. This was a way of protesting the oppressive nature of relationships without breaking them, and it clearly symbolized the girl's ambivalence toward familial connections.

Some evidence suggests that medieval fasters were involved in a similar struggle with their mothers for autonomy. Mary Magdalen de' Pazzi, for example, "waged her most severe emotional battles" against her mother and competed with her for holiness and her father's affection (Bell, 172). Bell says of Catherine of Siena, one of the most dramatic and influential of the holy anorexics, "In so ordinary and seemingly trivial a contest of wills as weaning, it had to be mother Lapa who triumphed over daughter Catherine, but as an adult this particular child made sure never to lose such battles, often redefining a situation in her mind so that what might appear to others as obedience in this world was to her a triumph in the next for the bridegroom with whom she was united" (32).

In medieval, Victorian, and modern families, fasting women are those with a special need for autonomy. Often they are particularly intelligent, striving, creative, or imaginative women who feel especially fettered by the confinement of their social role. Most contemporary anorexics are high achievers, ostensibly successful in school, sports, and life until the disorder takes over (Bruch 1978, chap. 3). Many of the holy anorexics were also uncommon women: ambitious, perfectionistic, articulate, poetic, capable of fanatical devotion to their religious fasting, cheerful, outgoing, and boisterous (Bell, 114). Although Bell documents a whole group of holy anorexics who turned to their behaviors after marriage and childbirth (chap. 4), most medieval (Bynum, 119), Victorian (Brumberg, passim), and modern (Bruch 1978, chap. 4) fasters appeared to begin or to intensify their extraordinary behaviors around adolescence, a time when the mother-daughter relationship becomes particularly difficult as the daughter begins to define her adult female identity. Because of the centrality and significance of food for women and their lack of other means (Bynum, chap. 6), women use its refusal as the central vehicle in their search for identity, relationship, and autonomy.

Traumatic feeding in infancy and early childhood may explain why some women become fasters where others, facing similar cultural and psychological problems, do not. Freudian psychology, as Brumberg (213) and Bell (11) both discuss, turned attention to this domain. In a seminal paper, Anna Freud (1946) extended many of her father's implicit notions about the importance of feeding in establishing a child's personality, relationship to the mother, and later attitude toward food.[10] Bruch (1973, chap. 4) discovered that parental failure to teach children appropriate recognition of and response to hunger and satiety was the basis of many of her patients' eating disorders. Bell believes that patterns for future relationships are determined by the consistency or inconsistency of breast-feeding. For example, he attributes Catherine of Siena's great capacity for faith to her "oral contentment" in infancy (30–35) and Catherine of Racconigi's psychological and spiritual turmoil to the fact that her mother lacked breast milk and "sent the infant around in her brother Luigi's arms to beg suckle from healthier village women" (159).

Anthropologists have provided data that give an interesting perspective on how traumatic early childhood feeding can affect adult personality and attitudes toward food without causing anorexia nervosa. Dorothy Shack (1969) and William Shack (1971) argue that the inconsistent feeding of infants and children among the Gurage of Ethiopia, including deprivation when hungry and forced gorging when satiated, is responsible for a host of personality traits prevalent among adult Gurage including selfishness, emotional detachment, passivity, dependency, feelings of worthlessness, and food anxiety. Low-status Gurage males, those most deprived of food and most subject to dependency-frustration by the mother, suffer *awre* spirit possession reminiscent of but markedly different from anorexia nervosa. It is characterized by loss of appetite, nausea, and stomach pains (Shack 1971, 35). The spirit is exorcised in a collective ritual where the victim's relatives feed him special ceremonial food until the *awre* spirit cries out from inside him, "I am satisfied" (36). The Gurage show that psychological disorders are expressed through eating in non-Western as well as Western societies and that psychological disorders centered on food can indeed be determined by inappropriate infant feeding and family dynamics, but they also show that the sex of the victim and the use of food to resolve the disorder depend on the unique cultural, social, economic, and psychological setting. Data on the Gurage support Brumberg's (24) claim that eating disorders are multi-determined and depend on "the individual's biologic vulnerability, psychological predisposition, family, and the social climate" (24).

CONCLUSION

The holistic and cross-cultural perspective of anthropology can help explain the prodigious fasting of Western women over eight hundred years by drawing into relief a similar, though not identical, array of cultural forces that have influenced their relationship to food and the body. An absolutist, dualistic worldview has established a context where total denial of appetite is a meaningful and admired path to perfection. Patriarchal society has relegated women to a secondary position by virtue of their sex. Some—perhaps particularly ambitious and striving women fettered by oppressive families—seek a voice and struggle against their subordination by refusing food. They choose fasting because of the Western belief that the mind should dominate the body and because of the centrality of food in their lives. It is the most important resource they control, even as they control only its consumption. Denial of food and appetite brings its practitioners moral worth, admiration, and the socially desired states of holiness, daintiness, or thinness, ephemeral states that can involve the fasters' entire negation through death.

The self-destructive relationship Western women have with the body and food is, I contend, significantly different from that of women in many non-Western cultures, for reasons that bear continuing investigation by both historians and anthropologists. We need more data to answer the questions opened by this essay: How has the development of capitalism affected and altered women's relationship to their bodies, food, and fasting? How has the commoditization of the body, especially the female body, through fashion and art (Berger 1972; Nochlin 1988), contributed to the ideological reinforcement of female subordination and to women's alienation from their physical selves manifest in extreme fasting? Does women's relentless fasting express their efforts to become significant social *actors* in the context of the economic superfluousness of their labor? Do women fast to death in similar ways in cultural contexts where they are economically significant actors? How can we explain the anorexia nervosa of contemporary Japanese women noted by Gordon (1988) and Brumberg (13, 280–81, n. 15)? To what extent is it caused by "rapid Westernization" (Brumberg, 13) or by other indigenous cultural forces, and what light does it cast on our understanding of Western women's food refusal? Finally, how do we explain anorexia nervosa in men without invalidating claims that fasting over centuries is intimately related to the specific experience of women? I believe that some men become fasters because they share female subordination, the lack of meaningful outlets for self-expression, and the absolutist moral ideology that puts a premium on asceticism, although other men may fast for different reasons that need further investigation. I fear that as long as Western culture denies many women (and some men) opportunities for self-realization, power, and meaningful connection; as long as it encloses them in oppressive families and trivializes the figure of the mother; and as long as it insists on an absolute standard of perfection, some women will continue to turn to the sometimes fatal manipulation of their own food consumption as a means of self-definition.

7

Food Rules in the United States

Individualism, Control, and Hierarchy[1]

> "For I have known them all already, known them all,
> Have known the evenings, mornings, afternoons,
> I have measured out my life in coffee spoons . . . "
>
> T. S. Eliot,
> "The Love Song of J. Alfred Prufrock"

INTRODUCTION

Rules about food consumption are an important means through which human beings construct reality.[2] They are an allegory of social concerns, a way in which people give order to the physical, social, and symbolic world around them. This chapter uses data from college students' food journals to examine rules about what and how to eat in U.S. culture. It argues that students' food rules convey a belief in self-control and individual choice and that they uphold hierarchical social relations.

College students' ideas about food are embedded in the value system of U.S. society. Unlike noncapitalist societies where food exchanges reduce social distance and solidify relationships (Mauss 1967; Sahlins 1972, 215–19), in our capitalist society, food is a commodity, an object whose exchange creates distance and differentiation. Through capitalist exchange, what Sahlins calls negative reciprocity (1972), individuals are separated from and placed in antagonistic positions toward each other. Some have control over access to food; others do not. Hence food becomes a vehicle of power.

For students, the ability to determine their own and others' food consumption establishes their place in the social hierarchy and their ability to be autonomous and independent. For male and female students alike, self-control is the ability to deny appetite, suffer hunger, and deny themselves foods they like but believe fattening. Individual choice involves determining for themselves what foods are acceptable and consuming them or abstaining from them when they wish. Together, these two values are part of the Euro-American cultural ideal. My informants share the perspective of Sidel's "New American Dreamers" who hold "that they can and must make their own way in life ... can and must take control of their lives. ... They believe success is there for the taking; all they need to do is figure out the right pathway and work hard Above all, they believe that they must be prepared to go it alone" (1990, 9).

The beliefs that success comes from individual hard work and taking control of one's life are manifest in college students' food rules. Their food rules embody these beliefs almost unconsciously and hide from young men and women the realities of class, race, and gender stratification that they uphold, reinforcing students' tendency to assume worth is earned by those with privilege, rather than seeing that privilege defines worth.

Because food has an unusually rich symbolic malleability (Barthes 1975, 57), it is a particularly apt medium for displaying widely varying cultural ideologies. In different cultures, people endow food with meaning on the basis of its primary qualities, such as color, taste, texture, or smell; according to its method of preparation or presentation; or by the manner and order in which it is served. Food may also take on the attributes of those who contributed to its preparation or production. In addition, food has meaning according to what it does to the body in terms of weight gain or loss, or feelings of strength or weakness. Anthropologists have studied food rules and taboos to explain cultural constructions of gender, class, nature, religion, morality, health, and the social order.[3]

Awareness of how eating is defined and evaluated in the United States is important. First, it enables us more accurately to study the meaning of food in other cultures with acknowledgment of the blinders provided by our own food rules. Second, the success of nutrition education programs depends on their ability to fit into cultural patterns. Finally, food rules are part of a usually unscrutinized cultural ideology that continuously leads to the reinforcement of life as it is. Because eating is such a basic condition of existence, people take their foodways for granted and rarely subject them to conscious examination. To use the words of Antonio Gramsci, food rules consist of a "language" which contains "a determined conception of the world" (1955, 3–4). Yet because they reflect and re-create the gender, race, and class hierarchies so prevalent in American society, deconstructing food rules is part of the process of dismantling the hierarchies that limit the potential and life chances of subordinate groups.

RESEARCH ON FOOD RULES IN COLLEGE CULTURE

Method and Study Population

My data come principally from food-centered journals kept by male and female students in my "Food and Culture" class over several years.[4] Keeping journals is a requirement for the class; students write twice a week on topics provided by me or of their own interest. Of particular relevance in this chapter are their writings on "good" and "bad" foods, food and gender, food and power or control, the meaning of "fat'" and "thin," food and family, food and the holidays, fasting, and binging. Data come from approximately 250 students at Stockton State College in southern New Jersey and at Millersville University in south central Pennsylvania. Students are predominantly working- and middle-class white Americans of European background. A significant minority are first-generation college students. The majority come from two-parent families, though divorce of parents is not uncommon. Often students' mothers worked only at home during their childhood but were employed outside the home before and after this period. In most cases their mothers were the primary food preparers.

In this chapter I do not focus on differences in the food rules of male and female students because, for the most part, they share a culture of food even as it differentially affects them and as it poses far more serious limitations on women than on men. In this respect, my findings conform closely to those of Holland and Eisenhart (1990) who, in their study of southern college students, found that male and female students held similar models of attractiveness based on different standards for men and women that "constrained women's lives more than men's" (1990, 94). Thus I will use quotations from both men and women to illustrate what I believe are food rules common to both and to a large segment of Euro-American society.[5]

Why Study College Students?

Present and past college students form a large segment of U.S. society. While not fully representative of the population, the fact that today "roughly half of American youth between the ages of eighteen and twenty-one" (Horowitz 1987, xi) attend college means that college students are worthy of study. They are particularly interesting for the purposes of this chapter because they are in a sort of long-term "liminal" state (Turner 1969), betwixt and between youth and adulthood. They are autonomous yet not fully responsible for all their needs (which are provided by dormitories and food services), and they are both enacting and challenging central cultural values.

As Holland and Eisenhart have convincingly demonstrated in their study of college students at one historically black and one historically white state university in the South (1990), the peer culture is the most important source of values, arbiter of behavior, and focus of interest (see also Horowitz 1987; Moffatt 1989). It is also a particularly "virulent purveyor . . . . of gender privilege" (Holland and Eisenhart 1990, 8). For most college students the "culture of romance" has an overriding importance. Within this culture "men's prestige and correlated attractiveness come from the attention they receive from women and from success at sports, in school politics, and in other arenas. Women's prestige and correlated attractiveness come only from the attention they get from men" (1990, 104).

As a result, ties to men are the most important social ties for women, stronger than and determinant of those to women. Academic studies are secondary to peer relations for most women. Participation in the culture of romance prepares women for and reinforces their subordinate social position, for it links their self-worth to men's attention rather than to their success in school.

Holland and Eisenhart define attractiveness only in relative terms as a woman's ability to command good treatment from desirable men (1990). It is clear, however, from my data on college students that a crucial absolute determinant of attractiveness in the peer culture is thinness. As will become evident below, female students' desire to be thin so as to be attractive reinforces their secondary position in the gender hierarchy below males while supporting their claims to higher status among females. Hence, my findings confirm and extend those of Holland and Eisenhart by providing data on food rules and meanings, areas not covered in their study.

At the same time as my data reveal a great deal about the college peer culture, they also provide information about U.S. culture in general, for students' ideas about eating reflect the standards and values learned through their family, friends, teachers, and mass media while growing up. To be sure, the student life imposes some special characteristics on eating behavior and attitudes. For example, the fact that most of my student informants live in dormitories or their own apartments rather than with their parents affects the meaning of "family" food which, through its absence, takes on greater symbolic import than when eaten every day. Students on meal plans must eat at specified times or miss meals; this sometimes forces them to eat when not hungry and to resort to junk or fast food when they are hungry outside of institutional meal times. They are likely either to eat alone in their rooms or to eat publicly in front of scores of peers in the collective dining commons, at parties, or on late-night pizza runs. The extent to which they eat in public and with people they know and want to impress probably exacerbates their concerns over eating properly and calls the food rules into more salient relief than might otherwise be the case. However, in spite of the peculiarities of living in a world populated almost exclusively by age-mates, I believe that the food rules espoused by students are highly revealing of central values and concerns in Euro-American U.S. society.

FOOD RULES IN U.S. COLLEGE CULTURE

The most important aspects of food in the meaning system of American college students are its vaguely understood nutritional qualities, particularly its caloric value; its power to tempt appetite; its ability to make one fat; and its emotional associations. Although students do articulate specific symbolic meanings for a few foods—for example turkey epitomizes Thanksgiving, and pork and sauerkraut eaten on New Year's Day bring luck to Pennsylvania Germans—their overall interest in food is not in its intrinsic properties, but in their relationship to it. Their feelings about their own bodies and about a standard of beauty based on extreme thinness are a result of the relationship to food.

Nutrition: Good and Bad Eating

One salient intrinsic characteristic of food in U.S. culture is its nutritional content; this fact represents the influence of the scientific mode of thinking on popular ideology. Rules for good food involve the notion of a balanced diet that is defined not in terms of hot and cold (Laderman 1983, Manderson 1986c), male and female (Meigs 1984), sweet and savory (Douglas 1974), or raw and cooked foods (Lévi-Strauss 1966), but rather in terms of the basic four food groups, defined according to their complementary nutrients (see Science and Education Administration 1980).

The principal goal of the scientifically defined balanced diet is to ensure adequate nutrients and calories according to individual needs while limiting damaging foods that are high in sugar, fat, cholesterol, and sodium. Students have a vague knowledge of scientific nutrition. Many learn at some point in their upbringing that everyone should eat something daily from the basic four food groups, although none is very explicit about specific recommendations. Many students condemn excess consumption of red meat, animal fat, cholesterol, sugar, junk food, and greasy food. They report as "good for you" vegetables, fruits, grains, low-fat dairy products, fish, poultry, roughage, and such anomalous foods as pancakes, corn, and lamb. In spite of the enormous publicity over oat bran in the late 1980s, students rarely mention it. Not only does student understanding of nutritional precepts seem rather sketchy (see Sobal and Cassidy 1987), but so does their perceived adherence to them as shown in their food logs and reports on meals (see Stasch, Johnson, and Spangler 1970). Students tend to eat too few fresh fruits and vegetables; to consume too many soft drinks, sweets, greasy snacks, and alcoholic beverages; and in general to lack precisely the "balance" in their diets that even they recommend. Nevertheless, they do not seem terribly upset by their failure to eat nutritionally.

In fact, college students express their individualism and independence by defining their own good diet. Over and over again, they write in their journals statements such as the following: " 'Good' and 'bad' foods are simply what you make them to be" (F/F 1990),[6] that is, not what scientists say they are. Women in particular are more concerned about calories than about vitamins, minerals, fats, carbohydrates, and proteins, as is evidenced in the following statement: "I always think of food in terms of calories. It's like I have a built-in calculator in my brain. Every time I eat something I automatically think about what I'm eating and how many calories I'm consuming. I don't seem to think in terms of nutrition, just calories" (F/S 1986).

What my informants think most about is how much and in what manner they eat. They are most concerned not with the food itself but rather with their behavior toward it. Personal expression of willpower and release of control only under certain culturally sanctioned conditions are the key issues in their relationship to food and in their overall ideology of life. Students believe "good" eating involves consumption of three meals timed to fall at appropriate intervals in the morning, midday, and early evening and limited to amounts just sufficient to satisfy hunger. As one student said, "I try to eat a healthy diet three times a day; cut down on snacking; exercise; and I stop eating when I feel satisfied" (M/S 1990). "Bad" eating is that done solely for pleasure (except in exceptional circumstances), in excess, in between meals or late at night, without control, and beyond the point of minimally satisfying hunger. Snacking, binging, eating on the run, eating alone, and stuffing oneself are all "bad."

There are many reasons for students' failure to conform to the rules of scientific nutrition. First of all, their behavior reflects their belief in the American dream: that each person can and should carve his or her own path to success. Eating should be as individualized as other pursuits. Furthermore, empirical evidence contradicts science and undermines students' faith in its tenets. This was beautifully expressed by one male informant:

> Bad foods. People say too much red meat is a bad food. Well I guess that's scientifically been proven. But, for example, my grandfather, who is eighty-four years old, has eaten meat and potatoes every day for years and he's in good condition. Another example of bad foods is fast food,

well do you know Hershel Walker, who is a great running back in the NFL [National Football League]? He eats one meal a day which contains four hamburgers from a fast food chain. And throughout the day he eats eight to ten candy bars. If you have ever seen this man you would realize he's in top condition with an excellent body with no fat. (M/S 1990)

Not only does experience contradict the scientific canons, but they themselves are confusing, sometimes contradictory, and perceived as ineffective.[7]

> What might be good for someone to eat to keep their cholesterol level down may not be good for their high blood pressure. . . . Food that is supposed to lower your cholesterol may in fact raise your level. . . . Both of these problems have happened to both friends and family. The foods that my father is told to stay away from for his gout are the foods that he is "allowed" to eat to keep his cholesterol level down. . . . A friend was rigorously following the advice of his doctor and faithfully watched what he was eating to reduce his cholesterol level, but instead of lowering, his level increased. So, who is to say what foods are "good" or "bad" for me? Maybe someday someone will convince me that they found the list of "good" and "bad" foods but until then, I'll just go with what I've been eating. (F/F 1990)

The confusion students perceive in the rules themselves contributes to the ease with which they break them.

Another reason why students do not eat according to the tenets of scientific nutrition is because they have what Laderman (1983, 3) calls "rules to break rules." These enable people to behave differently from ways professed as proper by the food rules, but to do so in culturally justifiable ways. U.S. college students have clear ideas about the circumstances under which it is all right to break their own food rules, and these are highly revealing about their attitudes toward self and eating. Rather than structuring their behavior primarily on the basis of what they know about nutrition, whether from science or from folklore, people eat according to the complex meanings food has for them.

THE MEANING OF EATING FOR COLLEGE STUDENTS

Food signifies pleasure and celebration. Because of these meanings, holidays are a justification for eating in ways that students define as bad. As one student said, holidays are an "excuse to overeat" (M/F 1990). Their ritual and social nature enables extraordinary behavior that is normally condemned and highlights a contradiction central to consumer capitalism: the tension between the pleasures of consumption and the moral superiority deriving from abstention. Whereas students who overeat alone in their rooms may feel immediately guilty, those who splurge at Thanksgiving or a party may not like their behavior, but will not feel as guilty: "I always stuff myself at restaurants or at parties. The temptations of the wonderful foods are too strong. . . . I do not become depressed or think constantly about what I ate. I just know I'll eat less the next day" (F/S 1986).

Students also define food as fuel for the body: "What does food mean to me? It means energy and without food I'm like a car without gas" (M/S 1990). Because of this belief, being in a hurry or coping with a life that is too rushed to eat "right" is another excuse to eat badly by grabbing some junk food out of a vending machine or stopping for fast food. The more convenient accessibility of bad foods compared to good foods contributes to students breaking rules and being able to justify the transgression.

Because food means comfort and love for students, splurging on sweets or other special foods is sanctioned as a crutch for dealing with emotional distress: grief, depression, anger. Students know eating certain foods makes them feel better, so they allow the emotionally therapeutic value of the food to override the possible nutritional drawbacks of eating too much or eating the wrong things. One female student wrote the following: "Around adolescence, I guess that I was going through some kind of a crisis. Food became my only consolation. While other people started smoking or taking drugs, I became addicted to junk food. I came to the point where I used to buy brown sugar, and eat it raw. Food is a friend, a consolation, a hobby, a companion. Whenever I feel lonely, down or depressed, I go to the refrigerator" (F/S 1986).

A very common explanation for students' food habits is their perceived contrast between bad-tasting foods that are "good for you" versus good tasting foods that are "bad for you." For example, one student said,

> What is good food? I'm assuming it's food that is healthy for your body. But what about bad food? Bad food is unhealthy food, and I've been known to like bad food for a long time. Why is the food bad if it tastes good? I know it clogs your arteries and your heart. But why does it taste so good? If junk food, as it is also called, would taste bad there would be no problem. I guess there is a reason why junk food tastes good! Aha I know why! Junk food is often a treat for us so we savor getting treats. If we don't always eat junk food or any food for that matter we become hungry for it. (M/S 1990)

Students eat "badly" because they love so-called bad foods, and they define these foods as "treats." Eating "badly" is consolation and reward.

Another reason why students transgress the rules of scientific nutrition in their eating behavior is because, as one student said, "there are no real consequences" (M/F 1990). Transgressors of food rules in other cultures may be subject to supernatural punishment (Mauss 1967,

53–59), illness (Laderman 1983), shame (Kahn 1986), or social ostracism (Young 1986), but in the United States there are few perceived consequences for not eating according to the canons of scientific nutrition. Any detrimental health effects take years to manifest themselves. And young Americans have a pervasive sense of invulnerability, "a belief, shaped by individualism, that they have some sort of personal exemption from the consequences that we are warned of.... Being young, in itself, gives special license to break rules.... Youth brings immunity from penalty" (Fitchen 1990). However, Americans do suffer consequences for eating the wrong way, that is, for eating too much. Eating is a behavior that constructs the self. It must be done in a proper and controlled manner lest one project an undesirable, immoral, or gender-inappropriate self.

Control

Eating sparingly is a measure of proper human behavior in the United States and in many other cultures (see, e.g., Young 1986). For example, Wamirans of Papua New Guinea fear greed and have deeply held social expectations that people be generous with food (Kahn 1986). Greed and stinginess are immoral because they threaten the fabric of community so painstakingly constructed through sharing food and feasting communally (see Mauss 1967; Young 1986). For U.S. college students, controlling greed is also important, but not to promote food sharing and the ongoing construction of community as in Wamira. In the United States eating properly promotes individualism and personal power. As one student noted, "I use food to sometimes show some control in my life.... When other aspects in my life seem to leave my control, I can always rely on food to bring back some feelings of self-control" (F/F 1990). College students value the exercise of restraint in eating because it is a path to personal attractiveness, moral superiority, high status, and dominance:

> Thinness, to me, is a symbol of control. This control is both applied over other people and to one's own actions and needs. Despite the role of heredity in the determination of one's body type, over which there is no control, I nevertheless have more respect for and am more attracted to those who are thin. My own preference seems to be that of most other people as well. I believe that to become and remain thin, in a society of excess such as ours, takes a great deal of self-knowledge and control. It seems so easy to give in to the powers of the palate and eat our way to ecstasy while ignoring our self-image and the image we present to others. Thin people are controlled by these images and thus rarely give in to excessive eating. Thin people also have control over those who are not thin. When non-thin people look at those who are thin there is usually resentment at what they are not and at those who represent this. With

this resentment comes a sort of "invisible" control exhibited by thin people since they are somehow more powerful and in control. Thinness is thus a cause and effect of control both over oneself and over others. This control arises from our own ideas about attractiveness and unattractiveness. (M/S 1990)

Hierarchy

The white working- and middle-class students who form the majority of my sample adhere to food rules that uphold a cultural reality based on stratification by class, race, and sex. Although some may individually challenge or subvert the rules on occasion, I found no evidence of a collective challenge of the rules or of the hierarchies they uphold. In fact, the only power that students frequently subvert through their eating habits is, not surprisingly, that of their parents.

Psychologists and pediatric health-care professionals have documented how food can become a battleground between parents and children (Bruch 1973; Freud 1946; Satter 1987). College students recognize the power parents can exercise through food: their control of what and how much is available, their efforts to make children eat what they do not want, their ability to reward with or withhold food, and their use of food as emotional power. Some students evince very strong positive feelings about home cooking and family meals, which seem to represent love and nurturance to them: "Another way I think of food is 'home' and 'love.' When my mom cooks something special, I know it's because she loves us and wants the best for our family" (F/S 1986). Others describe in dramatic detail horrible fights with their parents over how much and what they eat:

> It started again tonight—I don't know why I expected tonight to be any different. The dinner table becomes a battleground every night around 5 P.M. I'm not home very often for dinner, but when I am it's brutal. My mother is the worst. Every night at dinner we hear about how hard she works and how rotten we kids are. . . . Then she starts complaining how tired she is when she comes home from work and how she 'puts herself out' to make dinner for us, how ungrateful we are because we don't eat it. How does she expect us to eat after she's been bitching at us through the whole meal? (F/S 1986)

Some students delight in the freedom at college to eat when and what they choose; others miss family food deeply. If Holland and Eisenhart are correct that a common feature of student peer cultures is opposition to authority (1990), it is not surprising that many college students would desire to oppose parental authority and claim their growing independence through their eating habits (Counihan and Tarbert 1988). It seems clear, and the literature on eating disorders supports this assumption, that students who are most troubled in their efforts to achieve autonomy from their parents and control over their lives are those who may most dramatically oppose traditional family eating habits.[8]

For students the moral behavior of constrained eating places them higher rather than lower on axes of power. As research has shown, class status varies directly with thinness for both men and women, though more strongly for women (Sobal and Stunkard 1989; Stunkard 1977). The higher one's class, the thinner one is likely to be. By clinging to standards of thinness and control over eating, students are supporting a hierarchical social structure and their place higher up within it. They are concerned with not eating too much or not letting food consume them. They fear losing the moral authority that comes from self-control, and they fear the social condemnation that comes from being fat. Fat is not only supremely unattractive in our culture, but it is a clear symbol of loss of control. The thin body proclaims that its wearer eats "right," is good, and fits society's ideals. Thin people, as one student stated so eloquently, have bodies that symbolize their control. And thus they have power over others, the power that comes with self-righteousness and moral rectitude.

Students not only support the class structure in their adherence to the standard made famous by the duchess of Windsor that "you can never be too rich or too thin," but also in their belief that "the poor should eat differently from other Americans because they are different" (Fitchen 1988, 311). Students, particularly those who work as cashiers in food stores, often complain that people with food stamps buy junk or luxury foods, do not shop wisely, and do not stretch their limited resources. The USDA "thrifty food plan" that determines food stamp benefits is based on the expectation that the poor eat differently—less meat and high protein food, more breads, cereals, and beans (Emmons 1986, 1987). However, the poor try to eat like everyone else as a way of overcoming the feelings of deprivation and difference associated with poverty (Fitchen 1988). The claims of middle- and upper-class people that it is legitimate for them to determine the diet of poor people, that they have the ability to be choosy about food, and that they have a superior diet, define them as both more powerful and as behaviorally and morally superior to the poor.

Adherence to properly constrained eating behaviors also reinforces ethnic and racial hierarchies in U.S. culture. Researchers have noted that there is "a strong ethnic component to patterns and degrees of overweight among given subgroups of Americans" that is particularly salient among women (Beller 1977, 8). African American women (Parker et al. 1995; Styles 1980), Puerto Ricans (Massara 1989; Massara and Stunkard 1979), and Native Americans (Garb, Garb, and Stunkard 1975) all have and accept higher obesity rates than whites, especially rich whites (Sobal and Stunkard 1989; Stunkard 1977). By trying to control eating and body size, students can differentiate themselves from lower-status ethnic and racial minorities and—perhaps unwittingly—uphold U.S. racial hierarchy.

Similarly, men and women are defined as different and ranked hierarchically in many cultures, including our own, by rules about their food consumption (Meigs 1984). Adams claims that in the United States the "message of male dominance is conveyed through meat eating—both in its symbolism and reality" (1990, 189). While college students today express vague notions that "lighter" foods such as salads and chicken are female, and "heavier" foods such as beef and potatoes are male, they much more consistently define male and female eating in terms of how much rather than what is consumed. [9] The sexes are enjoined to eat differently—men to eat heartily and abundantly, women to eat daintily and sparingly. As one female student said, "It seems that if a woman eats a lot in front of a man she takes on some kind of masculine quality" (F/F 1990). Contemporary Americans tenaciously maintain gender difference and hierarchy by eating differently and appropriately for their gender. One female student described a fellow student who represented "the typical male attitude towards food and eating. [He believed that] females should 'watch what they eat,' whereas males can eat whatever they want. Also, men seem to feel that they have power to delegate to women what they can and cannot eat" (F/F 1990).

Students enforce gender hierarchy by notions about who has the right to control whose food consumption. Just as the well-off claim the right to decide what the poor should eat (Fitchen 1988), men are often the arbiters of women's diets. Women repeatedly note that eating in the presence of members of the opposite sex is intimidating; on dates they eat sparsely lest they be judged "pigs." Several female students reported male friends decrying how much other women eat, and others wrote about how their boyfriends or fathers harassed them about being overweight and eating excessively, experiences also reported by Millman (1980, 165) and Bruch (1973, 1978) in their research on eating disorders. For example, one female student reported:

> Ever since third grade my father and I would always argue bitterly about how much I weigh. He would always try to prevent me from eating certain things. It has always upset me that my own father could not accept me the way I was. I know he loves me but I wish he didn't feel like he had to make me change.... Even though he made an attempt to make dinner times comfortable, I still remembered how he felt about my weight and I tended to eat less in front of my father, then I would eat more in secrecy, late at night, at stores, at fast-food restaurants, or over at friends' houses. This

resulted in me gaining more weight. I resented my father putting restrictions on what I ate. Therefore, I ate more behind his back. (F/S 1986)

This student felt oppressed by her father's regimentation of her diet and dissatisfaction with her person; she rebelled by eating more when away from his authority.

Men gain control of women not only by making them feel insecure about their weight and food consumption, but by having the "right" to be judges of their weight. In fact, women are much more likely than men to be the targets of judgmental comments made by both women and men on all topics related to eating. The acceptance of this fact and its constant reproduction by women as well as men reinforces the subordinate position of women, who are judged, relative to men, who do the judging. Given the importance of being attractive to men in the college "culture of romance" (Holland and Eisenhart 1990), it is no wonder that my female informants devote a great deal of time and energy worrying about their weight and food consumption. They are very like Holland and Eisenhart's female informants, who "were constantly exposed to societal evaluation—to judgments of their worth—on the basis of their sexual attractiveness to men and . . . much of what they did was addressed to improving or avoiding that evaluation" (1990, 18).

The students' journals reveal that for men eating can be a path to size and power; for women it is a path to thinness and control:

> Being thin seems to be a common goal for women. Whether it is to become thin or to stay thin, women take great pains to moderate their figures. I think that women's struggle to be thin can be paralleled with men's goals to be strong. Not every woman cares about her weight just as not every man cares about his strength. On the whole, however, most women would like to be thin, being thin is attractive and shows control of one's own body. Strength in men is also considered attractive and shows control. It's ironic though, women eat very little to attain their desired state of being while men eat to "bulk up" and turn their fat to muscle and strength. (F/F 1990)

Although contemporary men, like women, are not supposed to be fat or obsessively voracious in regard to food, they can still eat a lot and be "big." As one student said, "I think my father shows some power and authority because of his big, round belly. It's weird, but I go after my mom more if I see her gaining weight than my father. . . . I agree that men can get away with being overweight more than women" (F/S 1986). Often male students report wanting to increase their size, whereas females want to reduce. Women are more likely to impose stricter standards of thinness on themselves than men do on either themselves or women (see Miller, Coffman, and Linke 1980). Women are also more likely to perceive themselves as fatter than they actually are (Mable, Balance, and Galgan 1986), showing their internalization of an unreasonable and oppressive cultural standard (Orbach 1978). The different eating behaviors associated with the different sexes parallel their cultural definitions: Men are still supposed to be big, powerful, free, and dominant; women are to be small, dainty, constrained, and submissive.

CONCLUSION: STATUS QUO AND RESISTANCE

In U.S. culture, food rules express an ideology of life that focuses on how and what is eaten. College students are primarily guided by their own definitions of good and bad food and are concerned with being in control of their eating. For them, eating is not a simple act of fueling the body; it is moral behavior through which they construct themselves as good or bad human beings. Class, race, ethnic, and gender boundaries are maintained by eating differences. Eating daintily separates women from hearty-eating men and concommitantly makes women less powerful. Voluntary restraint and freedom of choice toward food differentiate well-fed, well-off people from poor people with hunger and limited ways to satisfy it. College students eat to show they are individuals, to be special, to be moral; they eat to be themselves and to declare their place in the complex race, class, and gender hierarchy in which they live.

For the most part, working- and middle-class white students seem to uphold the food rules of their culture. Men's adherence to the rules makes sense, since the rules reinforce their privileged status in contemporary U.S. culture. But women are shackled by the accepted food praxis of U.S. culture. Their conformity to the rules that reaffirm their own subordination demands further analysis.

It is not that women never oppose the food rules; they do. But like Holland and Eisenhart's college students (1990), their resistance is individual and partial. They do not challenge the basic meaning system that oppresses them. Women subvert the rules by such behaviors as eating in secret, as did the student who rebelled against her father's imposition of a strictly limited diet by sneaking food or binging at friends' houses. However, the student realized she was harming herself by this behavior, for she did not stop her father's denigration of her appearance, she did not lose the weight that caused the denigration, and she felt guilty for secret eating. However, she did find some relief in the food and did gain some autonomy by her secret and limited rebellion.

Other students attempt to subvert the food rules by binging and purging in an effort "to have their cake and eat it too" (see Cauwels 1983; Gordon 1990; Boskind-White and White 1983). They eat enormous quantities of food in violation of the rules, but then throw it up, thereby maintaining a physical appearance in conformity with cultural standards. Unfortunately, however, they lose self-esteem by their devious behavior and may be trapped in a pathological psychological spiral that can lead to serious illness and even death. Some women become anorexic and reduce their food consumption to almost nothing, thereby subverting the food rules by taking them to a radical extreme (Bruch 1973, 1978; Gordon 1990; Lawrence 1984). They too, however, ultimately may place themselves in a life-threatening situation by this behavior, and they never manage to gain the autonomy and control that they so desperately seek. Other women opt out of the food game altogether by eating with abandon and getting fat. Few, however, manage to do so and maintain their pride and self-respect, so virulently enforced are the cultural codes of thinness and self-control (Millman 1980).

My female students do not show evidence of organizing collectively to throw out the whole food-rules system that enforces their subordination. There is no evidence among students of any movement such as the National Association to Advance Fat Awareness (NAAFA),[10] which challenges the cultural hegemony of thinness in the United States. NAAFA asserts that "fat can be beautiful, . . . it stresses how fat people and fat admirers are victims of prejudice, stigma, and consequent self-hatred. NAAFA's purpose is to call attention to the exclusion, exploitation, and psychological oppression of fat people and to press for changes in the ways fat people are regarded and treated. Its central message is that it's all right to be fat" (Millman 1980, 4).

Why don't female students collectively rebel against the food rules that oppress them? There are probably several reasons. First, they may not be able to see their own oppression, so thoroughly is the sex-gender hierarchy embedded in U.S. culture. Second, in the peer culture women's ties to each other are secondary to their ties to men (Holland and Eisenhart 1990), thus making difficult a women's movement. Third, the food rules embody central cultural values. Acceptance of responsibility for controlling one's own eating habits and weight fits in with the Euro-American cultural belief that all make their own destiny. Students repeatedly reaffirm this view in statements such as the following: "For many years I always felt that it was the person's own fault when they were fat and often wondered how they could do this to themselves. I often thought that they just didn't care about what they looked like and that they deserved to be fat for not taking better care of themselves" (F/S 1986). And even when students are able rationally to understand that fat may not be a person's "fault," they still are unable emotionally to rid themselves of the belief that fat is "gross" and due to the person's willful negligence.

Finally, collective opposition to the food-rules system is subverted because many female students gain some advantages from it. With careful monitoring of their food consumption, they can become "attractive," get men's attention, and achieve a certain status in their peer culture. Furthermore, such status is likely to determine their lives beyond relationships with peers: "Ranking by attractiveness and its associated constraints followed the women into the classroom and was likely to follow them into the workplace" (Holland and Eisenhart 1990, 107). Hence, rejecting the food-rules system is likely to be met with immediate negative consequences as women lose attractiveness, status, and potential success in the world of peers and work. Following the rules, on the other hand, is likely to produce positive results. It will be difficult for women to reject the food rules of American culture until they are in a position to challenge the sex-gender hierarchy in all of its manifestations.

8

Fantasy Food

Gender and Food Symbolism in Preschool Children's Made-Up Stories[1]

> "We'll eat you up we love you so."
> Maurice Sendak,
> *Where the Wild Things Are*

INTRODUCTION

This chapter asks whether children express clues about their gender identity through food themes in their fantasy stories. I came to ask this question out of a curiosity about the origins of the oppressive gender power relations encoded in foodways that I have discussed in preceding chapters. As we have seen, in Western cultures, eating habits and attitudes toward food are channels for expressing male dominance and female subordination.[2] Women are supposed to have slender bodies, eat little, and provide food for others, especially men. Men are supposed to have powerful bodies, eat heartily, and be served food. These different stances toward food and the body reveal different attitudes toward the self. Women's sometimes servile role around food and their concern with restrictive eating and thinness reveal an insecurity about being women and a sense of powerlessness and subordination, whereas men's attitudes reveal a sense of self-confidence and entitlement. This chapter was inspired in part by an effort to assess when and how gender differences and power imbalances in relationships to food emerge and whether they appear among three- to six-year-old children.

The data on how children use eating or food imagery to develop and signify gender is much more sparse than data on adults. While there is some literature on the eating habits, problems and needs of young children,[3] I have yet to find much research on gender differences in either their food consumption or their attitudes toward food. This study began with the notion that feeding and the ideas and values communicated through food *ought* to be important in children's development of gender identity because of food's social and symbolic significance. It addresses the following questions: Do food and eating encode gender identity and/or power for children? Do preschool boys and girls define themselves through concepts of fat or thin? Do children exercise power and control over their world through symbolic or literal control over food? Does food express and reflect gendered family connections and conflicts? What are the meanings of hunger, greed, and devouring for children, and do they reflect gender similarities or differences?

THE FUNCTION AND IMPORTANCE OF CHILDREN'S STORIES

In investigating whether young children use food as a marker of gender identity I ran into some obstacles. I had hoped to conduct participant-observation in a day care center and then tape-record interviews with the children. However, when I asked the children questions such as "Can you name good and bad foods?" "Are there boys' foods and girls' foods?" "What does fat mean to you?" and "What does thin mean to you?" they were generally uninterested and either didn't answer at all or gave short responses that led into topics they found more interesting. Stymied, I stumbled upon the methodology of tape-recording their stories and then later looking at the food symbolism.[4] The children told stories willingly and with fervent interest. At the day care center, the children may have been "primed" to tell stories about food because I had been asking them questions about their eating habits and sitting with them at lunch, but I also tape-recorded stories at a kindergarten without asking the food questions and found that a roughly similar proportion of the stories had food themes.

Listening to their stories is a good way to learn about young children, for they tell tales willingly, spontaneously, and with great pleasure. Unfortunately, I have found no anthropological analyses of story collections from children in other cultures, although there are several studies from researchers in a variety of disciplines of children's stories, language, and games in our own culture.[8] I have found no ethnographic studies at all of childhood linking children's stories to in-depth knowledge about their family and social life. Such ethnographic studies are sorely needed. My own ability to interpret children's stories was hampered by the lack of ethnographic context. For that reason in particular, this chapter aims to be suggestive rather than conclusive.

Researchers have investigated children's stories, fantasy play, and language use to determine how children think and whether they mani-

fest gender differences in early childhood.[9] My study continues this
work and adds a new dimension by focusing on food symbolism. It
draws on the work of others to establish the import of fantasy and language for understanding children.

Vivian Gussin Paley's work is a masterful, insightful, and humanistic
demonstration of the significance of children's stories. In over a quar-
ter century of teaching at the University of Chicago Laboratory School,
Paley has concluded that children know "how to put every thought and
feeling into story form" (1990, 4). Working chiefly with kindergarten
children, Paley has developed a classroom culture where the telling,
recording, and dramatic enactment of her pupils' stories is the basis of
learning, growth, and socialization. Believing that "the fantasies of any
group form the basis of its culture" (1990, 5), Paley shows how the children use their stories to grapple with conflicts, questions, fears, and
loneliness. They use the stories to learn, grow, and connect with each
other. In making up a story, the child "refocuses an event" and thus
makes it more comprehensible or real (Paley 1981, 158). In lucid prose,
Paley's many books demonstrate how children use their stories to make
sense out of the world, transform it in beneficial ways, and transcend
their own limitations.

Brian Sutton-Smith has been a pioneer in the study of children's
play, folklore, and stories (1972, 1979, 1981). He argues that children's
folk stories, although idiosyncratic, are like folktales in some fledgling
phase in that they "have the same basic plot structures and the same
general concerns with fate, fate overwhelming, and fate nullified"
(1981, 2). Their stories reveal children's cognitive organization and
show their "attempt to come to narrative terms with fateful, perhaps
conflictual matters" (1981, 9). Sutton-Smith affirms the major significance of children's folkstories by claiming that "it is reasonable to consider the mind as narrative, and therefore to consider our analysis of
narrative as an analysis of mind" (1981, 37).

Like the illustrious child researcher Jean Piaget, Sutton-Smith sees
the stories of children as a mediation between the satisfaction of their
egocentric needs and the accommodation of those needs to the constraints of social reality. Fantasy, according to Piaget (1962), is a way
for the child to relive experience to please the self rather than subordi-
nating the self to the demands and desires of others. Stories often
involve wish fulfillment—representations of the way children want
things to be—and thus are a path to empowerment and self-develop-
ment. All thinkers who have looked at children's stories concur that
they spring from, as Piaget put it, "deep affective schema" (1962, 175).
That is, children's stories deal with issues that are deeply felt if not
always clearly articulated in the child's conscious mind. They can

express inchoate feelings, thoughts, and conflicts that cannot be expressed in cognitive conceptual thought because they are either too threatening or too elusive.

Pitcher and Prelinger offer a fascinating Freudian analysis of stories collected from young children in the mid-1950s. They argue that stories are a solution to the conflict between children's unconscious desires and adults' demands that children behave in socially acceptable ways (1963, 216–17). Fantasy stories are an important way for children to act out their own untamed impulses as well as to practice and challenge adult roles. Rosalind Gould, influenced by Freud and Piaget, analyzes fantasy play and stories collected for her by preschool teachers (1972). Fantasy, Gould believes, involves the unconscious transformation of wishes, impulses, and emotions. It springs from children's efforts "to alter intolerable limitations and frustrations" in their lives and to defend themselves from the anxieties coming from their sexual and aggressive impulses. Fantasy provides for children a way of dealing with emotional conflicts, challenges to achieve mastery (e.g., to control their emotions or their bodily functions), threats to their self-esteem, or inscrutable mysteries. Gould suggests that children's fantasy stories and play reveal their "inner psychological processes" and enables the development of their "core self image" by allowing them to practice being who they wish to be and by freeing them somewhat from dependency on parent figures (1972, 54).

Bruno Bettelheim's (1977) study of the meaning and importance of fairy tales articulates the power of fantasy stories in unlocking troubling issues from children's unconscious and making them accessible to the conscious in a metaphorical form that defuses their threatening nature and enables them "to serve positive purposes" (1977, 7). Like Paley, Bettelheim sees separation anxiety, the fear of being abandoned, neediness, and dependency frustration as central issues for children. He finds these issues particularly well expressed in the story of "Hansel and Gretel," a story quintessentially centered around food and children's struggle to control and satisfy appetite. The story uses children's hunger as a metaphor for all their dependency needs.

Several recent volumes have published exciting articles exploring gender in children's stories.[10] Because fantasy stories express children's deepest conflicts and wishes, we can use them to see if boys and girls express the same concerns in the same ways. In looking at the stories, I focus on content rather than structure or context.[11] My study involves reading close to a thousand stories from children from the mid-1950s to the present that I interpret collectively as representations of evolving middle-class European-American children's culture.

THE SIGNIFICANCE OF FEEDING AND EATING
IN CHILDREN'S DEVELOPMENT

In all cultures, food plays a central role in mediating and expressing human beings' place in the world. Feeding is one of the earliest and most important ways in which adults establish relationships with children and impart their own "organized attitudes about the world," as Margaret Mead said (1967, 70). Adults communicate to the growing child through the ways they satisfy the child's hunger. Whether they hold the child a lot or a little, feed on demand or on a schedule, respond immediately to the infant's hunger or make it wait, feed in a calm or hectic environment, use feeding exclusively as nourishment or as a general comfort, express a pleasureful or utilitarian ideal of eating—all these practices communicate a sense of what the world is like to the infant. Many dimensions of cultural habits and beliefs are expressed in the feeding relationship (Du Bois 1941; Shack 1969).

Anna Freud has been a pioneer in explicating the importance of feeding in the normal psychosocial maturation of children (1946, 1968). Infants are largely motivated by instincts, and hunger is the strongest. Completely helpless to satisfy the distressing sensations of hunger, infants must rely on others, usually mothers, to relieve the painful tension by feeding them. The satisfaction of hunger is the basis of a strong emotional connection to the providers who introduce them "to experiences of wish fulfillment, contentment, and happiness" (Freud 1968, 443).

The feeding relationship becomes the primary medium through which the infant makes the transition from what psychologists call primary narcissism and symbiosis to separation, individuation, and object love, a necessary transition in psycho-emotional growth. At first, the infant loves the experience of feeding. Anna Freud calls this "narcissistic love," which is centered in the contentment of the self. Then, in a transitional phase, the infant comes to love "the food which is the source of pleasure," the milk provided by breast or bottle. Finally, the infant loves "the provider of food, that is . . . the mother or mother-substitute" (1946, 125). This final stage constitutes "object love," which is central to psychological maturation. For in object love, the child emerges from the feeling of oneness with the mother that characterizes the first four or five months of life and recognizes his or her separateness as he or she becomes capable of loving another as separate from the self (Mahler, Pine, and Bergman 1975). This transition from primary symbiosis to separation and individuation is essential in normal child development, and Anna Freud highlights the significant role of eating in this transition.

Eating is the first great source of pleasure for the child, and the frustration of hunger causes terrible discomfort. Anna Freud points out that infants and toddlers are incapable of delaying the satisfaction of hunger; its frustration causes great tension and suffering. Thus hunger results in either pleasure or pain, and it comes to stand for strong feelings of satisfaction or frustration for the child. "Eating may . . . become invested with sexual and aggressive meaning" (Freud 1946, 120). Eating also sometimes involves the child in a conflict with the caretaker because the child wants food immediately and the caretaker defines occasionally frustrating conditions for its consumption, such as suitable table manners or sequencing of foods. Training in proper eating is a main channel for child socialization, but it inevitably defers children's gratification and sometimes causes them rage that they express through biting, refusing food, or throwing food. Anger may also derive from children's jealousy of the feeding of other siblings by the parents. Closely related to this anger is "fear, the fear of losing one's special place" that Paley defines as a central concern in children's stories (1990, 157). This fear is an inevitable result of the necessary process of separating and individuating from parents (Piaget 1962, 175; Pitcher and Prelinger 1963, 218, 229). Because eating involves the first experiences of love and autonomy, the first awareness of pleasure, the first expressions of aggression, and the first dimensions of frustration and rage, it is a rich domain for children's self-expression.

Anna Freud suggests some of the ways in which children can use their relationship to food as a form of communication (1946, 126). Expressions of hunger in stories can represent children's neediness, which can be depicted as huge and overwhelming or as controllable and satiable. Greediness can be not only a response to loss of motherly love due to separation or perceived rejection but also an expression of sibling rivalry. Children can present themselves in stories as either the hungry one or as the satisfier of hunger and thus represent either states of neediness or of empowerment.

Children's fantasy stories are riddled with violence and aggression, and frequently these are expressed in oral terms: through images of gnashing, eating up, swallowing, being eaten, and so on (Gould 1972, 18–19; Pitcher and Prelinger 1963, 176). Ames believes that children are "by nature" violent (1966, 390), whereas other researchers link their aggression to Oedipal conflicts and dependency frustration—the inability to have all their needs satisfied by others or to satisfy them themselves (Gould 1972; Pitcher and Prelinger 1963; Bettelheim 1977). Clearly, this last explanation is directly linked to food as the vehicle for satisfaction of hunger, a primary need in children that can stand for all needs (Freud 1946).

Food symbolism provides a clear channel for identification with parents. As Gould (1972, 30–31) has pointed out, identification enables children both to become another and to claim the powers and attributes of the model. Thus by identifying with a bad guy, for example, children can be wild and scary and can externalize and diffuse their "personal demons" (Paley 1988, 21). By identifying with mothers, children affirm a deep connection to them that helps overcome fear of separation. Furthermore, children gain parental potency by taking on the mother's feeding role in stories and identifying with characters who nurture by providing food or exert arbitrary retribution by withholding it. Finally, children use food gifts or refusals in their stories (and in their daily lives, see Katriel 1987) to signify the making or breaking of relationships.

These symbolic attributes of food may be enhanced by mothers' tendency to "treat the food which they offer as if it were part of themselves" (Freud 1946, 126). Both Anna Freud (1968) and Hilde Bruch (1973) document how inappropriate feeding and its overloading with distorted psycho-emotional content can result in psychopathology in children evidenced in compulsive eating or anorexia nervosa. The feeding relationship is very important in children's psychological and emotional maturation, and because of this "the symbolic significance of eating plays a big role in the older child's fantasy life" (Freud 1968, 456).

FOOD AND GENDER IN CHILDREN'S STORIES: METHODOLOGY AND FINDINGS

I collected 129 stories from children, 71 during the fall of 1991 from three- to five-year-olds at a day care center and 58 during the fall of 1992 from five- and six-year-olds in a private kindergarten class in a day care center. Both centers were on college campuses in eastern central Pennsylvania, one a private liberal arts college and the other a public university. Children came from families affiliated with the two different colleges as well as from the surrounding community. Many of the parents were professionals; some were blue-collar support staff. All of the children were verbal and articulate. My subjects were of similar socioeconomic and racial background to those of the other studies I will refer to in this chapter. Almost all were middle- and upper-middle-class European-American children, and all were from families that were wealthy enough to have plenty to eat. Clearly, any interpretations made about the stories considered here are based on the understanding that these children are white, middle-class, and educationally privileged. Children of other ethnic groups with different food habits and symbolic concerns, and children who suffer chronic hunger or food deprivation will surely tell different kinds of stories needing interpretation. Other studies on children of diverse class, race, and ethnic groups are sorely needed. [5]

I gathered stories by visiting the classroom long enough so the children were comfortable with me and then simply asking them, "Would you like to tell me a story?" I carried a small tape recorder and turned it on if they said yes. Most children were eager to tell me one or several stories; some were indifferent. I did not pressure them and received several stories from some children and few or none from others. I transcribed all the stories from the tapes. Twelve boys told 47 stories and 19 girls told 82 stories that varied in length from a few sentences to more than a typed page in length.

To increase the numbers of stories available for interpretation, I also looked at other collections. Pitcher and Prelinger gathered 360 stories from 137 children (70 boys and 67 girls) during 1955 and 1956 (1963). Ames collected 270 stories from 135 boys and 135 girls from 1959 to 1961 at the same center where Pitcher and Prelinger worked, but she published only about 80 of the stories rather than the complete collection (1966). Sutton-Smith published 292 stories from 22 two- to five-year-old children, 180 from 12 boys and 112 from 10 girls, only including stories from the boys and girls in any given age group who told the most stories (1981).[6] Finally, I consulted the stories scattered throughout Paley's several books (Paley 1981, 1984, 1986, 1988, 1990, 1992).[7] In all, I read over 1,000 stories gathered over a thirty-six year period.

I did a simple count of food symbols in the stories collected by myself and Pitcher and Prelinger and have summarized the results in table 8.1. This table does not have statistical validity, for the sample of children was small and nonrandom and the counts were not verified. The numbers are merely meant to be suggestive about the frequencies with which boys and girls use certain images in their stories. The time span between my and Pitcher and Prelinger's story collections—thirty-five years—is certainly not irrelevant; however, for the categories examined here there appears to be quite a bit of similarity between the two collections. My analysis consisted of reading the stories for overall theme and content, as well as counting words referring to food; fat; thin; hunger; eating as consumption; eating as devouring; and food-centered activities such as meals, cooking, shopping, baking, barbecues, picnics, and so on.

Over half of the stories told by both sexes used food imagery, a particularly apt symbolic medium. Children use food in matter-of-fact ways to move the plot or provide props and they also use it to depict deep human dramas. They tell stories where wild animals eat people up, squalling infants cry for food, mothers feed babies, and children

TABLE 8.1

Analysis of Stories Collected by Counihan in 1991 and 1992 and by Pitcher and Prelinger (1963)

A   489 stories total
168 children
89 girls told 262 stories (i.e., 53% of the children told 54% of the stories)
79 boys told 227 stories (i.e., 47% of the children told 46% of the stories)

B   250/489 (51%) of all **stories** have references to foods and food-centered activities
134/262 (51%) of all stories by **girls** have references to foods and food-centered activities.
116/227 (51%) of all stories by **boys** have references to foods and food-centered activities.

C   total of 157 references to eating or drinking in **comestible** sense
girls have 99 (63%)
boys have 58 (37%)

D   total of 132 references to a **meal** or **food event**[1]
girls have 96 (73%)
boys have 36 (27%)

E   total of 106 references to **food tasks, food workers,** or **food places**[2]
girls have 74 (70%)
boys have 32 (30%)

F   total of 360 different references to more than one hundred different **foods**
girls have 237 (66%)
boys have 123 (34%)

G   total of 199 references to eating as **devouring**[3]
girls have 86 (43%)
boys have 113 (57%)

H   TOTALS:

954 references to foods, eating, food events, food activities, and devouring
592 by girls, 86 eating as devouring (15%), 506 food as comestible (85%)
362 by goys, 113 eating as devouring (31%), 249 food as comestible (69%)

---

1. Includes references to breakfast, lunch, supper, dinner, meal, snack, dessert, picnic, birthday party, cookout, and barbecue.

2. Includes references to baker, candy store, cook, ice cream man, kitchen, market, pancake store, and shopping.

3. Includes references to eats up, swallows, starves, bites, chews, poisons with food, and cooks.

greedily gobble up food. They express some central concerns and create meaningful ways of dealing with them through food symbols in fantasy stories. Feeding can represent all acts of nurturance. Hunger can stand for all wants. Eating can be a metaphor for satisfaction of desires, whereas devouring can symbolize aggression against those who fail to meet children's needs. Cooking and shopping can be vehicles for expressing children's identification with parents and their ability to fulfill their own wants. Food provides children ready symbols for expressing diverse messages in their fantasy stories.

Although the children I studied didn't seem terribly interested in talking about food in the abstract, over half of the stories examined in my and Pitcher and Prelinger's (1963) collections contained some mention of food (See table 8.1). I counted mentions of specific foods, eating events or meals, food tasks, food workers and food places, and eating in a devouring sense. Approximately half of the stories referred to food, and references varied from a single mention to an entire story built around food themes. Ames reported that food and eating themes were the second most common in the children's stories she collected, after themes of aggression and violence (1966, 344). There were both similarities and differences in boys' and girls' use of food symbols and eating themes in stories. References to fat or thin body states are very sparse for both sexes. Both use food themes to mark time, to sustain the plot, to introduce the child's family and central issues of parental identification and sibling rivalry, to exhibit neediness, to manifest nurturing and relation, and to express aggression. Both sexes often indicate through food imagery their fear of not getting enough to eat, but girls more often overcome neediness through social and alimentary activities (e.g., by feeding or baking), whereas boys more often cope with dependency frustration through hostility and violence in their stories (biting, chewing, or eating others up). Let me now present these findings in more detail and then offer an explanation for them.

Fat Symbolism in Children's Stories

In my observations of and discussion with children in the day care center and preschool, I found no clear differences in boys' and girls' physical relationship to food and their bodies. This is contrary to what one might expect on the basis of how differently male and female college students relate to food and body as discussed in chapter 7. There appear to be no obvious gender distinctions in what or how much preschool boys and girls feel they should eat. They showed little interest and no evident gender-determined differences in body shape concerns and stigmas associated with being fat, which clearly emerge more strongly in girls than boys by adolescence and that are evident in children as young as fourth grade (Thelen et al. 1992; Zaslow1986).

The random comments of the children I studied seemed to indicate the disparagement of fat typical of their culture, but it didn't seem that either boys or girls suffered more heavily from it. Children's disdain of fat was not surprising given the value of thinness in mainstream Euro-American culture, a value expressed in the media and reflected in many homes with dieting parents (Bruch 1973; Kaufman 1980; Schwartz 1986). Dyrenforth, Wooley, and Wooley report the results of a study in which preschool children prefer a thin doll over a fat doll and drawings of thin children to those of fat ones, with a tendency to "describe thin children as more competent than fat children" (1980, 35). Further-more, "thinner children tend to be liked more than children of average weight or heavier, a sign that it may be 'thinness' that is valued even more than 'the absence of fat'" (35). This study neither addresses nor reports gender differences in sensitivity to fat issues but concludes that children learn very early in life that fatness carries negative weight in our society.

In Thelen, Powell, Lawrence, and Kuhnert's study of 191 second, fourth, and sixth graders' ideas about eating and body image (1992), second-grade girls and boys showed no gender differences regarding weight concerns. But fourth- and sixth-grade girls showed more dissat-isfaction with body and concern with weight than the boys of their own grade and than girls of the second grade. Their study suggests that con-cern with body image strikes girls somewhere between second and fourth grade.

Although preschool children are apparently disdainful of fat in real life, fat imagery was strikingly absent in their stories. In fact, in the 129 stories I collected, only 2 contained any references to fat; in the 360 col-lected by Pitcher and Prelinger, only 4 had references to fat. Equal numbers of boys and girls mentioned fat in each collection, and the mentions of fat varied in tone and use, from being a positive attribute for a turkey to a neutral, negative, and dangerous state for a crocodile, dinosaur, and giant monster. Two of the children's stories with men-tions of fat referred to it as an unwanted characteristic. One boy's story referred to "two big fat Indians. They hurt us—Winsey and me. They hurt me" (Pitcher and Prelinger 1963, 45). This boy used "fat" as a generic insult rather than integrating it into the plot the way the fol-lowing girl's story does:

Story #1 She has her lunch and her daddy's gonna teach her how to swim and they ate on the beach. A picnic because it wasn't in the house. They ate sandwiches, hamburger, and drank each day outside, because they were going swimming each day and they didn't want to waste any time. They didn't eat, because they were getting kind of fat, and they wanted to get thin again. (Tess, 4:2, Pitcher and Prelinger 1963, 110)[12]

This was the only story that mentioned restricting eating to avoid getting fat, which was implied to be an undesired state. In the following story, the link between overeating and fat is made, but is value-neutral.

> **Story #2**   When Mommy and me went to my party, it was my birthday time then. The door opened and it was my Am [grandmother] and she tried to eat all the cake. And we said, oh my. Then the door opened quietly and here comes another mom-mom [grandmother], two mom-moms came and tried to eat all our cake up, 'cause they were both fat, these are different mom-moms. Then they turned in to be fatter. They started to be fatter and fatter and fatter because they ate more of the cake. And then they had seconds. Then they had more seconds because every mom-mom comes in and tries to eat the whole cake because they were all fat. (Leslie, 3:11, Counihan 10/91)

The grandmothers kept eating the cake and getting fatter, and then eating more cake. But Leslie stops short of condemning them for either eating the cake or being fat.

The following story by a boy defines fat as a necessary and positive characteristic, although for a Thanksgiving turkey, not a person:

> **Story #3**   One time there was a man. And he was looking for a turkey because it was Thanksgiving. And then he drived down in the woods to find one. Then he finally found one, but he wasn't fat, so he looked for another one. He wasn't fat. So he found finally one that was fat and he took it home and then ate it. The end. (Nate, 5:6, Counihan 10/92)

Fat may not be a good thing for a person to be, but in this story it is good to eat. In two boys' stories collected by Sutton-Smith (1980), fat appears as a result of excess eating and leads to blowing up—of the eater in one story and of his house in the other. Here is one:

> **Story #4**   Once upon a time there was a giant monster. When he was asleep his Mommy came in. She woke him up because she wanted to tell him that dinner was ready. The giant ate the first bowl of cereal and then he ate ten more. He got so fat that he blew up the whole house. (Brian, approximately 5, Sutton Smith 1980, 137)

Similarly, in Tab's story #19, printed in the "Aggression, Hunger, and Greed" section (page 147), a "terrible crocodile" eats to excess, gets fatter and fatter, and then dies as a result. In these cases, the narrator seems to make the excess eating rather than the fat itself the cause of disaster. Meanings associated with fat in preschool children's stories are occasionally but not consistently negative. The very few references to fat in the many stories I examined suggest that weight and body conscious-ness are not deep concerns or problems for preschool children. Further studies are needed on elementary school children to see when, why, and how girls and boys begin to think differently about their bodies so that by fourth grade, girls are already showing far more signs of body dis-tress and self-deprecation than boys (Thelen et al. 1992; Zaslow 1986).

Control of Food and Food as Control

In their stories, boys and girls have many references to foods, eating, and meals. Because meals and foods have a certain pattern and regu-larity in many families, children can use them to give order to the events in the story and by extension give order to their world. Witness, for example, the following story by a two-and-a-half-year-old boy:

> **Story #5**   Little boy goes home. He eats lunch. Then he bumps his head off. He goes bump, bump, bump. He gets into dishes. Then he's hungry. Then Mother comes. He just plays outside. (Tobias M., 2:6, Pitcher and Prelinger 1963, 33)

Here allusions to food serve to organize time, move the plot along, and provide key events and states. The following story I collected from a three-year-old girl uses food in a similar fashion:

> **Story #6**   Once upon a time, my dad ate supper and I had one ice cream sandwich and one day we went out in the woods, and there was a tractor with Uncle Steve and there wasn't a ghost. He ran into a bear, and you know what I found in there? Barbecue. And one day, one day, I had ice cream sandwich and one day my mommy told me and I watched Goldilocks tape, and when Goldilocks was laying with the baby bear one, he went wow. (Polly, 3:2, Counihan 10/91)

In the previous two stories, food is mentioned deliberately to order the narrative. Children also use food imagery to control the world by bringing about their own satisfaction as Max does in the following story about his birthday:

> **Story #7**   My daddy ate his supper all up and I eat my supper all up and my mom does and we play baseball and then we play volleyball and I have a volleyball net and I just punch it all over the net. And my mom and dad play baseball, in the alley, in the street, and under the car, and we found it. And, then we played, and then we played soccer and we ate our supper all up and my mom played her supper and she says, "Time for supper." And then after supper we go out to Campbells and then my

birthday comes and after that my birthday comes, then we ate my birthday, blew out the candles. (Max, 3:2, Counihan 10/91)

This story unites his family around playing sports together and ends with the birthday, which, Paley tells us, is one of the "great Ideas examined in play" (1988, 9). She believes that for children the image of the birthday—and, I would add, of the birthday cake—is "the affirmation of safety and power" (1988, 108), a haven of satisfaction and nurturance for boys and girls.

Whereas Max's story brings about satisfaction effortlessly, Leslie's evinces a more problematic resolution of her needs:

> **Story #8**   When Mommy and me ate pancakes with Reena, Reena and me and mommy went out to the pancake store to get pancakes, then we come back and eat them. Mommy and me went back to the pancake store but it was closed. So then we go to another pancake store, but every pancake was closed. So Daddy said, "I know a pancake store where it's open." Mommy say, "What pancakes are you talking about?" And Daddy said, "Down there in the forest." Then, then, mommy and me and No-nina, we went out to the forest, there was a pancake store, but it wasn't open, and we goed in there but there was monsters in there so we didn't go in it. We told daddy all about our story going through the monsters' home, then there was a big monster behind us, but it wasn't really a monster, it was Nina and Poppa, they scared us. "How did you trick us?" said mommy, "We just thinked you were the monster." "I wasn't," said daddy. (Leslie, 3:11, Counihan 10/91)

This story introduces some anxiety over getting enough food, a common theme in children's stories and one that sometimes concludes happily, sometimes produces anxiety and aggression. In Leslie's story, the search for pancakes is a long and somewhat frustrating one. It leads to dead ends and monsters who metamorphose into grandparents (Nina and Poppa), much more benign characters than monsters, but ones who in this story do not resolve the search for food. Anxiety over getting enough food can also reflect anxiety about getting enough love, care, or attention—concerns for both boys and girls. Raising this anxiety in fantasy may help tame or resolve it.

Food and Family: Connection, Identification, and Conflict

In Leslie's story, food is the centerpiece of social activities that involve the nuclear family and its extensions. The story plays with the idea of family members being monsters but then affirms they are not, demonstrating the ambivalence children feel toward their parents—an ambivalence often expressed by the splitting of the "good parent" and the "bad parent" into two different characters in stories (Bettelheim 1977). An important use of food themes in both boys' and girls' stories is to express the often intense and sometimes conflicting feelings the young child has about family members. These feelings include identification, love, connection, and hostility. The beauty of food symbolism is that it can convey all of these complex feelings simultaneously. Story details about food provisioning can symbolically stand both for identification with the parent and for nurturance of all sorts. But simultaneously, eating can be a violent and aggressive act because it involves biting, chewing, dismembering, and devouring.[13] Furthermore, the withdrawal of food can symbolize withdrawal of love.[14] My preschool and kindergarten informants used food messages to express identification with and affection for parents as well as hostility toward them. This oscillation between connection and opposition is part of the child's development of a separate and autonomous identity.

In identification with parents around food, girls have the edge over boys because of the fact that mothers still are the primary providers of food in the family (DeVault 1991; McIntosh and Zey 1998), as they certainly were in the 1950s when Pitcher and Prelinger collected their stories. In fact, the great majority of girls' food references were to its comestible and social uses (see table 8.1). Girls referred to meals or food events more than twice as often as boys. Girls spoke often of picnics, cookouts, and barbecues, whereas boys rarely mentioned these events. Witness the following story by a girl:

> **Story #9**   Once upon a time, my mother and me went out for a picnic. There was nothing in it, 'cause there was a hole in the picnic basket. Then they tied it and then they put some food in it. They tied the hole and then they put food in there but it didn't fall out. (Margaret, 3.9, Counihan 10/91)

Here, a girl seems to worry about having enough food and uses the metaphor of the picnic basket with the hole to express that worry, but she brings the powerful figure of her mother into the story and gets the hole fixed. Perhaps she uses a picnic—generally a fun food event—to diminish the anxiety over deprivation.

Girls made many more references to food tasks, workers, and places, than boys. Girls frequently spoke of themselves or others shopping, cooking, or giving food to others:

> **Story #10**   Once there was my mom and there was little cooking stove. She cooked all these hamburgers and bread. And one night she said, "What are you doing?" "I'm playing with toys. What are you doing, mom?" "I'm doing work." And that's it. (Katrina, 5:0, Counihan 10/91)

Here, Katrina juxtaposes and links her mother's work with her play through the image of her mother working on "a little cooking stove" that recalls a toy stove. Overall, girls are much more likely than boys to use food as a vehicle for enacting a social role (Pitcher and Prelinger 1963, 203), and this gives them a channel to power through the ability to withhold or give food.

One of Karen's stories shows a more fully developed sense of how maternal identification can grant the power to nurture and satisfy the self:

Story #11   Once upon a time my mom and my daddy went to the market and they bought lots of baby feeds for my aunt, because my aunt was a baby. And they went and saw at the market with my aunt and pop-pop. And I was still in my momma's stomach. I wasn't even born. And I went to the market with them. The next day I came out of my mommy's stomach, and then I saw that mom had me. I saw that my mom got married and I had a new baby wedding dress. The wedding dress had little flowers on it, and I had flowers on my head. I saw my mommy got dressed up into a wedding gown and then she got married. She got married, and then she wanted to see what else I did there at the wedding. I colored and I ate a cake. It got all over my face. I liked the cake, and I said, "waahh" and then they knew I wanted more cake. And then that was enough cake for me, 'cause my mom wanted to let me have no more, 'cause I was just starting teeth. I was just starting my teeth to come up, and whenever I started to cry, at the wedding, they knew my teeth were coming, they were coming out. Then I had to come home 'cause the wedding was over. I got lots of peppermints, and I took them home, and I got lots of butter and I got lots of milk, and I got lots of orange juice, and we took it home to our house, and we ate and we ate and we drank and then my mom put me in my cradle. (Karen, 4:11, Counihan 10/91)

In this story, Karen organizes her references to the nuclear and extended family around marketing, eating, being fed, and even being literally inside her mother's stomach. She also tells about her mother's wedding. She describes the wedding dress she wore and uses it as a form of identification with her mother, who was getting married and thus also wearing a wedding dress. The story is also about what it means to be a baby: a needy being who cries and eats and eats and eats. Paley tells us that babies are an omnipresent symbol in children's fantasy play and that they seem to embody children's anxiety about the struggle to achieve a secure autonomous identity: "The demanding, whining creature within seems to embody all the forces that resist separation and socialization" (Paley 1988, 108). For Karen, eating cake at the wedding is linked to her babyhood and to her growing ability to make her nurturing needs known by crying and asserting them.

Karen's story reflects the power gained in fantasy by identifying with the food provider, a power traditionally more accessible to girls than to boys in their identifications with their same-sex parent. Of course as fathers increasingly become involved with feeding and nurturing children, boys will have a chance to use identification with the father to gain this same power. The following rather unusual episode of fantasy play between three three-year-old boys shows them doing just this:

Story #12
"I won't give you any food if you're not good," Christopher threatens. He is the father and Stuart and Barney are his babies, crying and throwing off their blankets.
   "I'm good," Stuart says.
   "No, you're not. You're crying. Only good babies get food."
   "I'm good. Put my pie on. My pie! My pie!"
   "This is not what I'm cooking. The father says what's cooking."
   "Give me what you're cooking."
   "Only if you beez a good baby."
   "We won't cry, Daddy."
   "Wait till these are ready because they're too hot. But if the babies aren't good, no food."
   "We're laughing."
   "Okay. Here's some food, baby."
   "I'm good, right?"
   "Yeah, you're good now. Both of you get porridge that's just right."
(Paley, 1986, 129)

Here not only does Christopher express identification with his father by enacting his role of being in charge of food, but he also expresses a small child's awareness of the power of adults, who can nurture through giving or punish through withholding food. Christopher subtly manifests his understanding of what could be described from the child's point of view as parental aggression toward children by prohibiting them food, something parents of course do all the time, particularly by withholding especially desirable sweet foods defined as treats (Satter 1987).

Just as the previous story reflects awareness of the dark side of feeding, the following one demonstrates that although identification with the mother can be a source of power, it can also perhaps be threatening or dangerous:

Story #13   Once upon a time, me and my mom, me and my mom were honey bears. Me and my mom sticked our hands into the honey thing and a bee stung our hands. And we went "oooch, ouch" all the way home, and we made honey bread. (Karen, 4:11, Counihan 10/91)

Here, she identifies with her mother by being a bear like her and by getting honey and making honey bread. But she gets stung by a bee for being like and with her mother, and perhaps this image implies the potential danger of excessive attachment and identification.

Devouring as Aggression

Children very commonly use food explicitly to express aggression—sometimes against parents, sometimes against others in general. They tell many stories in which they use eating to represent devouring and use biting to stand for hurting (Freud 1947, 1968). The following is a representative boys' story told by Ben, aged almost five. The presence of monsters is typical of children this age.

> **Story #14**   Once upon a time a monster ate ten people and then yeaugh, yeaugh, and then the ghost ate the monster and the witch died. And they all ate another head off and they couldn't move and they couldn't get out. . . . And then the witch died and the ghost ate the witch and they were all dead. And then when the people, sometimes they were all huddled and they couldn't do anything and they were caught and they couldn't get up and then they were trapped and they were dead and they couldn't get out. (Ben, 4:10, Counihan 10/91)

Ben's story quite clearly refers to eating as devouring. It is an aggressive, menacing, and threatening act. There is no mention of real food consumed in an alimentary or nutritive sense in his story, and there is no reference to the social and quotidian nature of eating.

Winnie, almost five, tells a story where eating—although involving cooking—is also about devouring and death:

> **Story #15**   Once upon a time there was a farmer milking cows. A bad guy came and peeked behind the tree and was hiding there. A bad guy peeked there and saw the cow and wanted to shoot it so it shooted it, so the farmer shooted it and cooked it for dinner and ate it. The police came and arrested it and got it out of its belly but it was all broken in pieces. So they taped it back up but it died one day. (Winnie 4:10, Counihan 10/91)

The previous examples show the varied ways in which food and eating themes are used to express important and widespread concerns of both boys and girls, particularly their anxiety about dependency and autonomy, hostility toward parents, and aggression. As stated earlier, about half the stories told by both boys and girls have some reference to food, eating, or food-centered activities. But whereas girls make more references to food in its eating and provisioning senses, boys make more references to eating as devouring. Almost one-third of all boys' food references were to eating as devouring or killing, whereas only half as many of girls' were (see table 8.1). Boys were much more likely to have stories like the following:

Story #16 A wolf. And he starts to fight. Then he eats up the bear. Then he eats up the house. Then he eats up the grass, the dirt, the chickens, the bikes, the cars, the people. (Kip P., 3:7, Pitcher and Prelinger 1963, 50)

Aggressive imagery is not scary or discomforting for boys; on the contrary, they delighted in telling stories full of biting, dismembering, and devouring. The following story is a wonderful example of the pleasure boys often take in identifying with oral aggression:

Story #17 Then one man, a sheriff, that was me, and I killed them all up. And I ate them all. They tasted funny 'cause I love meat and blood. (It's just a story!) Then he ate his horse too, and he ate another bear. And the witch was eaten up because she was killing all the people. The cowboy ate the whole country. Then a giant came and killed the cowboy and the cowboy killed the giant. The cowboy was all bitted up. (Eliot M., 4:11, Pitcher and Prelinger 1963, 79)

Girls also use oral aggressive themes, but they use them only half as often as boys and they are less likely than boys to build a whole story around them.

Aggression, Hunger, and Greed

I wondered if boys' greater use of food imagery to express aggression might be related to their greater insecurity as some researchers suggest (e.g., Paley 1984). I decided to examine all the stories primarily about hunger and greed in my own and Pitcher and Prelinger's collections. I chose hunger and greed stories because I think they are about neediness and insatiability, central concerns of children. I defined hunger stories as those where hunger was either specif-ic-ally mentioned or implicitly alluded to and greed stories are those where a character eats to excess. I read through all the stories and inductively chose those I believed to be hunger or greed stories. Clearly this method is impressionistic, susceptible to distortion, and not scientific. My ideas are intended to be suggestive rather than definitive.

I examined 13 hunger stories, 5 by boys and 8 by girls. They show similarity among boys and girls in that they have diverse, ambiguous, and usually but not always benign endings. The 11 greed stories I examined, however, 6 by boys and 5 by girls, show suggestive differences and hint that neediness may be more problematic for preschool boys than for girls. Boys' stories of greed almost never end with a successful satisfaction of the need to eat. Rather the satisfaction is problematic: nonexistent, ambiguous, incomplete, involving the wrong substance (e.g., a tree mistaken for a rabbit, a dead mouse, a wooden duck and fox), or to such excess that harm results—throwing up and dying, blowing up, or harming property or others. All of the boys' greed stories result in harm as in the following where greed results in the eater blowing open:

> **Story #18**   Boy. He fell in the lake. He got on the land. He got his boat, put it in the water and got in it. He went fishing. Then he went home with one hundred fish. He ate them and blew open. They buried him. (Thayer, 5:11, Pitcher and Prelinger 1963, 132)

Perhaps this story reveals the boy's perception that excess consumption is dangerous. The following story also involves eating to excess, getting fat, and dying.

> **Story #19**   Once there was a terrible crocodile with sharp teeth. He saw a person, ate him up and he got fatter, fatter and fatter. He threw up and died. He was under ground. He couldn't get up, 'cause he was dead. He went back to seed; he has a little seed like you have a baby in your stomach. And he grew up to be a crocodile again—because he was planted in the ground and up came a crocodile again. And that's the end. (Tab 5:0, Pitcher and Prelinger 1963, 132)

This story is notable in describing death and regeneration and in metaphorically linking orality with birth, an occasional concern in children's fantasy (Freud 1946; Pitcher and Prelinger 1963, 230). This story illustrates not only the symbolic association of eating with pregnancy, but also the dangers of excess consumption and the role of wish fulfillment. A child may feel his own wants are extreme, dangerous, and difficult to satisfy. Tab perhaps uses the fantasy of rebirth to overcome anxiety over neediness.

Girls seem more successful in their stories at resolving neediness and are perhaps less threatened by it than boys. This may be related to the fact that girls' greed stories, like all their stories, tend to be more socially located, have more mentions of family members, and more often involve other characters than do boys' stories (Pitcher and Prelinger 1963). All of the girls' stories of greed end by satisfying hunger; none of them ends with harm. Contrast the following greed stories with those of boys', remembering that all the boys stories end in harm:

> **Story #20**   Little baby and she messed all over the place. Then the baby made a pie. Then she watched her eat it. Then she wanted to eat it all up.

Then she wanted to have a plate. Then she eat it all, all up. (Anita W, 2:10, Pitcher and Prelinger 1963, 34)

Anita's story expresses a desire and allows for the resolution of the desire with no negative consequences. There are hints of sibling rivalry in this story through the mention of the baby, but this emotion does not lead to a bad ending. The following story also enables the protagonists to revel in eating to excess with a happy ending:

Story #21   Kitty cat and a puppy. They were all alone without their mother and father. And they had too many cookies. They finished up the whole food in the kitchen. They made crumbs all over the place. And ants came and ate crumbs all up. So they went to the candy store, and they got all the candy out of all the shelves and ate it all up. Then they got back home and got more food. And they went to the circus and swinged in merry-go-round and went to school and write their lessons and had lunch and supper and went to bed and breakfast and no more school. (Bonnie C., 3:11, Pitcher and Prelinger 1963, 55)

This story shows a girl's conception that kitty cat and puppy can deal successfully with their food needs in the absence of parent figures. They eat cookies, candy, and "more food"—all without harm. Then they continue to show their self-reliance by doing lessons, having meals, going to bed, and eliminating bothersome school. They act auspiciously on their own.

The last story is one of the most fascinating because of the way it unites several themes around eating symbolism:

Story #22   Once there was a little girl named Betsy. And she played in the yard a long, long time. Her mother called her in, but she was having so much fun she said, "Mother, could I stay out a little longer?" She was hungry. She saw all the food. As soon as all the food was dished out—she went down under the table and tied all the spaghetti to hers; all the spaghetti from her brothers and sisters went into her mouth. Her mother said, "Some day you'll pay for this." But in her dream a little man made her walk and gave her an apron and then pulled the table food away from her. And he went in a little store that had machines' gears and he geared all of them and made them (the little girl) eat ice cream and cake. And when he came back to the chair she was so full. And she was still hungry; she took another leg of chicken. Then her mother called her for breakfast and she still didn't learn her lesson. And her mother called her for breakfast and she cooked up another idea but didn't know what that was. She still didn't learn a lesson in the dream. That's the end of my story. (Eleanor K., 5:2, Pitcher and Prelinger 1963, 137)

This story conveys a sense of neediness and insatiability through the girl's telling of getting "full" on ice cream and cake, but then in the next breath being "still hungry." The relationship between hunger and emotional needs is explicit in this story in the description of the protagonist eating all the spaghetti of her brothers and sisters and then being threatened by the mother for doing so: "You'll pay for this some day." A child may feel that she is not getting enough—be it food, love, or attention—because of rivalry with siblings. She may have a hunger that is insatiable and turns to greed because it is an emotional hunger rather than a physical hunger. The story shows the dependency frustration of children and the role of grown-ups in that frustration, for in the story there is a "little man" who forces food on the girl and then denies it to her. Adults control the satisfaction of children's needs, and they probably often seem arbitrary and mean to children as a result. But even in this story, where Eleanor makes explicit her dependency frustration and the greed that accompanies it, she does not describe a bad ending for Betsy. Eleanor merely says, "She didn't learn her lesson." This paves the way for future stories, where perhaps Betsy will learn her lesson. It is a more open future in contrast to the blowing up and dying that ends several boys' greed stories.

SUMMARY AND EXPLANATION

There are a few suggestive differences in food and eating symbolism in boys' and girls' stories. First, girls have more mentions of conducting food activities or filling food roles than boys. Second, boys have more mentions of eating as devouring than girls. Third, boys' stories about greed often result in harm, whereas girls' greed stories usually have benign or ambiguous resolutions.

The hints of gender differences in my analysis cohere with those of other researchers on similar middle-class white children. Others have studied competitive styles, argument, and play and found that boys are more individualistic, care more about establishing their position in a hierarchy, and display more aggression and violence than girls. Girls focus more on maintaining relationships than establishing rankings and are more sociable and less combative than boys. [15]

Pitcher and Prelinger, for example, categorize stories according to the themes of aggression and of hurt or misfortune; they say that oral aggressive themes are common. They find that boys' stories have significantly more manifestations of aggression, hurt, and misfortune than girls' stories and that boys' aggression tends to be more violent than girls' (1963, 176–77, 252). Ames found that the most common story themes for two- to six-year-old boys and girls were violence and aggression, and she also found boys' aggression to be more violent in general than girls' (1966, 342). In her recent analysis of children's conflict resolution in fantasy play, Sheldon found that boys have more conflict that is "more heavy-handed and more controlling" and more aimed at asserting dominance and individual ends than is girls'. Girls' discourse is more "collaborative," their conflict negotiation is "more mitigated" and they aim to communicate, respond to others' needs and to maintain relationships in the play setting rather than to achieve a place at the top of a hierarchy (Sheldon 1990, 28). Paley summarizes the boys' and girls' stories in her kindergarten classroom in the following way: "Boys narrate superhero adventures filled with dangerous monsters, while girls place sisters and brothers, mothers and fathers in relatively safe roles. If lost, they are quickly found, if harmed they are healed or replaced. Boys tell of animals who kill or are killed; girls seldom involve animals in violence. A bear or lion encountered in the forest is likely to lead a girl home and will not be shot and eaten for supper" (1981, 203).

The literature confirms that in middle-class European-American culture, as early as age three, the self-enactment of boys involves more aggression and violence, while that of girls reveals more sociability and nurturance. To explain these gender differences we must examine the culturally specific kinds of gender socialization, gender definition, and family structure experienced by the children. Detailed ethnographic data would maximize our ability to interpret story themes, but without it, the literature can provide clues. In the United States and many other cultures most boys are socialized to be more physically active, entrepreneurial, independent, competitive, and aggressive than most girls.[16]

Furthermore, in U.S. culture, male and female identities are defined as bipolar and mutually exclusive. Children, especially boys, adhere tenaciously to uncompromising definitions of themselves as male or female, which they perceive as opposites. To be a boy is, in large measure, not to be a girl, and vice-versa. As Paley says, "All opportunities to make oneself distinctly masculine or feminine are seized upon: If I am doing something only boys do, then I must be a boy" (1984, 18). This means that boys learn to identify only with men and masculine things: activities, toys, and colors. Similarly but not in quite such an extreme fashion, girls learn to identify with women and feminine things (Davies 1989; Paley 1984).

But the world of children is populated mainly with women. Mothers, baby-sitters, day care providers and elementary school teachers are predominantly female. This has two consequences. First, as Paley points out, boys' natural learning style, which is marked by physical exuberance, may be experienced as "discordant" to the female grown-ups and thus receive negative feedback, increasing boys' insecurity, whereas girls' learning style may more closely match that of the teachers and receive positive feedback (1984, xii and passim). Second, girls have many close same-sex role models available and boys have few. This may affect how they experience such challenges of growing up as separation anxiety and fear, processes studied by Nancy Chodorow and others particularly in regard to family structure.[17] In Euro-American and many other cultures, Chodorow argues, boys and girls experience an "asymmetrical organization of parenting" because the primary parent is female, and the male parent is usually rather remote (1978, 166). This is less true today than it was in the mid-1950s when Pitcher and Prelinger gathered stories, but it continues nonetheless.

Girls develop in closer relation with the same-sex parent throughout infancy and later with same-sex role models. Thus, "feminine personality comes to define itself in relation and connection to other people more than masculine personality does" (Chodorow 1974, 44). Boys' development of gender identity involves separation from the mother and rejection of the femininity she represents. Yet the father and other male role models are usually more distant and emotionally detached than the mother and female role models. Girls, on the other hand, can remain close to the mother, both in actuality and in identification, and thus do not undergo as traumatic a process of radical separation. On the basis of this scenario, we can see that separation issues can easily be more scary and threatening for boys than for girls, causing the greater fear, hostility, and self-definition in competitive terms that emerge in the food themes of their fantasy stories.

Furthermore, while boys experience a stronger sense of abandonment, they may simultaneously experience greater frustration of their dependency needs and less ability to satisfy them by themselves. Girls' proximity to the mother enables them to satisfy both their physical and their emotional hunger by emulating the mother's nurturing and food control behaviors.

Detailed ethnographic studies of individual children, their parents, and their socialization in a variety of cross-cultural settings are needed and will help explain the relationship between their gender definitions in fantasy and their family structure. Taggart argues that Mexican Nahuat men express a much more highly developed relational identity in their folktales than Spanish men do in theirs because of the more active role of Nahuat men in the parenting of young children (1992, 1997). His research supports Chodorow's (1974, 1979) and Ehrensaft's (1990) claims that increased involvement of fathers alongside mothers in parenting will enable boys as well as girls to develop identities based both on experiencing personal relationships and on emulating impersonal roles. This may also make separation anxiety less traumatic for boys and reduce male aggression. Further studies of the fantasy stories of children socialized in a variety of family structures will enable us to see to what extent gender definitions are affected by parental roles and to see if there are variations in children's food themes and self-conceptions related to parental involvement in feeding and nurturing in general.

The children who are subjects here, as I stated earlier, do not lack food. But cross-cultural studies show that in cultures where food is scarce, girls' closeness to their mother enables them to satisfy their hunger more successfully than boys, and boys and men are more likely to suffer hunger anxiety coupled with lifelong dependency frustration (Shack 1969; Shack 1971; Parker 1960). The psychoanalytic literature suggests that early dependency frustration—for whatever reason—makes the transition to comfortable, rational, and autonomous ability to satisfy one's own needs difficult.[18] Studies of hunger anxiety among the Gurage of Ethiopia (discussed in chapter 1, see Shack 1969; Shack 1971) and the Ojibwa of northern North America (Parker 1960) confirm this claim. The Ojibwa lived in a harsh northern climate with consistent food shortages. Child-rearing patterns exacerbated children's dependency frustration, particularly of boys, and in extreme cases resulted in what Parker calls "the wiitiko psychosis." Ojibwa infants were reared primarily by the mother, in a "permissive" manner, with breast-feeding on demand (1960, 605). However, between the ages of three and five, attitudes toward children changed, and parents weaned them harshly, exposed them to cold and solitude, and forced them to fast and endure hunger for hours at a time (605). Such harsh and early independence training was directed particularly strongly at boys and it sometimes resulted in lifelong "dependency cravings" (606) and an association of food with power, and hunger with weakness and rejection (607). In extreme cases of physical and emotional deprivation, some individuals—almost always male—developed the wiitiko psychosis. Basic to the disorder was hunger anxiety manifested in victims as depression, nausea, loss of appetite, and eventual possession by a cannibalistic figure known as the wiitiko monster. When possessed, the victim saw family and friends "as fat, luscious animals which he desire[d] to devour" (603).

Parker's explanation of the wiitiko psychosis is suggestive: "Studies of the psychodynamics of dependency indicate that frustrated and unsatisfied dependency cravings often result in repressed rage" that may be expressed in images of devouring or being devoured (611). Greater aggression and rage will occur in those members of the social group who are less able to satisfy their dependency needs. Among the Ojibwa, men are most vulnerable to wiitiko spirit possession. Ideals of masculinity demand prolonged fasting, long periods of time spent hunting in isolation away from home, and separation from the cooking work of women. Women, on the other hand, control access to food, are not as pressured to fast and deprive themselves as men, and are involved in more cooperative social ties than men. Throughout their lives females are better able to satisfy normal dependency needs than males and rarely suffer from wiitiko psychosis (617–18).

The Ojibwa and Gurage cases provide a channel to understanding boys' and girls' differential aggression in U.S. culture. In the first five years, girls may suffer less dependency frustration and have a greater ability to make a smooth transition to autonomous satisfaction of their own needs due to the presence of their mothers (and other women) as role models and figures of identification. By becoming the mother in fantasy, girls can gain power to satisfy their own needs and to overcome their anxiety about their needs being met. While both boys and girls are able to "use fantasy play to portray fear in order to prove that fear can be conquered" (Paley 1988, viii), girls are more likely to have available a close adult model who comforts anxiety and displays power. Boys cannot be mothers, so they become bad guys (Paley 1988). Bad guys are powerful, but through aggression rather than nurturance. Boys may have a greater amount of aggression and violence in their play because they suffer greater separation anxiety and lack nurturing close role models to emulate. As Paley says, "The more unprotected they feel, the louder they roar" (1984, 50).

This study has shown that boys and girls have both similar and different ways to use food themes to express and assert themselves in the world. While boys and girls use food in a variety of ways and demonstrate no absolute differences, boys more often use food symbols for aggression and violence through images of devouring, while girls more often use them for parental identification through food tasks and feeding. This study suggests that in early childhood, both boys and girls can use food to gain power. But the vexing question still remains: Why and how in adolescence and adulthood does girls' relationship to food become a vehicle of their disempowerment and insecurity while boys' is more positively self-reinforcing? At some point, girls and boys encounter beliefs that deny the power of cooking and feeding, activities normally performed by women. They learn that male activities are more highly valued, and that competition and aggression reap greater rewards than nurturance. At the same time, they learn that restricted eating, thinness, and denial of appetite are appropriate for girls, and that hearty eating, bigness, and expression of appetite are appropriate for boys. These different definitions manifest and reinforce the unequal gender relations of U.S. culture. One path to gender equality involves the struggle for cultural approval of women's appetites, their diverse bodies, and their cooking and feeding work. In the next two chapters, we will explore how Florentine women experience gender through food and body in ways that can provide models of difference and change for men and women in the United States.

9

Food as Tie and Rupture

Negotiating Intimacy and Autonomy
in the Florentine Family[1]

INTRODUCTION

This chapter examines how two Italian mother-daughter pairs negotiate the life course and their evolving relationship through food. Feeding is the first and most important basis of relationship between mothers and children.[2] In most Italian families, mothers feed and children eat. Mothers' feeding can stand for all forms of nurturance, and children's eating can symbolize acceptance of mothers' care. The fascinating paradox of family dynamics plays out in the feeding relationship, for the result of nurturance is growth away from the need for it. Mothers' feeding both acknowledges children's dependence and simultaneously advances their growth toward independence. As children mature, the feeding relationship must change to reflect their growing autonomy and ability to satisfy their own needs. The reciprocal giving and receiving of food can be a way for mothers and children to achieve the balance between assertion of self and recognition of other that is essential to relationships of equality, a way to move toward a mature relationship of independence while maintaining the emotional connection that feeding and eating provide.[3] Refusing to share food or to recognize each other's cooking are sure signs of problems in a parent-offspring relationship.

Here I examine the different ways two Florentine mother-daughter pairs handle the feeding relationship. One pair consists of the mother, Elda, and daughter, Gigliola.[4] The second pair is Elda's younger sister, Tina, and her daughter, Sandra. They were all born in Florence, Italy— Elda in 1918 and Tina in 1920, Gigliola in 1945 and Sandra in 1943. Their story is part of a book I am writing entitled *Food at the Heart:*

156

Gender and Family in Florence, Italy, 1908–1984. The subjects of this book are the twenty-five members of a family I knew well for thirteen years. Data consist of tape-recorded food-centered life histories and an extensive collection of their home-cooking recipes.

FOOD AS TIE: ELDA AND GIGLIOLA

Food has been a lifelong link between Elda and Gigliola and an important force in reinforcing their positive relationship. As soon as she became pregnant, Elda began to connect with her baby through the feeding relationship, linking her great hunger during pregnancy to her daughter's hearty appetite, and her specific pregnancy cravings to her daughter's favorite foods. For both women, Elda's feeding and Gigliola's eating were important forms of connection. Later on, Elda's appreciation of Gigliola's cooking marked the growth of their relationship toward the reciprocal giving and receiving of food that marked a broader mutuality.

At the time these data were gathered, Elda still lived in Florence in an apartment where she moved after her husband, Gastone, died in 1978. Gigliola was her only child, and she had moved permanently to the United States in 1967 after marrying John, an Italian-American engineer employed by a major electronics firm. Gigliola had two daughters, Gloria and Sandy (named after her cousin Sandra), born in 1967 and 1970. Gigliola graduated Phi Beta Kappa from an American college in 1976, received an M.A. in International Relations in 1985, and was teaching high school in a suburb outside of Boston when I interviewed her. She made regular extended visits to Florence during summers.

Elda's parents ran a bakery in Piazza Donatello in Florence from 1936 until 1964. She lived with her husband Gastone, daughter Gigliola, and her parents in an apartment behind the bakery, where she worked as a sales clerk from her early teens until she was forty-six, when her family sold the bakery. Elda became engaged to Gastone when she was eighteen years old and he was twenty. They married in the thick of World War II on January 23, 1943, and Gastone had to return to the front again right after his short wedding furlough. He finally returned from war late in 1944 and shortly thereafter, Elda became pregnant. Her pregnancy coincided with the final months of World War II, when food was extremely scarce (Wilhelm 1988). During this terrible time of widespread hunger, Elda was in her second trimester of pregnancy with an enormous appetite:

> I remember waking up during the night to eat with desperation because I was so hungry. Oh yes, I remember eating many boiled chestnuts in those

days, because they were never lacking. I gained fifty pounds when I was pregnant.[5] In fact all those women that I had around me—my aunts, my mother, my grandmothers, my great-grandmother—they all said, "You've got to eat for two. You can't eat for one, you've got to eat for two." And because I had a great desire to eat because I was always hungry, I really threw myself into eating.

Elda's memories of her pregnancy portrayed a tight bond between mother and baby steeped in traditional beliefs about what a pregnant woman should eat. Elda was certain that specific hungers and eating behaviors during pregnancy had direct effects on her daughter Gigliola, as shown in the following story of *le voglie*—"the desires" of pregnancy. Florentines held beliefs common in Italy that if a pregnant woman craved a food and didn't eat it and then touched herself, her baby would get a birthmark in the shape of the desired food in the place where the mother touched herself. Elda said,

I remember that when I was pregnant there was little to eat. I had to eat whatever we could find. One time my father managed to buy a whole large salami.[6] I remember that he hung it on the kitchen wall. I was just pregnant, only two or three months, and I looked at that salami and I said, oh I remember it well, "Oh my God, that salami will be good. Oh, that salami will be good." And then, as soon as they found out I was pregnant, they sliced it right away and gave me a piece. But it was too late and my baby was born with the birthmark of that salami. She was born bald, completely bald, you know, without a single hair on her head. And right here on her little head, where I always touched myself to push back my hair, she has a birthmark exactly in the shape of a slice of salami. Thank goodness I touched myself up here.

Yes, because I always remember that a neighbor woman had repeatedly said to me, "When you become pregnant, listen well, if you see something that you want to eat, don't ever touch yourself on your face, always touch yourself where it won't show. Remember, always do this. Because then the 'desires' will come where you cannot see them."

And instead with this salami, I longed for it and thought, "Oh my God, who knows how good that salami will taste?" And then when Gigliola was born, a tiny little thing just born, you could barely detect it, but I definitely could make out this little birthmark in the shape of a slice of salami. And I said, thank goodness I touched myself where it wouldn't show.

Interestingly, salami was one of the foods that Gigliola craved when she returned to Florence. Elda said that she would buy two or three whole salamis before her daughter arrived, and Gigliola constantly snacked on them.

She goes to the refrigerator and cuts herself a couple of slices of salami, not at meals, but during the day, between one meal and another. As soon as she gets here, she begins to feel a craving for salami.

Gigliola bears the literal mark of her mother's craving on her head and carries it in her own fervor for salami.

Just as Elda's "desires" in pregnancy affected her baby, so did her hunger, for Gigliola was always a hearty eater. Elda remembered her daughter's eating with fondness, and she breast-fed Gigliola with enormous pleasure.

> I loved it; for me it was such a beautiful thing that I never would have stopped, never. I had a lot of milk, even though I was slender and not very big. I had so much milk that I could nurse as many babies as I wanted. And I found other infants to nurse whose mothers didn't have any milk. They asked me if I would nurse them and I was so happy to do it. I would have nursed all the babies in the neighborhood I liked it so much.[7]

Elda attributes her abundant milk supply to the foods her mother and grandmothers gave her to eat and linked her own food consumption to the success of her baby's nursing, again emphasizing food ties:

> You know Gigliola had six grandparents who all told me what to eat. I had to eat *farinata*. Next to the sink. My grandmother told me, "Go and eat it next to the sink. That will make your milk come," she said. Every morning I ate *farinata*—flour cooked in water and flavored with a little olive oil. They thought that this made good milk, sweet-smelling and nutritious milk. And you had to eat it next to the sink. You had to eat fennel because it also made the milk smell good. You couldn't eat beans, nor pork, because they said that those foods would give the baby a stomachache. You couldn't eat onion either, because they said that the baby wouldn't like the milk because it would stink of onion. Everything that the mother eats, they said, shows up in the milk. The milk takes on the taste of our foods, like when we eat asparagus, the milk comes out sour, distasteful. So I followed their instructions and ate everything that the baby loved, and it worked because she really sucked.
>
> Oh yes, she was a really good nurser. My milk spilled out from my breasts. I remember that the baby slept in her bedroom back behind the bakery, between one breast-feed and another, while I stayed in the shop and waited on customers. I used to make mad dashes back there every little while to check on her because her room was a bit removed from the bakery. But I continued to work in the bakery, and at one point I remember a customer saying, "Signora Elda, your baby is hungry."
>
> "Oh God," I said, "Do you hear her crying?"
>
> She replied, "No, no, no." She said, "It's you who are losing your milk."

They could see the milk coming out onto my apron, the white apron that I always wore in the shop. They could see the milk coming out.

And so, "Yes," I said, "Yes, it's time, it's time for her to eat." It was beautiful.

For Elda the milk leaking from her breasts was an integral part of her joyful nurturance of her child. The following quotation reveals one of the main reasons she loved breastfeeding:

Because at that moment, the baby belonged completely to me, that's why. In that moment, she was really all mine. And I thought about it, I said to myself, look, the baby is growing because I am giving her my milk, because I am giving her life, I am giving her nourishment. And it seemed to me to be such a beautiful thing that I never would have stopped. And you know, when I should have stopped, I didn't because I liked breast-feeding so much. So then my grandmother said to me, "Stop giving that baby your milk. It's not doing anything for her any more, it's water." But instead, every night before putting her in bed I loved to give her a drop of milk. I realized that it couldn't be of much nutritive value, especially because the baby ate everything already, she ate everything. I breast-fed her just for love.

But then one day, exactly the day of her birthday, her first birthday, Gigliola said, "Mommy, no more." She didn't want it any more, really. "No more, Mommy," she said to me. Oh how I cried that night. Oh God.

And there was my husband Gastone laughing. He said, "But how long do you want to continue nursing her? She walks by herself, she talks, she says everything, she eats everything, and you want to continue nursing her?"

She said to me, "No more, Mommy." Exactly on the day of her birthday, her first birthday.

Elda didn't want to stop nursing, for it symbolized her life-giving power and connection to her child. But Gigliola refused the breast and took her first step toward autonomy; in this she was supported by her father, whose attachment to her was loving but less intense than that of her mother. But although Gigliola gained some distance from her mother by eschewing the breast, she stayed connected to her by a continuing and enthusiastic consumption of Elda's food. Elda described her daughter's appetite thus:

She really loves food, and she eats everything I cook for her. I remember when she was a little child and a young girl, she ate so much. As a result, she had a tendency to get fat. So one time her father said, "Look, listen, you know what you should cook tonight for dinner for Gigliola, so she won't eat so much, you should make her a big plate full of boiled zucchini. For you know," he said, "they're still only zucchini, they're not even really very good, boiled zucchini, and then you just dress them with a little olive oil, you'll see that she eats less, that girl." *Mamma mia*, those zucchini! Do you know what devoured means? Devoured with bread. She loved even those. She loved everything.

And then she would never finish eating. For example, I don't know, take cheese. We gave her a piece of cheese together with a little bread. So then maybe she finished the bread and said, "Mommy, will you please give me another little piece of bread to eat with this last bit of cheese?" And so we gave her the bread. And then she finished the cheese but had a little bread left, "Mommy, will you please give me another little piece of cheese so I can finish this bread?" Always like that. So she tended to be a little plump. But then, little by little she slimmed down. We weren't worried about her because she was always healthy, but she ate so much, really a lot. Bread, especially bread. You can understand that, in that environment, the bread was born there, that warm bread just out of the oven, smelling wonderful. Nobody could resist, and she really threw herself into it.

Gigliola's love of eating reflected her mother's hunger during pregnancy and matched her mother's love of cooking. When Elda retired from the bakery at age forty-six, she devoted herself to the kitchen.

Look, for me, cooking was my greatest satisfaction. I loved to invent new dishes, to re-elaborate all the recipes of the foods I knew how to make, and to make new things. I found great satisfaction this way for me and for the family. I saw how much they appreciated it, all that I did for them. And so I invented, I tried to make new little things, to vary my cooking, and that too was a beautiful thing.

Clearly, through cooking and eating, Gigliola and Elda had a close and pleasurable bond of nurturance. But over their life course together, Gigliola and Elda had to confront a challenge common to all mothers and daughters—that of establishing the separation and autonomy essential to a daughter's growth (Chodorow 1974, 1979). One of the ways Gigliola did this was by learning to help out and take care of herself. Elda recounted one aspect of this experience:

Well, Gigliola had to learn to be self-sufficient at a very early age because I couldn't be there, I had to be in the bakery. Hence from when she was very small she had to go out and get the milk, prepare her breakfast, wash herself, dress herself, and go to school. Because I just couldn't do all these things. She had to manage by herself. Cooking, oh Gigliola learned to cook, oh yes, yes. She's a little like me; she's always had a passion for cooking. In fact, she has learned so many things. As far as cooking is concerned, I don't think that she found herself uncomfortable with that after getting married. She knew how to make many little things, yes, yes, she had a passion to learn.

I asked Elda whether she thought it was a good thing to develop independence in children, and Elda's answer demonstrated conflicting feelings:

> Yes I do. I find it a good thing, absolutely, like they do in America. They get the children used to being self-sufficient very early. This is a good thing. It is absolutely different from how we do things in Italy. For children in Italy, at least during the time when I was growing up, were much too spoiled, much too closely watched over in everything—in their needs, in their lessons. But I find it a great thing to let children be—or at least to try to let them be—as self-sufficient as possible. But Italian mothers seek to keep the umbilical cord as tightly attached as possible to their children. They don't cut it. I too was like this, apprehensive, for my daughter. It was my husband who restrained me and who said, "But let her go, let her be, she has to have her own experiences." And I have always had so much fear, so much terror of anything happening to her. Unfortunately, I've always suffered great anguish about this, and I've never known how to conquer it.
>
> I was always terrified that something would happen to Gigliola. When she was a baby, sometimes we thought about going to the movies, and we went. We left the baby with my mother and father, and they were two valid people, still in good shape. However, I had no peace. I began thinking, "What if the house catches on fire, what if something falls on her, what if something happens to this baby, if she gets suffocated by something?" I was continually thinking like that. So I couldn't wait to go home because I couldn't stand it anymore.
>
> I couldn't say this to my husband, because he would scold me and say, "But now you never enjoy anything anymore. Don't think about it; the baby is in good hands." Yes, but still, even though babies are carefully watched, things still happen. From the day she was born even up to today it's the same. Even though she's far away, it's still the same. It's a continual worrying about everything, about how she is, what she's doing, is she well, is she sick, you know; it's just a continual preoccupation.
>
> At a certain point, I had a lightning bolt of intelligence, and I said to myself, "I've got to learn to control myself, otherwise I'll make my daughter miserable," and it was true. And naturally I was encouraged by my husband, who counseled me as best he knew. I tried to check this desire I had to keep her always here.

Elda struggled mightily to control her fear of separation from Gigliola and to let her grow and go. Her words revealed her conflict between wanting her daughter to be self-sufficient and fearing letting her out of her sight. Elda said that her husband helped moderate her excessive attachment to her child. In fact, psychologists have noted that often the mother-daughter tie is particularly deep and problematic for the daughter as she grows. Identification and connection with the mother are very important for a young girl, but they can be suffocating in adolescence. Fathers often present an alternative figure of identification and attachment that helps girls gain distance from mothers (Chodorow 1974, 1978; Ehrensaft 1990). In Gigliola's case, this was definitely true. She said,

> I loved my father so much. In fact, my father and I were twin souls, and I missed him very much when he died.

Gigliola seemed to have used her identification with her father, and her father's more balanced and less clinging relationship to her, as a wedge to gain distance and independence from her mother. Elda metaphorically demonstrated this familial equilibrium in the following story about *baccalà*[*8] —dried codfish:

> Gastone loved all foods. There was only one thing that he didn't like—*baccalà*. He never learned to like it. This was perhaps because when he was a boy he took so many blows in being forced to eat *baccalà*. A bit of *baccalà* and a slap, a bit of *baccalà* and a slap—from his father. Because he had to learn to eat everything. The child learned, but he just really couldn't ever stomach *baccalà*. I tried the same thing with Gigliola. Then it just made me upset. I said to myself, "Why in the world am I doing this, if she doesn't want to eat it, she won't eat it." Understand? Gigliola was just like him. She didn't like *baccalà*, only that; she was just like her father. And instead I intended to teach her to eat it too. The first few times, I gave her a few slaps to make her eat it, but then I was sorry, and so I said, "But no, let it go if she doesn't want it." And you know, I think she still doesn't like *baccalà*. She is really her father's daughter, the same, the same. But, look, for me, *baccalà* is the best thing to eat in the whole world. That's why I couldn't understand why she didn't like it. Me, for *baccalà*, I would do crazy things for *baccalà*. I love it to death. I dredge it in flour and fry it in olive oil. Then I prepare tomato sauce. I chop up garlic, parsley, and a touch of hot red pepper, and then I put the tomatoes in and cook them a while, and then in goes the *baccalà*. But oh, it is something great—it is superlative!

Elda adored *baccalà*, but Gigliola aligned with her father and detested it, thus distancing and differentiating herself from Elda. Separation from the mother was problematic for the daughter, especially under conditions of fierce attachment like Elda's. Gigliola expressed her anxiety about separation and her efforts to combat it thus:

> I remember from the time I was a child I was always afraid of ending up alone. I had this fear of being abandoned, of not being able to be part of—how can I say it?—any social context. From this I developed a need to have a certain independence, not just material, but also spiritual. I needed to know that all right, if I find myself alone, I'll be okay just the same, understand? The fact of being independent, self-sufficient, has always strongly appealed to me. I don't know what caused this fear of being alone—maybe not having any brothers or sisters. The fact is that

yes, friendship is important, but you can count on friendship only up to a certain point. Eventually you realize that your parents are getting old and sooner or later you're going to lose them, and then you can end up alone, understand?

Perhaps Gigliola's fear of solitude was the mirror image of her mother's fear that something would happen to her; their reciprocal eating and feeding may have been paths to overcome and transform their fears into a pleasurable connection. Perhaps Gigliola had to go all the way to the United States to escape her mother's excessive attachment, but she returned to her mother to find a sure love that she could count on and that she expressed through hunger for and consumption of her mother's food. Gigliola reinforced her connection to her mother and to her Italian identity by eating Elda's delicious Italian cooking. She said,

> I get fatter here when I come to Italy, because I rediscover all the flavors of my childhood, and so for this I eat, because I eat the things that I can't easily find every day in the States. I get fat here, do you know why I get fat? Because there's this pressure to eat, from my mother. She pushes me to eat because I'm here, because she likes it, and because she also fulfills herself doing this for me, do you understand? It gives her pleasure. And finally, there's the fact that if you cook for yourself, as you well know, you always eat less. But when your mother cooks, well then you eat more.

And Elda knew exactly what Gigliola wanted. She always went to Florence's famed San Lorenzo market before Gigliola arrived to stock up on Tuscan salami, prosciutto, fresh fruit, fresh vegetables, and her daughter's favorite cuts of meat. Elda recounted,

> Listen, when Gigliola comes here, she seeks out all kinds of foods. Oh how Gigliola likes that vegetable *minestrone** so much. She has such a desire to eat it when she visits. I make her pot roast—*lo stracotto.** She always wants me to make her rolled veal flanks—*la pancetta di vitella arrotolata*. I don't know if you know this cut of meat; it's a piece of veal, a small piece from outside of the ribs. It's not an expensive cut, oh no, but it is very tasty. And here we cook it like this. We roll it all up, really, really tight, and we tie it up and we cook it. I cook it on the stove top very slowly with broth, water, everything. There are those who put it in the oven, but in the oven it doesn't come out as well. It comes out better on the burner. Well look, Gigliola goes crazy for that. But the only trouble is that since it is a cut of meat marbled with little pieces of fat, little ones, eh, the others in Gigliola's family don't like it. Only Gigliola and I like it. As a result I haven't been able to make it yet.

When Gigliola returned to Florence, Elda cooked for her, and Gigliola ate with gusto the flavors of her childhood. Food was a literal connection between Gigliola and Italy, through which she reaffirmed her Italian identity, especially by eating dishes that Americans, even Italian-Americans, often don't enjoy, like the *pancetta di vitella* mentioned above.

Food was a literal tie between Elda and Gigliola, where Elda nurtured Gigliola and Gigliola accepted her nurturance with appreciation. They established a balance with each other that altered when Elda visited Gigliola in the United States; there, Elda still often did the cooking, but Gigliola was more in charge because she shopped and also sometimes cooked.

Gigliola's description of her cooking style demonstrated its Italian roots, its typically Italian inventiveness, and her own self-confidence.

> Well, being Italian, and being used to having a little of this and a little of that, if I'm at somebody's house and I'm eating something I like, I'll ask them, "What did you put into it?"
>
> And of course the answer will be, "Well, you do a little bit of this, and a little bit of that, and you add a pinch of this, and a handful of that." And I then go home and duplicate it, and sometimes I change it, and sometimes I don't even write it down. I guess I just invent a lot. When I cook, most of the times, I pop it out of my head. Sometimes I make a mixture of vegetables with tomato sauce or—a lot of times I just make it up. Or it's something I've made before; it's something I've seen my mother make. Even when I make, for example, minestrone, it's everything. And people say, "How much of this, how much of that?" Well you put as much of it as you like. You go by trial and error, the next time you omit something, the other time you may want to add something else. So that's the way I cook, really, most of the time. I guess I do cook Italian, but I don't think I make a big deal out of it. I actually like an awful lot of American dishes; for example, I love corned beef and cabbage.

Elda admired and enjoyed Gigliola's cooking, which had taken on a distinctive hybrid nature of its own. She elaborated,

> I have realized that over there in the United States, Gigliola has learned to cook many new dishes, even, for example, Irish ones. They have a cooking system completely different from ours, but even so their foods come out well for her. For example, I see that she prepares a big pot of meat, a cut of meat that I don't remember, and she puts with it all kinds of vegetables: cabbage, turnips, carrots, and you get a broth with this beef inside, and I'll tell you that I really like that dish.

Not only did Elda love Gigliola's corned beef and cabbage, but she also liked her adaptations of Italian cooking to fit American palates and meal structure.

> You know, I've seen Gigliola cook pasta differently from how we do it. She cooks the sauce with meatballs, and pigs' feet, and sausages. She

puts all this stuff into a pot and then she adds the tomatoes. She gets a thin sauce, kind of watery, and that's what they call a *pomarola* sauce.*[9] In Italy we make *pomarola* with no meat, just tomatoes. But in America they make it with all that other stuff. Even sausages, meatballs made out of hamburger. They pour all this sauce on top of the spaghetti, and they eat these sausages and meatballs as their second course, all together on one plate. They really love eating this. And you know, I like it too. That sauce really comes out well.

The fact that Elda appreciated this food was particularly significant given how headstrong and even arrogant most Italians were about their way of cooking being the best and only way to cook. It showed a mutually respectful balance between mother and daughter around the sensitive issue of cooking, one in marked contrast to Tina's lifelong disparagement of her daughter Sandra's cooking, discussed later. Elda managed to overcome her excessive attachment to Gigliola and let her develop her own individuality. But by allowing Gigliola her own wings, Elda lost her to the far-off United States and ended up alone, especially after Gastone's death in 1978.

Elda and Gigliola's relationship demonstrated many issues of separation and intimacy where Gigliola's eating and Elda's feeding played a central role. Gigliola, always an enthusiastic eater, expressed her continuing connection to her mother and Italy by eating her favorite foods with great gusto when she visited Florence. Elda always enjoyed feeding her daughter yet had twinges of concern that Gigliola ate too much. Gigliola's appetite perhaps expressed her neediness and hunger for connection, typical of all children. Elda's desire both to feed and limit Gigliola expressed her struggle both to nurture and establish independence in her daughter, a challenge to all parents. Eating tied them together and was a channel for female identification. However, it also served as a contested domain through which Gigliola struggled for autonomy and Elda for control. By identifying with her father through food, Gigliola established some distance from her mother, but after Gigliola's move to the United States and Gastone's death, that distance became overwhelming to Elda. Their story marks the difficulty for parents and children, and for mothers and daughters especially, of staying connected yet reaching autonomy, of maintaining a close emotional connection yet not being swallowed up by it, of achieving separation without rupture.

FOOD AS RUPTURE: TINA AND SANDRA

A focus on feeding and eating reveals a very different relationship between Elda's sister, Tina, and her daughter, Sandra. Their food interactions defined a more emotionally distant and less nurturing relationship. I didn't know Tina and her husband Mario very well for, as Elda said, "*Stanno su le sue*—They keep to themselves." In contrast to Elda, whom I interviewed five times, and Gigliola and Sandra, whom I interviewed twice each, I only interviewed Tina and her husband Mario once, and Mario dominated the interview. As a result I lack detail from Tina, and the description of Tina and Sandra's relationship is largely from Sandra's point of view.

Tina was born two years after Elda on December 5, 1920. She worked in the family bakery until she married Mario, a silversmith, in 1942. Tina gave birth to Sandra on September 28, 1943, during the German occupation of Florence. They moved into the bakery with Tina's family to be together and ensure themselves food in those horrific times of danger and hunger. Mario began to help out in the bakery and eventually took over its management after Tina's father died in 1947. Whereas Elda worked full-time in the bakery every day for thirty years, Tina worked little after her marriage. Gigliola said, "My aunt Tina didn't come to the bakery very much. If she came in the morning, she didn't come until around 11:00 or 11:30, because she had to clean her house first. Understand? And then she didn't come every evening, she only came once a week to work in the shop. She worked very, very little in the bakery." After her marriage, Tina devoted herself primarily to caring for her home, her husband, and her only child, Sandra.

Sandra had a teaching certificate and taught physical education for three years until she married Rolando and became a full-time housewife in 1967. Rolando was a self-made successful businessman from Prato and co-owned and ran a dyeing factory (*tintoria*) outside of Florence. They had two daughters, Elena born in 1970 and Olivia born in 1972. They lived in a beautiful, completely modernized, stone country farmhouse on several acres of rolling Tuscan countryside just outside of Florence, and they employed a peasant couple who produced most of their food.

Sandra's memories of her childhood had a bleak and lonely cast, as exemplified in her recollection of meals.

> When I was little, I had to be quiet at meals, and that was all. Me, quiet, mute, listening. I was an only child. I didn't like meals then, as a child, and I couldn't leave the table, because my parents' upbringing was that the child had to stay seated until the parents had finished. And in those days they loved to sit at the table, as they do today; they love to spend hours at the table. Therefore I had to stay there and wait until they finished, and I had to shut up. *Mamma mia*, what torture! Then, I'll tell you, look, I got this knot in my stomach; I didn't eat, my stomach closed up.
>
> When I was already getting older, when I was at that critical age of thirteen or fourteen years old, I went days without eating. So I asked, "Mom,

can I take my plate and go out into the garden to eat?" So I went into the garden, and then I would eat. When I stayed with them, no, I couldn't. I was so thin. So thin, look, you could count my ribs. Depleted. Then little by little after I got married, I began to sort things out. I needed two or three years, because even then during the first years of marriage, my stomach closed up and I couldn't eat, really. It was crazy. There were continual problems to confront—cooking, the household tasks. I had never done any of them.

Sandra's description of painful meals and inability to eat reflected her uncomfortable childhood. Eating problems in childhood very often reflect emotional distress and problems in the family (Bruch 1973; Minuchin, Rosman, and Baker 1978; Palazzoli 1974; Thompson 1994). She described her parents as overly protective and suffocating but not nurturing. Sandra seemed to be defined as a reflection of her parents, and she had to conform to their expectations without regard to her own aspirations. Gigliola said,

> You know, when Sandra was a little girl, my aunt was absolutely clean, a person of utmost cleanliness, impeccable—and so Sandra also had to be immaculate. They always dressed her in these beautiful little dresses so she couldn't go out and play with the other children because she couldn't get dirty. Understand? That was a problem. But Sandra has made gigantic progress from the time she has escaped from the chains of her parents—in independence, let's say.

Not only did Tina and Mario confine Sandra's play, but they also raised her very strictly, without any freedoms and without any friends. According to Elda,

> Sandra was raised to be very diffident towards others, because she was always taught that friendship doesn't exist. Be careful, even with relatives, because they will turn face on you. They'll do this to you; they'll do that to you. Sandra only has short-lived friendships, because earlier, when she was a girl, watch out. She absolutely was not supposed to have friendships; she had to mistrust everyone.

Sandra's description of her schooling reflects the overbearing influence of her parents, who insisted she follow a career path suitable to them and who thwarted her own ambitions. In answer to my question about what she thought a woman should be, Sandra replied,

> Listen, I would like for a woman to have a certain intelligence, also a mental independence, to be able to move around with tranquillity and to work with tranquillity, without the need to succumb to her family. I would like my daughters to be women who work, maybe because I don't work and I'm not independent. I would like to work, I would like that; if I

could, I'd like it. But I would like to have work that suited me, that was chosen by me.

That's why I have allowed my daughters to be free to choose their own studies. My daughter Olivia loves to play the piano. For now, that's what she's studying; later we'll see, I don't know, I'm not forcing her. My other daughter Elena said, "I want to go to the Arts High School."[10] You know, I had wanted to go to the Arts High School, but my parents wouldn't let me do it, because they thought it was frivolous.

So then I said to Elena, "All right, I'll enroll you in the Arts High School."

Later she said, "No, Mom, I'd rather do the Science High School."

As an alternative, I had said to my parents, "All right, I'll do the Science High School if you won't let me do the Arts High School."

And they responded, "No, Science High School no, because when you finish you won't have a diploma in hand. If you don't want to continue your studies, what will you do? How will you get by?" They said, "You do the Teacher Training High School." And they made me do this teaching track. I did the Teacher Training High School, these studies against my desire, and I did well because I put all my force of will into them. I graduated right on time with good grades.

After the Teaching High School I wanted to do something like biology—which I had wanted to study at the Science High School—or anatomy, these things really intrigued me—chemistry also, all the scientific fields. But I couldn't do it, because after the Teacher Training High School you couldn't at that time enroll in the University. So then I found myself with a trade in hand that I hated. At that point, I had to do the Higher Institute of Physical Education. Still a teacher, but at least of physical education, better than being an elementary school teacher, but still a teacher. I don't like teaching, no; I really don't like it. It doesn't give me satisfaction; it doesn't stimulate me. In short, it doesn't do anything at all for me. So I found myself with this trade that I can't exercise.

Fortunately I found a husband who has enabled me to stay at home because otherwise I would have had a nervous breakdown from trying to teach. Yes, it's extremely important for a woman to realize herself with her work. I'm not saying that I haven't realized myself, not at all. I've realized myself somewhat through my family. Yes, but after all, it wasn't what I wanted. I could have done both things.

I was always glad I had Gigliola. When she married thank heavens I was already engaged. The idea of having a cousin who was like a sister to me really lifted my spirits. I said, "I'm not alone; she's there." Even if we didn't see each other that often, at least I knew she was in Florence, like me, getting desperate, looking for a husband, and that's it. Really, that's the way things were. Our goal in those days was to find a husband. In the past if you weren't married you were looked at with different eyes. You had to find a husband. In those days we thought, I'll get married and finally I'll do what I want.

Sandra and Rolando had a whirlwind courtship that began in August at the beach, and they married within eight months of their first real date. Sandra recounted,

In September we saw each other often. Then he said, "I want to get engaged to you." Because in my house there was no way to go out in the evening. I had to be home before 8:00 P.M. If I returned at 8:10, even though I was twenty-four years old, it was a catastrophe. I was all by myself, fighting against my parents, and I couldn't keep it up. I didn't want to fight. I couldn't be angry, and I'm the type of person who can't stay mad. Maybe I make a big scene, I fight, I scream, if they really make me mad; however, afterwards it passes, because I feel horrible if I stay angry. So I had to endure my parents, and that was that.

Rolando and I ended up being engaged for a very short time; we couldn't stand it. At midnight the alarm clock went off because he had to leave, and they wanted to go to bed. We were in the parlor, and the door was always open, there was no way ever to close it—that was impossible. They patrolled up and down in the hall. So Rolando said, "Listen, I want to get married." I found myself after eight months with this man, married. I didn't know how to cook; I didn't know anything about the house. It all got to me; listen, it made me feel really stressed.

I was already exhausted beforehand, but when we set up the house, we had to get all the furniture, little by little. As soon as the mattresses and the box springs arrived, I could no longer go to my house to see what the workers were doing. Nothing. I could not go alone to that house. "Oh Mom," I said. "But the carpenter is coming—I want to go—but do you realize?"

She said, "No, you can't go, the bed is there." As if in that house we had nothing to do but to lie around on that bed. Do you realize what I had to deal with? I returned home, and they looked me in the face, both of them, as if to say, let's look and see if she lowers her eyes or not. They made me feel guilty even when I didn't do anything. They made me feel guilty even if we exchanged a kiss, for goodness sake. I had so many friends, oh, I knew so many women my age who were free and tranquil. I was twenty-four years old. Oh my God, who was there still like me at twenty-four years old? The only one left was me.

Sandra felt extremely anxious about getting married because she lacked confidence in herself, had never been given any freedom or responsibility, and did not know housewifely skills.

I didn't know anything at all about cooking. I had never cooked. I had always studied and worked, never cooked. Furthermore, in my house there was no way to stand at the stove because I would always be criticized. Every now and then my father said to my mother, "But let her be, teach her, but nicely." There was no way.

The day of my marriage approached, and I didn't know what to do. So every day that my mother cooked—because she was not a good teacher—

every day that she cooked I asked her, "Mom, what is that?" I wrote what she did in a notebook. Little by little I wrote down the ingredients as she added them, because if I had asked her just to dictate the recipe, she would have forgotten something for sure. I have a notebook full of basic recipes: roast chicken, spaghetti sauce, beans, all the things that are central to Tuscan cuisine. I had to write them down because my cookbooks didn't have the home-cooking recipes that I had always eaten.

I said to myself, okay, if Rolando wants to marry me, he'll take me as I am. Oh, I threw away a lot of those dishes, so many, believe me. Oh, huge pots full of minestrone; oh dear, it was crazy. Let me tell you this story. One of the first days after my marriage, I invited my brother-in-law to dinner when my sister-in-law was on vacation at the beach. I made him a salad with cucumbers. Cucumbers—I thought you didn't have to peel them, because they're like zucchini, and you don't peel zucchini. So I cut them all in little slices with the skin on them. I saw this man begin to slice all around the outside of the cucumber slices with his knife and fork. The shame I felt. These are just stupid little things, but if you've never done them before. Oh there was no way I could learn to cook with my mother, even though I got married on the late side, at twenty-four years old, so there would have been all the time in the world to learn. Never, there was no way to do it the way she does, but even now, you know. When she comes to visit me here, I always let her cook because never has she said that I could make something well.

Once when we were at the beach together, the very first time, I said, "Mom, let's take turns cooking. You can stay late at the beach, and I'll do the cooking. The next day or the next week, I'll stay on the beach late, and you do the cooking." No, she wanted to do it all herself.

I learned to cook with this little notebook full of recipes I wrote down as she cooked. Little by little I learned; however, I am not a great cook. I make really simple things—home-cooking, roasts. It's not like I can lose myself in it very much. I don't like to cook, no, no. I like to eat, but cooking very little. I'd rather sew; I'd rather iron and wash than cook. I think it's because I've always been criticized from the very beginning by my mother, and so I've still got a sort of complex about it. When friends come to dinner, I'm always in crisis, because I say, what can I make for them now? Usually I make just normal food and I succeed, without a doubt I succeed. But I still have that worry. Listen, I'm a housewife; if I don't know how to cook, you tell me, what else is there? At least if I worked, understand? It's important for a housewife to know how to cook, to know how to do other things too, but cooking is the essential thing.

But my mother always said, "You don't know how to do anything." What could I do, will you tell me? How could I learn? When she had a kidney operation, she stayed a week in the hospital. I made a *pomarola**
sauce. I'd never made it before, and I made a *pomarola*. When I didn't have her in the house, I managed to make something. But with her around, there was no way ever to do anything.

Let me tell you the story of the rice fritters—*le fritelle di San Giuseppe.**
Listen to this. Well, one year for the Feast of St. Joseph, my mother made

fritters according to the custom and invited me to her house to eat them. I replied, "Mom, I can't come because I too made fritters. This evening Rolando will be coming home, and then some friends are coming over."

"But you can't make them as good as I can," she retorted. The recipe is the same, identical, because I copied it exactly from the one they gave to her. So now, can you believe it? She even made me have a complex about my fritters.

There could be many reasons why a Florentine mother would not pass on cooking knowledge to her daughter. In some of the families discussed in chapter 3, the young women didn't care to learn to cook. They were busy going to school and working, and as long as their mothers or grandmothers cooked, that was fine with them. But Sandra wanted to learn and was blocked. Perhaps this was because cooking was so central to her mother's identity that she feared having her status in the family usurped by her daughter. Tina didn't work outside the home after marriage, and cooking was her pride and what her husband touted as the reason he had married her. During our interview, Tina said to me, "Ask Mario if he likes my cooking; go ahead and ask him."

"Of course I like her cooking," Mario replied. "If not, I never would have married her. I already tried her out first. Before marrying her, I looked carefully at how she cooked, and then I said, yes, it's fine. I married her willingly because she is a good cook."

Tina playfully bristled at that comment and said, "I'll leave you, after forty years of marriage I'll leave. You married me only for that? In the kitchen, I'm in charge."

Mario added, "Look out. She's in charge in some other place too, in some other place too. But when it comes to paying, I pay."

"When it comes to paying, he pays," Tina echoed.

Their words imply that Tina's status in the family comes from her cooking, which carries over into "some other place." But Mario paid. He had economic power, and they both knew it. Perhaps in their traditional division of labor, where he paid and she handled the household, Tina felt that cooking was the backbone of her status and that if she shared cooking skills with her daughter, she would lose her indispensability.

Sandra described the impasse her parents created for her. By forcing her into a career she hated and not teaching her the skills to be a housewife, she was neither fish nor fowl, neither working woman nor housewife. She could not find a satisfying source of self-esteem in either domain. She had to find a way to break free from her parents and their undermining attitude, and Rolando was essential to that process.

Luckily for me I found an intelligent husband who made me get—listen, right away—driving lessons. Something that I had asked my parents I don't know how many times. "Absolutely not," they said. "A woman does not need to know how to drive." For me, a woman without a license is not independent. Oh, they didn't want me to get it, the fights we had! They did not want me to get my license, you know. I asked them repeatedly.

Finally one time my father let me drive his car. Naturally I made a mistake, of course. The car took off with great hiccups and lurches. My father yelled, "Get out! And never get back in!" He left me right there in the street. Luckily I was near my house and could return on foot.

I said to myself, "*Mamma mia*, for heaven's sake. Let's not talk again about getting a license." But later Rolando made me get it, always with the idea of emancipating me. A license is necessary, are you kidding? In today's world, it's indispensable.

When I got my license I can't tell you how my parents flipped out. "Oh *mamma mia*, now she got her license. Look out. Oh that man is crazy." But Rolando tried, he tried to help me unburden myself as much as possible. He forced me. He made me grow.

Sandra's husband Rolando described the first months after they got married this way:

Tragic. Oh those times were tragic. Because she still had to find confidence in herself. She found her equilibrium and a little more self-assurance after the birth of our first baby, which we had put off for three years, eh. But then, luckily, something that she thought she couldn't do, she did, tranquilly, and all her fears have passed, all her insecurities.

Having children gave Sandra a boost in self-confidence and a new family to replace the one she lost; however, the transition to motherhood was not without its difficulties. One of these appeared in Sandra's negative description of breast-feeding, which contrasted dramatically with Elda's rhapsodic reminiscences. After the birth of her first child, Elena, Sandra didn't have enough breast milk—a common problem for new mothers, especially anxious ones. Mothers must develop their milk supply in response to their baby's needs. Unfortunately, Sandra's doctors told her to supplement with formula, a practice which breast-feeding advocates oppose, because only the infant's sucking will build up the mother's supply (La Leche 1981). In Italy at this time, many breast-feeding mothers, including Sandra, had a scale on which to weigh the child before and after each feeding to make sure it got enough, a practice that easily created anxiety and stress for the mother. Getting up in the middle of the night to weigh, nurse, weigh again, mix adequate formula, and feed again, was exhausting Sandra, so she gave up the breast and put Elena totally on formula, after which both mother and daughter did fine. When Sandra's second daughter, Olivia, was born two years later, Sandra only nursed her once in the hospital, then gave her formula. She was sure that formula had been fine for her babies, and because she disliked breast-feeding, it was much better for her. Sandra recounted,

Breast-feeding Elena really bothered me. First of all, I didn't like it at all—I didn't like it; it bothered me. I felt badly, I don't know; it bothered me. This sensation of this baby who was sucking at my breast was just something that I didn't succeed in—maybe because I didn't have milk. In fact my mother always said to me, "Do you feel the let-down reflex? You have to feel it, you have to feel the need to give your milk." I said that I didn't feel it. Hence it could be that it all depended on this.

Furthermore, I was very, very anxious, I don't know. In short, I didn't like it at all. No, no, breast-feeding was a negative experience. Perhaps I disliked breast-feeding because I was so anxious, perhaps it was because I was exhausted by everything that went before, all those preceding years. It bothered me. I felt weaker. I couldn't hold myself upright; I didn't have energy to do anything. You know, breast-milk is a food, eh, you've got to regenerate it yourself, with your organism. If you physically don't have sufficient strength, you can't. In fact, I didn't have any milk, which shows that I just couldn't do it.

I've never heard anyone say that it's beautiful to breast-feed. I'll tell you how ugly it is. I didn't like it. I really didn't like it. It was an unpleasant sensation. To me it was disgusting. I found no pleasure in it. They say it's something natural, but I find it absolutely against nature. Imagine how it felt to me.

My mother always said to me, "It was beautiful when you suckled at my breast: You really latched on; you really liked it you know."

And when she used to say this, I answered, "That's disgusting, Mom, what disgusting things I did." Understand? Thus I never saw it, not even before having children, as something pleasurable, this union between these two things.

Sandra mentioned her mother twice in this denunciation of breast-feeding. First, she implied that her mother made her feel inadequate by telling her that she should have been feeling the let-down reflex when she did not. Second, she found the thought of herself suckling at her mother's breast unbearable—"disgusting," she said. Perhaps the thought of herself being utterly dependent on her mother was terrifying, for she was trying so desperately to separate from her mother so she could grow into herself. Perhaps similarly, after her daughters' births, she could not bear the thought of such an utterly physical dependence of her babies on her; it overwhelmed the fragile sense of autonomy she had managed to gain.

Eventually, Sandra's relations with her parents deteriorated to the point that she had to cut off relations completely in order to gain confidence and independence and to rid herself from their criticisms.

The last step was to take that decision, to say, "That's it. Enough," to my parents. That was the last definitive act, and I have no regrets. I'm no longer so attached. There was an umbilical cord between me and them. If

I didn't call them every day they yelled at me. They felt free to criticize me at every moment. Now they can't do it any more because I don't see them. They don't criticize me any more. As soon as they open their mouths now I don't let it pass. I've become really mean, even too mean. As soon as my mother opens her mouth, everything she says bothers me, and I have a thousand arguments and fights because I have to react. They made me stand too much. Enough, you reach a point and then enough.

I have arrived at this conclusion, that they don't really love me. Even when I was a child, they never had much affection—well, I got some from my father. He gave me courage and a little confidence. But my mother—no way. I have never understood her. I'm a mother; I know what it means to be a mother and no, no, a mother who is a mother does not do what my mother did. A mother who loves her child, or a father, they don't make their own child suffer. I have never understood my mother. She is not at all a mature woman. She has not succeeded in getting mature and in using her brain. It's probably also my father's fault. But she—when she says things, it means it's because she believes them. She does not keep them to herself, no; she says them. When it comes to buttering up her husband, making him feel like a king, she doesn't keep quiet. Or the time she wanted the washing machine at any cost, oh how she badgered him. Madonna, she wanted that washing machine, and she went on and on about it; and she got the washing machine even though my father didn't want to buy it for her. But when it comes to me, she doesn't go on and on, understand?

Sandra gave up trying to establish a reciprocal balance with her mother around cooking or anything else and cut off ties with her parents. Unlike Gigliola, she didn't have the positive support of her father to help balance her relationship with her mother; Sandra's parents maintained a strong allegiance to each other at the expense of Sandra's needs for support and autonomy. Breaking with her parents was necessary for Sandra to rebuild herself. She developed her own way of cooking and enjoyed it more, though still not very much.

Sandra's cuisine was based on simple, excellent-quality, traditional Tuscan foods produced on her and her husband's farm. They went halves on the harvest with a peasant couple who raised the animals, cultivated the vegetables, and took care of the tree crops. They had every kind of fruit and vegetable common in the region: pears, apples, peaches, apricots, figs, grapes, cherries, olives, cantaloupes, watermelons, tomatoes, eggplant, lettuce, radicchio, zucchini, artichokes, basil, parsley, carrots, and so on. They raised rabbits, pheasants, and chickens, and they paid a nearby farmer to raise and slaughter a pig for them, so they had their own sausages, salami, prosciutto, and pork. With these foods, they could eat wonderful meals and entertain their group of twenty or thirty friends:

We get together often, and I make things that they can't make because they live in the city—charcoal grilled meat, pork when we kill the pig, things they can't eat because they don't have any way to make a fire. During the winter, we build a fire in the fireplace and we roast meat. When we slaughter the pig, we give them a couple of fresh sausages; they stick them onto the forks, and they roast them on the fire—that's what we do, understand? It's not that I make great things. For the love of God, if I had to go in there and cook! These friends of mine, when they cook, they make a thousand sauces, all these sophisticated things; I don't know, now I can't even remember what. I wouldn't know where to begin, listen, not at all.

Sandra still felt insecure about her cooking, perhaps because it represented mature independence, something she still struggled to attain. She expressed her anxiety and lack of self-esteem in her inability to eat as a child, in her insecurity about cooking, and in her distaste for breast-feeding. Sandra made a gigantic effort to build herself up by marrying a man who loved and supported her, by cutting off her strangling relationship with her parents, by having children who provided her with a new family, and by developing her own new relationship with feeding based around genuine traditional Tuscan foods produced on her farm. She enjoyed having meals with her children and ate much more contentedly than in the past.

I sit down there, tranquil, at the table. I am much more relaxed today, psychologically, you know. I was more anxious as a child, so I ate differently.

Sandra found a way to reconstruct herself with her management of food and has attained a new balance with her parents—a balance based on distance and mistrust, but one that enables her to nurture herself. She and her mother were not able to establish a give-and-take relationship around food, probably because cooking was so central to Tina's social position and marriage that she could not give it up without feeling threatened. But in the case of Elda and Gigliola, Elda worked for years in the bakery and thus had an identity as worker as well as of wife and mother. Elda embraced cooking when she retired and found it intriguing and novel but willingly shared cooking with her daughter. Gigliola was able to feel confidence in her own cooking because her mother had taught her how, respected her skill, and willingly ate her dishes. Gigliola, like her mother, had a career in the workplace that gave her a sense of identity and meaning outside of the home, hence the two did not threaten each other in the kitchen.

These two stories indicate the challenges to mothers and daughters to reach mutual respect and independence. Where a woman's status is weak because she does not hold a respected place in society outside the home, she may feel threatened by her daughter. She may need to hold her daughter back and fear her independence. But where a woman's place is strong in the workplace, she may be more able to respect her daughter and grant her independence. The lifelong balance between a mother and daughter can be seen through their relationships around food. To attain mutual respect, food must pass not only from mother to daughter, but back from daughter to mother. Parent and child must maintain a reciprocal relationship around the activities of cooking, feeding, and eating.

10

The Body as Voice of Desire and Connection in Florence, Italy[1]

INTRODUCTION

Why write about the body in Florence? Scholars have observed from many different perspectives that the body is a vehicle of the self and that conceptions of the body reveal conceptions of the self—particularly the self as male or female.[2] In this chapter I explore how the Florentine body represents the Florentine self. Florentines define the body as a source of pleasure, a reflection of family, and an active agent, yet they also contend with increasingly prevalent images of the body as an object and a commodity that are typical of late twentieth-century capitalism. Although Florentines' culture is quintessentially "Western," their body conceptions are different from those prevailing in the United States and offer new perspectives on them.

In the United States, attitudes toward the body are characterized by mind/body dualism—the belief that mind and body are separate and that the true self lodges in the mind, exercising control over the errant body. Mind/body dualism supports gender inequality by associating men with the exalted, controlling mind and women with the lowly body subject to control (Bordo 1992). Such attitudes mesh perfectly with the need of consumer capitalism to sell products because the body, especially the female body, is constantly defined as an object to be worked on and improved by buying things. As Anne Becker says, we define the body as a legitimate object of "self-cultivation" (1995, 36).

One of the most important ways Americans, especially women, "cultivate" bodies is through the pursuit of thinness.[3] We seek physical perfection defined as a level of slenderness that is metabolically impossible for most people, leading those people—usually women—to feel worthless because they do not fit the ideal. Furthermore, by being urged to diet, women are really being urged toward masochism

178

marked by denial of pleasure in eating and by the nagging pain of chronic, low-grade hunger. We tend to take our body attitudes for granted and rarely examine them, but in other times and cultures, different notions of the body have prevailed. Medieval Europeans, for example, defined the body as a site of fertility, decay, and holiness. They controlled, disciplined, and even tortured the flesh to pursue a "horrible yet delicious elevation" toward the divine (Bynum 1991, 162). Victorians reinforced women's subordination by defining the female body as weak, sickly, and without legitimate desires (Brumberg 1988). On Fiji, islanders define the body socially, as a legitimate object of social concern and social cultivation. They fortify each other's bodies through feeding and thus value an ample body as a sign of social success (Becker 1995). What about Florence? How do Florentines define the body? Is it a site of power or domination for women?

My discussion of the Florentine body is part of a book I am writing entitled *Food at the Heart: Gender and Family in Florence, Italy, 1908–1984*. The subjects of this book are twenty-five members of a family I knew well for thirteen years. All came from peasant, working-class, or artisan backgrounds. They were all born in the province of Florence, some in the countryside, others in the three main provincial cities of Florence, Prato, and Empoli.[4] None of the older generation had more than a ninth-grade education, and most reached only fifth or sixth grade. They ranged from working class to upper middle class and were blue- and white-collar workers, artisans, clerks, retirees, and housewives. They were born between 1908 and 1972 and ranged in age from twelve to seventy-six when I last interviewed them in 1984. All lived comfortably and with adequate income and housing, but none belonged to the Florentine economic, social, political, or intellectual elite. My data consist of over a thousand pages of transcriptions of food-centered life histories as well as field notes, observations of scores of shared meals, and an extensive recipe collection.

GOLA: DESIRE FOR FOOD

One of the most striking things about Florentines is that they celebrate the physical pleasure of eating. Men and women alike develop a positive and active relationship to their bodies by enjoying eating and self-nurturance, and they proclaim the pleasures of eating over and over again. Eighteen-year-old Paola said,

> I love to eat. I don't say no. Because for me, going out to eat—I feel great when I go and eat—*sto bene io quando vo a mangiare.*

When twenty-eight-year-old Cinzia explained why she was tired of dieting to lose weight, she said,

> I need to give in freely to my desires. For God's sake, you can't eat just because you have a mouth! You have to eat for the taste, for the pleasure.

Florentines name and celebrate their love for food. They call it *gola*—"desire for food." *Gola* means both craving and relishing a specific food. Someone who really appreciates eating is called *golosa/o*.[5] Dictionaries translate *golosa/o* as "gluttonous," but this implies a despicable excess of greed that distorts the Florentine meaning, which I translate as "really loving or desiring food."

Gola means "throat" as well as "desire for food." The throat is the passageway both for food to enter the body and for voice to exit. The implication is that the actions are reciprocal. The food goes in and makes the person; the voice goes out and externalizes the person. Because *gola* implies both "desire" and "voice," it suggests that desire for food is a voice—a central vehicle of self-expression, an animated manifestation of life and personhood. The Italian word for "waist" is the same as that for "life"—"*vita*."[6] This etymology further emphasizes a conception of the body as vital rather than inert, self-expressive rather than self-reflecting, and active rather than passive, a point that I discuss in detail later in the chapter.

In their concept of *gola*, Florentines defined the self as having a legitimate right to love food but also a moral obligation to eat judiciously and avoid excess. They recognized their special passion for certain foods by saying they were *golosa/o* for them, as fifty-four-year-old Bruno said,

> *Sono goloso di pane*—I really love bread.

Forty-eight-year-old Loretta said,

> I am *golosa*. I am *golosa* for pasta and I am *golosa* for sweets.

Eating the foods they desired made people feel good and they celebrated this feeling. As Vanna said,

> Just thinking about eating a good meal gives me satisfaction.

Florentines approved of this love of food, but they also believed in a sense of measure and disdained excess consumption. For example, twenty-one-year-old Alessandro said,

> Look, as far as desire goes, I'm the type that until I'm full, really full, I would keep eating. However, I try to brake myself a little.

He uses the word *frenarmi*—"to brake myself"—which is the same word sixty-six-year-old Elda used in describing her desire:

> Yes, I'll tell you, I'm a little *golosa*. I'm *golosa*. I try to brake myself [*frenarmi*], but I'm *golosa*. Every now and then I feel the desire to eat some-

thing sweet. So I go in the kitchen, and I look for, I don't know, the jam jar, a candy, something, because it is clear that I need something sweet. If I don't have anything, I have to put my shoes on and go out and buy myself something sweet. A couple of pastries or something like that. Maybe I eat that and nothing else, but I feel the need to eat it. Maybe my blood sugar falls or something. Sometimes I make a rice cake—*torta di riso**—which is delicious. It is just a simple home-style dish, but it is good. I cook rice in milk, add eggs, sugar, a pinch of salt, and grated lemon peel. If I have some, I add candied fruits or a little bit of rum or other liqueur or sometimes some cocoa to vary the color and flavor.

Elda respected the compulsion of desire and described in loving detail how she satisfied it, but she also felt it had to be controlled. Giving in to excess desire was not good, for two reasons. First, excess consumption destroyed desire and pleasure. Elda revealed this belief in the following story about her father, a baker:

I remember that at one point my father decided to sell pastries as well as bread in our bakery. He hired a highly skilled confectioner—a *pasticci-ere*—who made exquisite pastries. Imagine, Sunday we had a line of cars in front of the bakery filled with people who came to buy our pastries because they were so good. I remember that on the first day that the pastry baker began with us, my father said to my sister Tina and me, "Girls, here are the sweet pastries, eat as many of them as you want. Don't hold back, go right ahead and eat as many as you want." And off we went, eating, eating, eating, eating—so much that the next day we couldn't even look at a pastry. And then we realized why he had urged us to dig in. Oh we had such a nausea—we couldn't even look at those sweets. That was it; we had had enough, because after that, we could never eat another one.

The moral of Elda's story was that uncontrolled gluttony was bad because it destroyed the pleasure of eating. Measured behavior guaranteed that foods would retain their delectation.

A second reason why Florentines disapproved of giving in to excess desire was because it broke the balance between desire and control that Florentines valued, and as a result made a person fat. Elda made this point by describing her daughter Gigliola, whose appetite she described in chapter 9:

Look, take Gigliola; at a certain point she says, "Enough, I'm not hungry any more," but she continues to eat and it's that eating that hurts her. That eating after no longer being hungry. Because when a person reaches the point of saying, "Enough, I'm no longer hungry," then that should be all. She shouldn't eat any more. Instead she continues. I have a friend who is the same. She was visiting me for lunch the other day and she said, "Enough, I won't eat any more." Instead, when I put a plate of cookies out, she took one cookie after another until she had eaten a good part of them. She shouldn't have eaten because she was no longer hungry. Eating out of desire, that's what makes a person fat, eating out of desire.

Elda's words expressed a cultural belief in enjoying food greatly but consuming it moderately. I shall discuss later Florentines' complex feelings about body shape, but suffice it to say here that they did not at the time of this study castigate fat people. They did not make moral judgments about a person's size but about his or her behavior. Desire was legitimate, but gluttony was bad.

Florentines focused on how eating gave the body not only pleasure, but also consolation.[7] They recognized that eating made a person feel good and for some it was a major source of emotional comfort. Fifty-year-old Vanna related:

> You see, I have the kind of nervous system that I don't get mad, no no, but I eat and eat in continuation until food comes out my ears. It's not hunger because I feel uncomfortably stuffed, but it's stronger than me; I can't help myself—I have to eat. It stems from my nerves—a doctor told me this. I feel that I have to eat, it doesn't matter what, as long as I eat. I went through a period when I used to eat in the middle of the night—I had to eat. When I go through these periods, I go in the kitchen with the desire to eat. I know I shouldn't; I know it's bad for me, but it's stronger than me; I can't help it. Then maybe an hour later, I go back and I get something else. It's not like I eat huge sandwiches, but I snack [sper-luzzico]. I am capable of eating four or five cookies in the middle of the night. In short, I eat things that I shouldn't eat, especially at that hour. I feel badly afterwards because I feel stuffed and uncomfortable, but at the same time I always feel the craving for food, especially in these anxious periods. I don't know why. When I'm in a state of anxiety, the need to put something in my mouth is overwhelming.

Eating helped her because of its gratifying effect on both body and soul, which for her took precedence over the fact that it made her fat. She absolved herself of responsibility for her girth by defending her behavior. She didn't eat that much, she said, but she just had the sort of body that got fat easily.

> It's not that I eat so much, honestly. If I sit at the table, I bet I'm the one who eats least of all. Oh I have these days that I told you about that I eat all day long. But that's not usual. That happens when I am really tense. But if not, I sincerely think that I don't eat that much; I don't eat any more than others and in fact sometimes people say to me, "Well for heaven's sake, you don't even eat very much."

Vanna described herself as fat, but she did not feel evil or worthless as a result; for she felt she had a legitimate right to take pleasure in food, as did most Florentines, and she did not eat to excess.

Vanna's niece, eighteen-year-old Paola, expressed a similar conviction that she had a right to take pleasure in food even if her weight was not the ideal:

I'm a little bit plump [*cicciotella*] but nothing extreme in short. I could be a little thinner, I should be a little thinner, but if I can't do it—well, it's not like I want to pass my life suffering. Furthermore, if you don't have the tendency to lose weight, you won't resolve anything by dieting. That's my opinion. Sure, I can diet for two months and lose ten pounds, but then if I start eating normally again, I gain them all back. I can't pass my whole life eating what someone else wants me to eat. I can't spend forty years eating nothing but grilled meat, for heaven's sake!

BODY AS PRODUCT AND REFLECTION OF FAMILY

Florentines defined the body not as a product of personal moral concern but as a product and reflection of the family, given by nature through the family. Vanna's family members were almost all on the plump side. She said,

> Nature made us this way. There are those who can eat as much as they want and they keep their shape just fine. Instead there are those who watch what they eat, who suffer, and still get fat. My children are like me. Many times my daughter Cinzia has said, "I don't know, both Alessandro and I take after you. All we have to do is eat a little and we gain weight."

Her son Alessandro echoed his mother:

> All of us in this family have a large body build and so I think it is just something that we carry with us.

And his sister Cinzia said,

> We are all fat in this family.

Their cousin, Paola expressed the same idea:

> All of us in the family are nice and plump—*bell'e pasciucuti*. Our cousins in Florence too. We're all nice and abundant—*bell'e abbondanti*. I don't know. It's our constitution; it's logical. A person has to eat something.

They concurred that one's body was given by one's family, as were one's eating habits. As Paola said,

> In this family we eat; we don't hold back.

Living in families like those of Vanna and her sister Loretta led them inevitably to reconstruct their families through pleasurable meals and to enjoy the meals even more because of the company.

Just as commensalism—eating together—reproduced the family, it was also a primary means of forging and soldering extrafamilial relationships. Couples marked their official engagement—*fidanzamento*—by having a special meal with each other's families, and then they began the regular, lifelong habit of eating together that continually reaffirmed their connection. Friends got together for *scampagnate*—outings to the countryside—where they ate and drank in raucous company and had a great time together. They loved going out to eat with friends—for the simultaneous pleasures of food and conviviality—and were not willing to give them up to lose weight. When explaining her problems with dieting, Cinzia said,

> I'm not going to go out to eat and sit there having broth when everybody else is eating lasagna.

Similarly her cousin Paola said,

> For me, if we're all in a group on a Saturday or Sunday evening and we decide to go out to eat, am I going to go out to eat and then I can't eat? I have to eat a little salad with no dressing? No, I like to *eat* the way everybody else is eating. I can't suffer my whole life just to be thin.

Florentines linked the sensual pleasure and the sociability of eating. They could not imagine one without the other, and they eschewed sacrificing commensalism in order to mold their bodies.

Florentines recognized and gave precedence to the social bonds enacted through eating rather than to the body that resulted from commensalism. In fact, a body that was too thin aroused concern; Florentines especially loved fat babies and plump children. Like the Fijians described by Anne Becker (1995), Florentines defined the body as a reflection of nurture. Excessive thinness revealed problems with nurture and psychological distress, as the following story by Elda revealed:

> I remember when I was little, I entered my house and I smelled from afar the fragrance of the broth that was cooking on the stove. I loved that smell, in spite of the fact that I didn't eat the soup. As a young girl I never ate. I would go even a week without eating. You see, I realized as an adult why I didn't eat—because in my house there was discord between my father and my mother. I felt so much anguish, so much fear, and I have this defect that when something bothers me, my stomach closes, and I can't eat. That's what happened to me then, without my knowing it. I heard my parents arguing and my stomach closed and I couldn't eat.
>
> So then my parents were extremely worried about me—not eating today, not eating tomorrow—it was bad. But I realized later that I didn't eat precisely because of my parents' disharmony. I am frighteningly emotional. So much so that from not eating—because I ate nothing—I found myself in bad shape. I mean that my health promised nothing good. I always had a fever. I was continually losing my voice. So they took me to the doctor, and he found that I had swollen glands which were of course due to my bad nutrition—to the fact that I didn't eat, in short. So my parents were really worried and they cried from desperation, even more so

because in the family there was an uncle, my mother's brother, who had died from tuberculosis. So they had a terror of that illness, especially because I was so thin, I was like my little finger. I realized later, however, that it would have taken nothing to cure me—just having harmony in the family. For me, that was everything.

Elda expressed the widely held Florentine belief that excessive thinness represented physical illness and/or emotional upset. Hence Florentines did not think exclusively or primarily about the body as an aesthetic object, but as a symbol of inner states—of mental and physical health. They derived this belief out of a past where infectious disease and poverty were chronic and where a thin body represented vulnerability. Furthermore, not eating was a supremely antisocial act because of the importance of commensalism to social relations.

THE BODY AS ACTIVE AGENT

In their beliefs that the body gave legitimate gustatory pleasure and simultaneously represented and re-created the family, Florentines defined the body as an active agent of a person's self, not as a passive object to be molded into the abstract commodity of beauty. This belief can be seen by noting how often Florentines spoke about the body in language that prescribed *doing* rather than *appearing*. When describing the body, Florentines much more often used *fare* "to do," *dare* "to give," or *stare* "to be doing," rather than *essere* "to be."

Florentines described the body as *making* children—*fare bambini*—and this was a widely respected source of female status. "Making children" happened principally through feeding them, first and foremost from the very body of the mother. In chapter 9, Elda described the pleasure and satisfaction she took from nursing her baby and emphasized that she was "giving her [baby] life." Vanna expressed a similar idea when she described her babies: "It seemed like I was giving them life when I nursed them." Most women took pride and pleasure at being able to nurture their babies from their own bodies, and they described over and over how feeding was a tie to their children, one that made mothers special. Their emphasis on using their bodies for creation enabled them to accept the bodily changes often accompanying the birth of children. As Elda said:

> I've heard of some women who don't like breast-feeding. I think it's because they are afraid of ruining their figure; I don't know, that might be the reason. I can't see any others. It doesn't seem like a good reason to me. If a woman ruins her shape, what's wrong with that? What kind of a reason is that? I'll tell you the truth. I nursed Gigliola and I would have nursed her a lot more, but I never ruined my figure. I stayed the same as before, and I never even thought about the possibility that breast-feeding

would have ruined it. I stayed the same as before. Even in regard to the husband, have a little patience, if a woman's figure is ruined, it's because she had a baby, because she nursed it. That should be a reason for tenderness from the husband towards the wife in my opinion. It's not her fault; it's nature.

Florentines gave priority to the wonderful creation effected by the body and dismissed its shape as both secondary and given by nature.

Florentines also described themselves as *doing* work—*fare il lavoro*. Particularly among those Florentines descended from *mezzadria*[8] peasant culture, women were valued for using their bodies to work hard. Their tasks were physically demanding: cooking for large households, tending chickens and rabbits, gardening, preserving food, working in the fields, boiling laundry in ashes, and looking after children. As Vanna said, "In the old days, it was enough for a woman to take care of her family and her children, even if she was enormous [*una valanga*]. But today, the women pay much more attention to their shape. It's a whole different way of life."

One main characteristic of this whole different way of life was the reduction in physical activity, and Florentines of all ages explicitly recognized that the lack of exercise and physical labor was causing increasing weight problems. Eighteen-year-old Alessandro stated the problem,

> We don't get any exercise. Walking? If we go shopping in Center, yes. We drive there in the car and park, and then we have a little walk from store to store. Look, that's the only time we ever walk, otherwise, we're always sitting on our behinds in the car, always. We buy the paper, we buy the bread, always in the car. It's different from the old days.

His mother Vanna said,

> In the old days we didn't get fat because we used to walk so much. Today who walks? They all go in the car or the motorbike. We used to walk kilometers and kilometers to go dancing. We danced until it was time to go home, and then we walked all the way home.

In addition to describing the body as making babies, working, and walking, Florentines defined cooking as *making* the food, or literally "making for eating"—*fare da mangiare*—a turn of phrase that makes use of two active verbs.[9]

Florentines talked about the body in a way that emphasized its agency and reflection of inner states, not its appearance. They rarely used the verb "to be"—*essere*—to describe their bodily state. Their common mode of informal address was "How are you doing?"—"*Come stai?*"—rather than "How are you?"—"*Come sei?*"—which sounds very awkward in Italian. They emphasized health in their discussions of the body. In fact, they had an expression, *"Basta la salute"*—"health is enough"—that implied that if you had your health, you had everything essential. As discussed earlier, an excessively skinny body represented ill health and was considered ugly. As forty-five-year-old Rolando said,

> Some people take thinness to absurd extremes. If a person tries to get thinner than his or her constitution permits, it interferes with the bodily equilibrium and health so much that it is difficult to recover. Getting that thin is not worth it.

A plump body signified both health and fertility. Their emphasis on health reduced Florentines' emphasis on appearance and made their standards for body attractiveness more flexible.

In fact, even when Florentines were commenting on a woman's appearance, they often used active words rather than the verb "to be." They often said that a woman *"fa bella figura"*—"cuts a beautiful figure," or "makes a good impression"—rather than saying she *"is"* beautiful." An attractive woman was described as *"messa bene"*—"well put together." These expressions implied that any woman no matter what her shape could pass muster by dressing in a seemly and stylish manner. In fact, overweight Vanna said,

> I like to wear dark colors, because I think I look better. I have to dress to fit the person I am, in short. I think I look better in dark clothes, less showy. I always try to make myself look a little bit thinner. That way, I think I look more seemly when I go out.

Florentine women focused on fashion as a path to attractive self-expression. While fashion pushed them constantly toward thinness and objectification, it also provided a means to use the body as an active vehicle of self-expression. Elda's daughter Gigliola married an Italian-American and moved permanently to the United States. On her visits to Italy she had a sharp eye for cultural differences:

> Here in Italy, the women don't seem excessively preoccupied with thinness. They are more concerned with buying a beautiful dress, even if it is in a more substantial size, than they are with losing five or six pounds to fit into a smaller size. No, I don't think there is as much emphasis on thinness in Italy as there is in the United States. But just as there is conformism in the U.S. around body issues, there is conformism here in Italy around dress. Hence it seems to me that the two things—thinness in the United States and fashion in Italy—are parallel. Here in Italy, conformism in dress has always been very strong. For everyone, in all classes. Italians are much more fashion-conscious than Americans. I don't know why they have always been this way, but they have. Perhaps

it's related to the old Italian proverb that says, "*L'occhio vuole la sua parte*"—"the eye wants its part."

BODY: COMMODIFICATION, OBJECTIFICATION, AND RESISTANCE

In many discussions of the body, Florentines emphasized the pleasure of eating rather than the moral benefits of dieting, bodily action rather than appearance, and the body as a product of family nature rather than of individual will. By having a legitimate right to take sensual pleasure in food, women were on a par with men at the table, and this parity carried over into other spheres as well.[10] Florentine women were empowered by the way their culture defined the body as a social product out of their control—the result of family heritage and habits—rather than as an always imperfect demonstration of individual moral failings. Florentine women were also empowered by the active and agentive definition of the body prevalent in their culture, which emphasized doing—working, having children, making food, wearing beautiful clothes—rather than having a perfectly sculpted body. Florentine women were able to feel positively about themselves and their bodies by using them, whereas in the United States there is a disempowering narcissistic focus on appearance.

However, Florentine women also struggled with increasingly prevalent images in the media and fashion that proclaimed thinness, female objectification, and beliefs that women should cultivate their body to please men. Whereas older people cared more about good food and convivial meals than about staying in shape, younger women—especially those of the upper middle classes—expressed a strong concern with body beauty and thinness through dieting and visits to the spa. Forty-one-year-old Sandra said that some of her friends who were unemployed and living with high-earning husbands felt worthless and worked on their bodies to attain satisfaction. Sandra recounted:

> There's a lot of talk about being thin in this culture. If you open the newspapers, the magazines, they are all about shape and diet. They are full of the little image of the little lean woman. When you look in the mirror, you see her and you say to yourself, "*Mamma mia*, how fat I am." You feel like a traveling ball of lard. You see images of beautiful clothes worn by beautiful little women. You see advertisements for hairdos and shampoos all with these very thin little women. This tells you that you are out of this world if you are fat.
>
> I have many friends who diet occasionally, almost all of them. They eat these powders instead of food. Many, many friends are careful about their weight. Now at this time of the year, as summer approaches, almost all of them diet. They slowly lose a little weight because they feel ugly, they don't like themselves. If they have to put on a bikini, they don't like

themselves at all. It's not that they really need to diet, but they think they will be more attractive thinner. They all want to have a lean silhouette. They play tennis to sweat and to lose weight. They do aerobics to keep their thighs and bellies from sagging; they do massages. The goal is always this—to have a beautiful body, to be presentable, to wear pants with tranquillity, and to put on a bikini without fear. Yes, these women are all wealthy, very well off. This has a lot to do with it. Those with less money don't have the time or the resources to go and waste on massages and tennis. Furthermore, the wealthy people frequent certain ritzy environments where there is a certain competition in clothes, fashion, and body beauty.

My friends pursue dieting to be admired because they are always dependent on men. They can't live without men courting them and making them feel like women. They need this because they are unsatisfied in life. To feel like women they need to feel loved, pleasing, still attractive. They need to feel that even at forty years old they can still make a conquest of some young man. Perhaps the women who are most unsatisfied and thus most restless always want to realize themselves through their body. They have no other way to fulfill themselves. The life of a housewife is oppressive, so they go out with a beautiful body and they feel compensated.

Sandra recognized that the patriarchal media used women's bodies as commodities and that women were complicit in their own objectification.

Seeing women's bare breasts has become normal in Italy—on television, in magazines. Ever since it has become accepted for women to sunbathe topless, you've seen a lot more breasts in advertising. Yes, it is a form of exploitation to expose women's breasts in advertising. It makes the woman into an object, of course. Just like the issue of going on all these diets turns us into objects too. There's no way out. But it is women themselves who go along with this. We women turn ourselves into objects. It comes from advertising and these models who are paid millions to objectify themselves. It is men who put it all into action, no? In these newspapers it is the men who initiate it all—the photographer and the writer who use the women. The women go along with it to get paid or show themselves off, or who knows why? It begins with men, but the women go along with it. That's the way it always is. The women do it because they need the money.

Advertising objectified and exploited women's bodies, but women were complicit because men still held power and women's access to power depended on pleasing men.[11]

Florentines knew that the objectification of women's bodies made them, as Elda said, "vulnerable." They said that their contemporaries were worrying about being thin and dieting whereas in the past they thought mainly about being housewives, workers, and mothers and didn't have a thought for cultivating their bodies with exercise routines and diets. My subjects suggested that the pressure on women to mold their bodies to please men is directly linked to women's economic dependence and lack of self-fulfillment. Men's cultural power was manifest in their caring less about their weight and being defined as the pleased rather than the pleasers. Sandra described male body ideology:

> Men don't worry about their weight the way women do, but, you know, large men aren't unattractive. Plus men don't have all the competition in newspapers that women have. Women continually confront an image of how they are supposed to be, but men don't see images of other men in the press. Men are allowed to be normal like so many you see around. It's more the women who have to be perfect. I don't think men with a little extra weight get a complex about it the way women do. But you know— women have to attract physically and sexually as well as in other ways. But men can attract even if they aren't great looking. I don't think women focus on men's looks alone. Men can attract with their character, their behavior, their way of looking at you, and in so many ways. It isn't necessary for a man to be beautiful.

Sandra's opinion was confirmed by male subjects who expressed a general sense of well-being in their bodies regardless of their shape.

Older Florentines believed that bodies had their own equilibrium and natural shape. While none of my male subjects admired extreme fat, several said they preferred a woman on the plump side rather than on the thin side. Seventy-three-year-old Renato said that he didn't approve of the superthin television models and called them *questi grissini*—these breadsticks. Rather he admired a woman who was "a little more well made, more robust, more shapely." He also expressed his belief that fat was a part of a person's nature—*"il grasso è di natura"*—and that there really wasn't much of anything a person could do about it:

> *Quello nasce per essere grasso*—A person is born to be fat. We certainly can't all be thin, or all be tall, or all be short.

Older Florentines believed that the human body was variable and that it was useless to try to contradict nature. Their beliefs revealed a cultural tolerance for diverse body shapes and a preference for amplitude. Fifty-four-year-old Roberto said,

> I'm a man who goes for a pound or two extra more willingly than for a pound or two less.

His brother-in-law, fifty-four-year-old Bruno, preferred a woman who was *grassocella*—pleasingly plump. He decried the fact that the dieting industry was reaping enormous profits for multinational corporations and creating body images totally unrelated to natural bodies:

For God's sake, at the beach you see certain bags of bones. Desire to be that thin is launched by the fashion industry, which has always begun from the concept that a beautiful woman has to have a certain shape—always thin rather than fat. But for me, they are all illusions.

Florentines acknowledged that stringent bodily standards existed, especially for women, and that those standards, which were motived by fashion and television, seemed to be getting thinner.

I have been unable to find reliable statistics on the extent of anorexia nervosa in contemporary Italy, but anecdotal evidence indicates that the disorder may be on the upswing and that there may be increasing numbers of Italian women striving for extreme thinness.[12] Sandra spoke at length about one friend of hers who had suffered for years from anorexia nervosa.

I had this friend who went on a diet and couldn't stop. She and her husband don't talk. There was a long awful period during which he just put on a sulk for two or three months—that's a long time. She too let things be and pretended that she didn't give a damn. She went off and played tennis. Here's what happened with her diet.

She used to be a woman with a great appetite. We used to play tennis together and in the morning before tennis she used to eat sausages and spinach, a big plate of them left over from the night before. She arrived and said, "I had some sausages." She was beautiful—full and firm. She was beautiful naked, and she looked great in a bikini. But then all of a sudden she decided to go on a diet. She also went and did massages and so many other things to firm herself up and rejuvenate herself. She saw that the years were passing and she was starting to crumble. You have to know how to age, no? She couldn't accept it, and she still can't. She still does special baths and massages. She says she feels so much better.

I don't really know what made her start on the diet, maybe she wanted to be more attractive. So she started eating this diet stuff and taking pills before meals that took away her appetite. Then I don't know if it became a kind of habit or if her organism just lost the desire, but she didn't eat anything more. Her husband was really worried. For several months she didn't eat. She said that she wanted to return to the shape she had as a girl, exactly like that. She was reduced to skin and bones, truly. So he took her to various doctors and they did a restorative cure. Little by little she made progress but it has been hard for her to get her health back.

Sandra's friend sounds like she was engaged in "the relentless pursuit of excessive thinness," Hilde Bruch's definition of anorexia nervosa (1978, ix). She clearly had a serious eating problem and chose thinness as a means of coping. She had many characteristics of anorexia nervosa: her use of appetite as voice, her inability to stop her food refusal, her cadaverous thinness, her upper-middle-class status, and her desire "to return to the shape she had as a girl."

Sandra was the only one of my Florentine subjects in 1984 who knew someone who had anorexia nervosa or an extreme obsession with thinness. The situation may be very different today. One of my students spoke with horror about the cult of excessive thinness she noticed during her study-abroad year in Florence in 1996–97, among her Italian relatives as well as among college students. She insisted that this obsession cut across a wide array of ages, backgrounds, and social classes. Further research into this topic is sorely needed. If in fact eating disorders are on the rise in Italy, it would be a great shame. It may, however, be a symptom of women's continuing struggle for gender equality—not because anorexia nervosa is liberating, but because it very often increases at times when women are seeking and having a hard time achieving social parity with men (Chernin 1981), a situation that might well describe Italy today (Passerini 1996).

Although my subjects in 1984 did not report any symptoms of anorexia, they did belong to a culture where men still had the upper hand in some important ways. One way was that although men were broad-minded about women's body shapes, they still claimed the right to judge women at least in part by their looks. Twenty-one-year-old Alessandro said,

> It is logical that a really fat person is less pleasing than someone who is trim and in shape. Women should be appropriate—I'm not saying like a model, but in the middle, neither too fat nor too thin. A woman should have a suitable shape.

Rolando, Sandra's husband, said,

> I think that at our ages of forty-five and forty-one, Sandra and I are just fine. Even though Sandra has gained, she's still within acceptable limits in my opinion. If in five years she weighs ten pounds more, I don't know. You'll have to ask me in five years. However, I would prefer that she stay within these limits; that's what I think, if you want my opinion.

There was an imbalance in Florence between men and women around body issues, for men worried little about what they looked like and women worried more. Women had to please men with their looks, but not vice-versa. Men had an implicit cultural right to judge women by their looks; women did not have the same right to judge men. Fifty-four-year-old Bruno explained:

> Men are less obsessed about being thin than women. A woman who is fat is afraid that she won't find a husband. But a man even though fat doesn't have this fear. He says to himself, "I can always find a woman who is fat like me. On the contrary, the other men will leave her for me, they will shun her." That's the way it is. The first worry a girl has when she reaches

age twenty is, "I won't find a husband." Even the thin ones have this fear.

Women felt that they had to please men to get husbands and have access to a decent life, a situation ensured by the Italian economic imbalance favoring men.[13] Bruno expressed clearly a double standard for men and women in regard to bodily beauty that defined women as supplicants for men's approbation. This belief was most explicitly voiced by twenty-eight-year-old Sergio:

> Our mentality about men and women may be wrong, but it persists. Women worry more about how they look. It comes from the fact of wanting to look a certain way as a person and of wanting to be pleasing in a general sense, not necessarily pleasing to a specific person. This comes from an old idea, a mentality persisting from the beginning, that it is the woman who has to please the man and not the man who has to please the woman.[14] Maybe nowadays we are both doing everything to please each other and maybe this old mentality is changing, but it still endures. I know many women who are obsessed with being fat but instead they are not fat. Men worry less; in fact, men are more likely not to give a fig about how they look. This is just due to the old mentality that is beginning to change, but it has always accompanied the woman. The woman has to please the man; it is not the man who has to please the woman.

Sergio articulated a viewpoint that not all of my female or even male subjects embraced, but they did still all define women as nurturers, principally responsible for feeding others, a cultural practice that paralleled men's legitimate claims to be served, and hence pleased.[15] But while some of my female subjects accepted men's right to judge their body, others did not. Twenty-year-old Paola commented about her generation, born in the 1960s:

> I know men who harass their wives or girlfriends about their weight. I wouldn't stand for it. It wouldn't be the thing for me. They badger their girlfriends to lose weight. The girls pay attention to them, but if they said it to me, after two days, they would be out the door. But their girlfriends pay attention. And the girls aren't even fat, they are just sick in the head in my opinion. And even if they were fat, so what? It's not something to harass them about. I don't know why they do it because it has never happened to me and it never will. It would be impossible for me. Yes, it's a form of male power. They make their girlfriends uncomfortable. My attitude is, if you want me, I'm like this. If you don't want me, you don't want me no matter how I am. You just can't marginalize what you are.

Paola projected a strong sense of self and rejected the idea of a man controlling what she ate or how she looked. She affirmed her self in her body. Yet she was not completely happy with her weight and wished she weighed less. Her ambivalence about her body mirrored broader cultural concerns. My subjects were passing through a transition in notions about the body. They were losing touch with old theories about food, body, and health. They were focusing less on the body as the vehicle of self-activation, and more on the body as aesthetic object, especially for women. Men and women related differently to their own bodies, and to each other through the body. For women, their body was a source of anxiety as well as pleasure; men had less anxiety about their body. This imbalance was related to another, cultural, one: that women had to please men yet men were not required to please women in the same way. Thus, because many women felt they had to please with their body, men had the power to judge women's bodies with freedom from having their own bodies judged. Yet women resisted the beliefs that subordinated them, and they gained support in their resistance from other cultural traditions, which emphasized the pleasures of eating, the active nature of the body, and the body's derivation from and connection to family. It remains to be seen if Florentines will continue to resist definitions of their bodies that are disempowering and demeaning to women.

11

Body and Power in Women's Experiences of Reproduction in the United States[1]

"The true focus of revolutionary change is never merely the oppressive situations which we seek to escape, but that piece of the oppressor which is planted deep within each of us."

Audre Lorde[2]

INTRODUCTION

In this concluding chapter of the book, I try to chart an empowering relationship between women and their bodies. In previous chapters, I looked at food and body across cultures—both in the literature and in my research in Florence. In this chapter I use my own research to ask whether women's experiences of reproduction can contribute to a positive construction of the female body in the United States.

As earlier chapters of this book have shown, many women in the United States, especially white women, have feelings about food and body that involve objectification, inadequacy, and powerlessness.[3] Many women dislike their bodies, relentlessly worry about their shape, and try to change themselves by toning up, eating less, and losing weight. The effort to reduce the body stands for women's efforts to reduce the self; it is a form of self-oppression. In the spirit of the above words by Audre Lorde, I write to challenge women's self-abnegating body attitudes and root out these "pieces of the oppressor" from deep within our psyches. This is an essential step toward gender equality, for women need the power that comes from being at ease within their bodies.

In the United States the objectification of the female body is a key

195

piece in upholding the race, class, and gender hierarchies essential to American capitalism. As Black feminist Patricia Hill Collins (1990, 69) has said, "Domination always involves attempts to objectify the subordinate group." The female body is defined as an object in thousands of different ways, most notably in advertising but also in daily parlance and action. The continual fragmentation of the female body into boobs, butts, legs, and crotches erases women's personhood and turns them into disembodied parts. These dismembered and sexualized fragments are used to gratify and sell.[4] Turning women into objects is one central means of ensuring their subordination. Women of all races and colors are objectified, but the ranking system gives women of different groups a different place in the beauty hierarchy. At the pinnacle is the white, Northern European beauty with a tall, long-legged, slim, spare, linear body—a body some approach more closely than others, but which almost no woman ever feels she matches.

The most "beautiful" body is the most objectified, most falsified, and most ornamental. To be beautiful, women are exhorted to a continual self-manipulation that involves their own fragmentation and objectification as they fix their nails, do their hair, compress their butts, push up their boobs, shave their legs, deodorize their armpits, paint their faces, perfume their wrists, and on and on. A woman with a beautiful body is constantly bombarded with leers, whistles, and comments that further emphasize her body and detract from her individual personhood. Women cannot achieve self-esteem or power as long as they strive to fulfill an unobtainable ideal based on their own passivity and commodification.

CAN REPRODUCTION BE A PATH TO BODILY EMPOWERMENT?

Women need visions of bodily agency to supplant their objectified self-images. They can seek new relationships with their bodies in many ways, for example through exercise, sport, bodybuilding, dance, yoga, sexual expression, therapy, and many other channels whose exploration and study are needed.[5] They can also seek positive constructions of the female body among counter-hegemonic groups in the United States, including people of color, feminists, lesbians, and fat liberation groups such as National Association to Advance Fat Awareness (NAAFA).[6] NAAFA claims that fat is beautiful. Some lesbians, in contrast, reject the fat-thin dichotomy entirely. They hold a "naturalist" body ideology in opposition to the skinny sexualized ideal that suits patriarchal heterosexist values. They extol physical strength, filling up space rather than shrinking, and a self-determined body (Crowder 1993). Another counter-hegemonic body ideal is held by Puerto Ricans in Philadelphia, for whom a fat woman symbolizes beauty, tranquillity, prosperity, fertility, and her husband's competence as a breadwinner (Massara 1989). For these Puerto Ricans, and for many African-Americans as well, a too thin body signifies physical, social, or psychological distress. Among many African-American women, an ample body can signify beauty, power, and victory over racism in keeping alive food traditions through consumption of soul food.[7] More research on body ideology among women in diverse ethnic groups, fat liberationists, lesbians, and others on the margins of mainstream white culture is deeply needed to uncover potential models of bodily empowerment.

Here I ask if and how women can develop a positive relationship to their bodies and counter bodily objectification through pregnancy and birth. I ask this question for many reasons. In birth, women use the body for the awesome creation of another human being, and thus birth can provide a possible channel for learning to value one's body. My own birthing experiences radically altered my relationship to my body. The miracle of growing a baby, the catharsis of birth, and the thrill of breast-feeding all made me proud of what I could do in my body and much less concerned with how I looked.

Pregnancy is a natural rite of passage. It is an extended period of being "betwixt and between" one state and another (Davis Floyd 1992; Van Gennep 1960), what Turner calls a "liminal" or threshold time when great growth or change is possible (1969). Emphasizing the transitional quality of pregnancy is the fact that the body boundaries are continually changing and that another is within and will soon pass outside; birth is a literal passage of boundaries (Young 1984, 49). Furthermore, pregnancy and birth can put a woman deeply in touch with her body in new ways as she monitors the growth of the fetus, thinks about food as a source of energy and life rather than of fat, and marvels at her own ability to create life.

Let me emphasize that I am not implying reproductive reductionism or essentialism. Not all women give birth, and my intent is not to say that they should. Rather, my point is that the ability to give birth is part of being a woman, and I want to ask how it can become a source of empowerment—not just for women who go through it, but for all women. Pregnancy and birth are one possible path through which women can challenge their objectification, but they are by no means the only path.

This chapter explores how and why women's relationship to food and body in reproduction is sometimes a source of power, sometimes of oppression. I examine how pregnancy, birth, and lactation foster or hinder women's transformation from object to subject, a central step toward empowerment. My data come from interviews with fifteen diverse women during pregnancy and postpartum. Subjects range in age from eighteen to thirty-eight, in family income from $23,000 to $130,000, in occupation from full-time homemakers to partially employed high school and college students to retail workers and professionals. They identified their ethnicity or race as African-American (1), Puerto Rican (2), Hispanic (1), Jewish (1), Italian-American (1), and mixed European ancestry (9). All were heterosexual. Eleven were married and living with husbands; four were single and living with their parents.[8] Seven had desired and planned their pregnancies, eight became pregnant accidentally. Some embraced the pregnancy wholeheartedly, while others felt ambivalent all the way up to the birth. Most informants were interviewed twice, once during pregnancy and once postpartum.

Here I present a narrative based principally on two of my subjects whose stories were particularly rich. They reveal a range of experiences of body, pregnancy, birth, and transformation. While presenting their stories, I will bring in some of the other thirteen women where relevant, but full discussion of all the women awaits another forum. First I will describe Jodie and show the pain she experienced by having an objectified, disparaged, and sexualized body. Pregnancy helped her step out of that objectification and that pain, but not totally and not permanently. Then I will describe Karen to show how pregnancy was a turning point in her self-confidence and power. I will discuss the conditions that facilitated or hindered Jodie's and Karen's different abilities to come to personal power through reproduction.

JODIE

Jodie was of working-class, Italian-American, New York City background and, when I interviewed her, was employed part-time in a profession and getting an advanced degree. Her husband was also a professional, and their combined annual income was just under $40,000. When I first interviewed her, Jodie was 35 and pregnant with her first child after a somewhat nerve-wracking year-and-a-half of trying to conceive. Having had several abortions in her twenties, she feared that her "wild past" would prohibit her from getting pregnant. But after eighteen months of trying to conceive with increasingly calculated effort, she succeeded. Her words describe a conflict between her own subjective connection with her body and her doctor's objectification:

> I tried to get pregnant for nearly a year, with the ovulation tests and the temperature charts, all this very scientific stuff. I was so distraught that I wasn't getting pregnant, and I was sometimes crying and feeling upset, and very depressed, and blaming myself for my past gynecological history, and all this other stuff, you know, the things I did in my twenties, the men I slept with, the whole nine yards. And one day I was working at

the mall and I went out to get a lemonade, and I was standing there, and I heard this voice say in my head, "You know, everything's going to be all right, and you don't have to worry about it, you can get pregnant," or something to that effect—"Everything's going to be all right." And it was this overwhelming feeling of my whole body just relaxing.

When I thought about it afterwards, I realized that this happened on the day I think I conceived. That day before work Jim and I had had sex, and interestingly, it was a day when I had said to him, "I'm not going to do these damn temperature charts any more; I'm not going to do this ovulation test. If it happens it happens; if it doesn't it doesn't." And it was this very passionate love-making, versus the very mechanical love-making that we'd been doing for the past eight months. Oh, you know, it had been like—quick! the ovulation test turned pink—and laying there afterward with my butt up on pillows, up in the air; I mean there wasn't much passion. It was very mechanical, and then here was this passionate moment, where I just said, forget it, I'm not going to play this game anymore. And I think that's why it happened. I'm convinced. The doctors don't believe me, but I'm convinced it happened.

When I showed the doctor the temperature chart, I said, "I got pregnant here."

She said, "Oh no, no no, you got pregnant here," which was a week after I said I got pregnant.

And I said, "No, no, no, it's here."

And she said, "No, no, no *because*—" and gave me all this scientific data of why it was here, because the temperature was way down, it was just at the right moment.

And I said, "Well, no. That's not the way the human body works." You know the egg comes down, and it just happens when it happens.

Jodie's pregnancy began with a conflict between her sense of her body and its ineffable mysteries and the doctor's reduction of her body to a scientifically programmed machine, a conflict that emerged later in her pregnancy as well. Jodie had trouble transforming her body into a subject during pregnancy—as many women do—because scientific medicine continues to treat the human body as object (Martin 1987).

Jodie not only contended with the medical objectification of her body, but with lifelong sexual objectification. She was a full-breasted woman who matured early and suffered harassment centered on her breasts for years. She related her objectification in the following way:

My breasts were just burdensome and burdensome because, until the day I had my breast-reduction surgery, people would stare at me. It was uncomfortable as a student to have professors talk to my breasts. It was uncomfortable to have people, men and women both, talk to my breasts. You know, I just wanted to point out that I have a mind, I have a face. Talk to my face, look at my eyes, not at my breasts.

Jodie's remarks show the extent of women's bodily objectification in U.S. culture, for women and men both fixated on her breasts. She draws attention to the fact that women reproduce their *own* subordination in body attitudes and thus that transformation must take place within women as well as within men and in the culture at large.[9]

When I asked Jodie what her breasts symbolized, she said,

> They symbolize a lot of years of pain. In this society, on the one hand, big breasts are fetishized, and on the other hand, they're resented. It's this contradiction, if you have them, you know, you're this commodity. There's this fetishization of breasts, while at the same time there's this resentment and anger and hatred of women with large breasts.

Jodie's remarks about her breasts being fetishes invoke both Marx's concept of commodity fetishism and Freud's notion of sexual fetishism (Freud 1962, 17–19; Marx 1967; Willis 1991). Under capitalism, Marx observed, all things become commodities, objects to be bought and sold. The human beings who make and exchange commodities become identified and interchangeable with the objects they produce, exchange, and consume. The commodification of women and their bodies is particularly prevalent in the United States through advertising, where women's bodies are routinely used to sell things and thus become things for sale. Breasts become disembodied objects, valued for their size and shape and detached from the woman herself. They are not only commodities but also sexual fetishes because they stand for and concentrate abstract, depersonalized, alienated sexual desire.

Jodie's efforts to hide her breasts and escape constant stares and pinches led her to a lifelong obsessive struggle with being fat:

> I was always a fat child and a fat teenager, and I think I was fat because I was trying to hide, to make the breasts somehow disappear. Yes, I definitely used fat to hide my body.

Being fat was a matter of survival because it protected her from sexual harassment and because eating was a source of comfort. She said,

> As a high school student, I used food to feel good.

But food and body also caused Jodie deep misery:

> I was a pariah in high school. No one liked me; they just called me a big fat cow. I had no friends. I was forty pounds overweight. I was horribly miserable. I was really unhappy.[10]

Jodie needed her fat for protection, but she hated and feared it because of the pain it caused her.

> I've controlled the fear of fat. There was a time where it just terrified me, the idea of being fat again. And now, I haven't really felt that way since

I've been pregnant. And that's why I think I like pregnancy, because I haven't had that fear, but occasionally before, and certainly I'm sure it will come up again after, there's this fear of being fat, and it's terrifying. I'll look at myself in the mirror and see cellulite and fat, and I'll get really upset and it will be very painful to look at myself.

Jodie explained how pregnancy changed her relationship to her body and breasts:

When I was pregnant I loved my body, and I loved my breasts, because I was allowed to have big breasts. Because I was pregnant, society allowed me to have big breasts.

During pregnancy, Jodie was no longer always and exclusively defined as a sex object. This enabled her to begin to look at herself in a new way:

I love pregnant bodies, and I love the way pregnant women look. I would stand in front of the mirror and look at myself and touch my belly. I just like the way I look pregnant. I like the way pregnant women look; I think they're beautiful. I had no problems with my body image; I really loved it. And I never understood women who hated their bodies when they were pregnant. I think it's a neat way to look. Actually I feel more attractive pregnant, and I think that part of that is that when you're pregnant people don't look at you and say, "Look at that fat cow."

Because pregnancy made her invisible as a sex object and allowed her to be ample, it liberated Jodie from a lifetime of deprecation. She could relate to her body more positively because she was free of the negative societal gaze. But she does not seem to have liberated herself from viewing her body as an object; she still stood in front of the mirror and assessed herself, but at least she was able to like that objectified self.

Jodie's invisibility during pregnancy reveals the desexualization of the pregnant woman in U.S. culture. This is, of course, a paradox, for who is more obviously sexual than a pregnant woman? But patriarchal definitions split sexuality from women's fertility and power of creation. Some of my subjects found this desexualization threatening. They talked of becoming invisible and losing their identity because they were no longer attractive to men. For example, twenty-seven-year-old Debby expressed her feelings about being pregnant thus:

I do have to say I feel a lot less attractive pregnant. I feel more matronly, I guess, is the word, instead of sexy. When you're not pregnant, you're used to that being your goal. You want to be attractive to the opposite sex. Where when you're pregnant, you're definitely matronly. You look matronly; you are matronly. I'm getting used to it, but at first I wasn't taking to it very well. People look at you differently; they treat you differently, like you're a different person temporarily. People ignore me.

Whereas if I was dressed up a little nice before I was pregnant and I was walking down the street maybe a guy would turn around and look at me, where now it's like I'm waddling down the street and nobody pays any kind of attention. I feel not sexy at all.

Whereas Debby felt erased by no longer being attractive, other women thrived on the desexualization of pregnancy. Jodie found it made her able to feel better about herself and gave her more personhood. Jodie's most striking words were:

I think I feel more beautiful pregnant because no one is looking at me.

Reproductive processes involve a fundamental and unstoppable change in the body to a form that is no longer of prime sexual interest or commodity value. As twenty-two-year-old Effie said,

I have this idea that a pregnant body is not a sex goddess body. I'm comfortable with the whole Earth Mother kind of thing but I think there is a definite feeling that it's not the sexy body.

Furthermore, the body in pregnancy insists on its own dynamic as it grows and hungers and suffers in insistent and unfamiliar ways. This can both make a woman more in touch with her body and also free her from the constant worry about shaping it to abstract standards. As thirty-eight-year-old Arlie said,

I don't have a good image of my body I would say, at the best of times. And now pregnant, I just sort of mentally throw up my hands and say, well, it's sweat suits for the next whatever. I don't feel wonderful about it, but I guess I feel I have an excuse so that I don't feel like there's something I should be *doing* about it. Whereas normally I would. Now I feel like my body has taken over. I don't feel like I have a lot of conscious control over how much I eat. I feel less sexy definitely, less attractive. But I don't feel like I want to be attractive. I just want to be left alone.

Reproduction enables women to disappear from the stage of objects. It also gives them a chance to redefine the body and the self through action—growing a baby, giving birth, and feeding a baby. In pregnancy, birth, and breast-feeding, a woman's body is acting, instead of being looked at, assessed, and appraised.

Breast-feeding was highly charged for Jodie, not surprising given that her breasts had caused her lifelong pain. She had wanted to do breast-reduction surgery for years but had held off because she thought she might want to breast-feed some day and felt "that's what boobs are for." She had troubles breast-feeding, however, because her baby had a very weak suck due to his prematurity. She said,

I remember saying to a friend, "You know, I kept these big breasts to breast-feed and now, it doesn't work."

She described her complex feelings thus:

> It was wonderful when it was going well, you know. When all this bad stuff happened, and he stopped gaining weight, and the breast milk dropped, I started to hate it. But I think I didn't hate breast-feeding as much as I hated that it wasn't going right. Now I love it, because it's going right again. I like breast-feeding. It's nice.

After she had finished nursing she decided finally to do the breast-reduction surgery. I interviewed her at length soon after the surgery about how she felt now about her new breasts. Her answer revealed her ambivalence:

> I feel fine. I like them. It's funny, I was thinking the other day I don't even remember what it feels like to have big breasts physically, but I remember emotionally. I don't know yet, I'm not sure, it's not been that long so I don't know if I feel like a different person. I do know I feel like people respond to me differently. There are two ways of looking at this. One is that I'm thrilled not to have the physical burden of big breasts any more, and the other way is that people just don't look at me the same way, and it was really a burden to have people just look at my breasts all the time. It's sexual harassment—no matter how you try to intellectualize it. The bottom line is, whether it's coming from men or women, it's sexual harassment. Because the breast is sexual in this society.

Jodie used the process of going through pregnancy, birth, and breast-feeding as a springboard toward diminishing her own objectification, literally cutting off the source and symbol of her worst bodily objectification and humiliation. Yet a month after the surgery, she was not yet able to speak about what she might become without those breasts. She could still only bemoan their past existence. Perhaps in time, Jodie will be able to redefine herself through her body in more empowering ways.

When I asked Jodie what the most significant change in attitude toward herself and her body was from pregnancy and childbirth, she responded,

> I don't think there is any. I don't think I've changed in how I look at myself. In terms of my body, I don't really like it right now because it's fat and out of shape. I feel like my hips are bigger, and I don't know that they'll ever be the same again. So I'm kind of bothered by that. I think a lot about liposuction.

A pamphlet from the American Society of Plastic and Reconstructive Surgeons describes liposuction (1988). It cost $1,000 to $3,000 "or more" and is not normally covered by insurance. It is performed not on obese patients but on patients "of relatively normal body build and weight to reduce disproportionately large hips, buttocks and thighs, a protruding abdomen or 'love handles' above the waist." The surgery is performed with either local or general anesthetic, and the recovery period is from several days to several weeks. The surgery begins with incisions of one-half inch in length into the fatty area. A blunt-ended tubular instrument with a suction unit attached is inserted into the incisions. Then the following procedure takes place:

> The surgeon manipulates the instrument in the tissue under the skin, separating the amount of fat to be removed. High vacuum pressure is created and the fat is suctioned off. Occasionally an additional incision is required to gain access to all unwanted fat deposits.... After surgery, pain that can be controlled by medication may be present for several days. Numbness or discomfort may be experienced for varying periods of time.... Some swelling and skin discoloration will exist, but usually will subside within six to eight weeks.... In some cases, permanent sagging of the skin may occur when the fat removed from the area exceeds the capacity of the skin to contract.... The decision on when to return to work depends on the individual's degree of swelling and discomfort.

Considered out of the context of the American "tyranny of slenderness," this sounds like a barbarous act of torture. That Jodie considered it voluntarily shows how terribly she feared fat.

She did not do liposuction but instead she began to take a high-energy aerobics class twice a week and on several occasions remarked that she was toning up, getting into shape, and losing inches from her thighs and butt. But two months later, after a very busy and stressful time, Jodie was lamenting her weight and size. She told of bursting into tears in a trendy clothing store because the smallest clothes she could fit into were a size fourteen. During her pregnancy she had managed to escape her fear of fat and love her body, but she could not keep these feelings after pregnancy. Why? Why did she still objectify, hate, and want to reduce her body? Why did she consider going through the pain, expense, and long recuperation period of liposuction to rid herself of a few pounds and a few inches? Why was she not able to develop a more permanent sense of her self and body as integrated subject, and why did she still perceive her body as an object to mold into a more perfect piece of work?

I believe that there are three main reasons: first, the depth of her bodily objectification; second, the difficulties of her pregnancy, birth, and lactation; and third, the deep-rootedness of women's bodily oppression in U.S culture.

Although Jodie had a three-page birth plan specifying as little medical intervention as possible, she unfortunately ended up having a great deal due to problems with both the birth and the breast-feeding. Her waters broke six weeks before her due date, and she had two scary and miserable weeks of bed rest during a scorching heat spell, trying to give the baby as much time as possible to grow in utero. She had blood tests every other day of the bed-rest period to make sure she was not developing an infection. She had repeated scares about the results of those tests and about the leaking of the amniotic fluid. Eventually, she had labor induced with pitocin and a pain-killing drug to deal with the severe pains of induced labor.[11] She described her birth experience in ambiguous terms.

> I kept my strength. I just got tired. I was in control. The baby's birth was this really wonderful experience. It was the most relieving feeling I have ever felt. It was like, "AH!" It was magical. Very magical. I remember saying that I would only do this again just for that one particular experience. It was very relieving, very nice, and I liked it. It wasn't really bad until transition. That was the worst; to me, that was the worst part. The pushing didn't hurt. I didn't scream hideously. I did a lot of loud yelling, and after a while I was really tired. I mean I just couldn't do it. Evidently, according to my husband, the nurse and the doctor were great at pushing.

Note that she remarked that "the nurse and the doctor were great at pushing." She gave agency to them rather than to herself, showing perhaps her inability to completely shake off her self-definition as object. This is not surprising, given that the American way of birth consistently reinforces the birthing mother's passivity and emphasizes the agency of the machines and the medical staff (Jordan 1993; Martin 1987; Rich 1986; Rothman 1982).

Right after the birth, Jodie wanted to hold her newborn and nurse him. However, she said:

> The nursery nurse kept saying, "Can Jodie nurse him; can she hold him?" and Dr. ——, the neonatalogist, I can't remember his name, kept saying, "Well, no I don't want the baby to get stressed." And finally he let me hold him for five minutes. I couldn't nurse him, because he was afraid that the baby would get stressed out, which was a concern. They had to take him in and put him on the monitors.

The implication here is clearly that it was more stressful for this newborn, who weighed a substantial 6 pounds 2 ounces despite being four to five weeks early, to stay near his mother's familiar body than to be rushed off to an impersonal bassinet in a sterile nursery and hooked up to lots of wires. This assumption is based on a cultural acceptance of medical "authoritative knowledge," which is often unsubstantiated by any scientific data, as Jordan has convincingly argued (1993). It is an assumption that robbed Jodie, the already insecure mother of a premature baby, of the ability to reassert her connection to her baby and of her achievement in giving birth.

Jodie found breast-feeding to be an important way to reclaim her ties to her baby, although it too was fraught with ambivalence. Throughout the several days her newborn was in the neonatal intensive care unit at the hospital, Jodie pumped her milk at home with an electric breast pump, and she and the nurses fed it to her baby through an eye dropper or a spoon. She felt really good about producing breast milk:

> When you have a premature baby, that particular issue is the most important thing, because that is the only thing you can do for the baby that the nurses can't do for the baby. So I pumped every two hours when I wasn't with him. And I had to pump after I breast-fed him because he didn't have a really good suck. I'd bring my milk in every morning, and there was this whole ritual of pumping at night and putting it in the refrigerator and bringing it to the hospital in this little ice bucket for him to have at night when you're not there, so they can cup feed him, or with a syringe feed him your breast milk.

Fortunately, the baby was fine and went home with Jodie and her husband after a week in the neonatal unit. Jodie breast-fed the baby at home, and although she had some trouble finding good positions because of her large breasts, she eventually developed a good routine. But later the baby developed breast-milk jaundice, and Jodie's doctor told her to stop feeding her baby for twenty-four hours. She was not advised to pump her milk, and over the twenty-four hours her supply dropped slightly. The baby was too weak to pick up the supply by himself, so he didn't get enough food and began to languish. This caused great anxiety until Jodie figured out the problem and began giving the baby formula to build up his strength. From that point on she alternated between breast- and bottle-feeding for the next several weeks until the hassles of doing both overwhelmed her and she weaned him.

It seems that Jodie's encounters with the medical system robbed her of agency and initiative, fouled up the natural process and didn't fix it, and robbed her of self-confidence. She said,

> I feel guilty about the problem I have about breast-feeding, and the fact that he's premature.

Her guilt and self-doubt may have made it difficult for her to use pregnancy, birth, and lactation as a path to self-esteem and bodily confidence.

A second possible reason for Jodie's reversion to bodily despair after birth is that her bodily objectification was too long-standing and too deeply entwined with her identity to be easily shed. Remember that Jodie had long contended with fat, bodily self-hatred, and a fetishization of her breasts. She made the following remark after her breast-reduction surgery:

> I don't know that I'm a different person for it. I don't know that I changed who I am. I think if I had had this done in my twenties it would have

changed me a lot, but at thirty-six I'm sort of set in my ways and certainly I still have a lot of weird feelings about my body. I just never have felt thin enough.

Jodie's lifelong anguished battle with her body and her fat was deeply and painfully meaningful:

> Fat symbolizes all the disfunction in my family. It symbolizes that disfunction, the whole ugly mess that is my family. It has come to mean that.

Jodie's mother was alcoholic and her parents' marriage was rocky during her childhood and adolescence. Both of her siblings were extremely overweight and had troubled marriages. Because Jodie linked her troubled family to her negative self-esteem and fear of fat, working through her troubled family relationships may be essential to overcoming her internalized bodily oppression.

Finally, shedding bodily oppression was difficult for Jodie and is for many women because it is a fundamental challenge to a prevailing cultural ideology that constantly re-creates female subordination. This ideology associates women with the inferior, objectified, controllable body and results in the erasure of their agency and personhood. Notwithstanding this major obstacle, some of the women I interviewed have come out of pregnancy and childbirth transformed in their self-attitude and feeling newly empowered.

KAREN

My second story is about Karen, whose pregnancy and birth enhanced her positive sense of self. Karen grew up in a comfortable working-class setting in southern California. She described her background as Irish, Scottish, French, German, and Native American. She grew up as one of few Anglo children in a predominantly Chicano community near Whittier, California. She expressed admiration for Chicano culture, saying,

> I grew up like being the *güera*, or the white girl in my class, in third and fourth and fifth grade. You know that was cool; I think I really benefited from being exposed to the Chicano culture, a culture I love. It's a wonderful culture, and I really felt close to it.

She was twenty-five and in her eighth month of pregnancy when I first interviewed her. She was working as a short-order cook up until she gave birth, and her husband was an iron caster. Together they had an annual income of between $20,000 and $30,000, depending on how much Karen was working and on how much overtime pay her husband

John was making. Karen spoke of her pregnancy and birth experience as a significant transition in her life. While pregnant, she had many anxieties and concerns, as well as much hope and optimism. She said,

> I am excited and typically frightened and scared to death of stuff, like can we do it and all that kind of stuff. I'm mostly really, really excited.

One challenge for Karen was putting her own life on hold and losing the economic independence that she had had since she was eighteen. She felt lucky that she could afford not to work for a while because her husband made a steady income as a welder, but she also felt anxious about losing her independence.

> I'd like to not work as long as possible, but part of me wants to; part of me is used to taking care of myself, and working, you know, and paying my own way and all that kind of stuff, so that is going to be a big step for me. The value of the non-dollar hours day, you know. John doesn't have a problem with it at all, but I think I do.

She also felt anxious about the lack of security and stability in all of her life plans at that time. When she found out she was pregnant, she had been intending to go to vocational school to take some classes in "welding or some commercially profitable skill, like going into printing or something like that, something besides making food." She expressed her career dreams thus:

> I guess I'd like to have my own ceramics studio. That's what I'd like to do. But getting to the point of being able to do that all of the time or most of the time is going to be a real challenge. It's like mom, wife, pay the bills, you know, and do what I want to do.

Karen's feelings about herself before, during, and after her pregnancy were mirrored in her expressed feelings abut her own body. At eight months pregnant she said,

> I think that I felt overweight and out of shape before I got pregnant. I've got one of those butt/thigh/hip emphasis bodies where if you are in good shape and eating right and really active you just look really good and round and sexy. I like having a really full body, but I only like it when I am fit. Sometimes I think that I look really good and sometimes maybe because of my attitude or because I didn't get enough sleep or I am worried about money or our sex life, or about how the child is going to affect our lives, then I don't. When I feel happy or excited I think I look sexy and when I feel neurotic and fearful I think I look crappy, so that is about it.

Unlike Jodie, whose body represented objectification, pain, and family disfunction, Karen had a more fluid relationship with her body. Her feelings about it were malleable and often positive; they reflected the current state of her self-esteem rather than a congealed negative sense of self. She also felt good about her body when she was using it through being fit and active.

The pregnancy was accidental and a shock, because she and her boyfriend had just gotten back together again after being apart for several years. She said,

> It was really frightening, extremely frightening. I felt overwhelmed. I cried when I found out that I was pregnant.

But later, her feelings changed:

> Now I think we are both really excited, and I just tried to feel that it is supposed to happen now. There is a reason for it to happen now. And we don't understand why. We can't always control things—you know, life is just life.

She defined her pregnancy as sometimes a difficult challenge, sometimes an exciting opportunity, always as a process of transformation:

> Every week there is a new discovery, and something that I learn how to accept, and that has been a really, really good thing. I think that I am learning more patience than I have had before. I am a pretty patient person with everyone except for myself. That is the main thing. That is the big issue with the body stuff and the food stuff—everyone looks great but me. And sometimes I think that is related to a self-esteem thing; but I think my self-esteem is pretty good, but I am just harder on myself than on other people. I don't cut myself any slack, which is kind of a nonproductive attitude. So our relationship, John's and mine, has benefited I think in a lot of ways from the pregnancy because it forced us to deal with certain things and it will continue to evolve.

She loved her husband and said he was "the best person in the world" for her, but throughout the pregnancy she worried about whether they could manage to sustain their relationship, raise the baby, and deal with the new economic and emotional challenges. Karen's need for reassurance was expressed as a strong sexual desire, which was rebuffed by her husband:

> During my second trimester, when I was super amorous all the time, I was putting a bunch of pressure on him, which of course did no good at all, you know? But I was going totally insane. It was winter; I was pregnant; I was incredibly horny all the time.

Her husband, she said, was reluctant to have sex with her not because of her or her body, but because "it's just like, there is an intruder there." Karen's sexual desire seemed to be—among other things—a search for reassurance and consolation in her worried state. Her husband's inability to satisfy her sexual needs was perhaps a reflection of his own ambivalence and anxiety about the pregnancy. Sexuality was the terrain through which they struggled with the changes represented by the baby.

Karen felt that her husband's attitude reflected his worries about her vulnerable state:

> It's like he's trying to care for the baby and therefore sometimes he's not treating me like a grown-up in some ways. That is my main irk with him. It's just like, "Talk to me like a regular person; you don't have to coddle me." It's just this certain very soft, walking on eggshells type of thing which is not him at all. But he is trying to be really careful, and it is bugging me even more. So that was a thing, and the sex thing was—I was trying to be cool and casual and not put any pressure on him, but I was also really in need of physical contact that was intense. Like there is cuddling and stuff, but I needed an outlet.

Eventually, she stopped putting pressure on him and accepted the hiatus in their sexual activity. After the birth, Karen told me of her husband's rekindled sexual desire. When I asked her about why she thought their sex life was better now, she answered:

> A major part of it was just the bonding experience of giving birth, you know, and without any words or anything, it was like logically cognizant during the birth process. Just going through that together, you know, we had increased trust, and increased intimacy, and increased respect for one another. He was really proud of how well I did, and I was really proud of how well he did and how much he supported me. So I think that's really a major thing. There's just this much more love, you know, twelve and a half more pounds of love between us. I think that's the major thing. I think giving birth was a definite big self-esteem boost that I needed. I know that that always makes someone feel more attractive and more capable, and that's more attractive to your mate and all that stuff.

For Karen, giving birth was a triumph, carried out with the support of her husband. It made her feel really good about herself as well as stronger in her relationship. She had a completely natural birth with no complications and with minimal medical intervention and no drugs of any kind. Like Jodie, she had learned a lot about birth beforehand and desired a natural birth, but unlike Jodie, she was able to fulfill this desire. She gave birth in the hospital, but felt fully in control of her labor and expressed that control through constant movement:

> I did everything. I got in the shower, I got out of the shower. I sat on the toilet, just to sit there. I got up and walked around. I was on the rocking chair; I was on the bed laying down on my side. I was moving the bed up and down. Lying up, lying down, moving the feet up, turning around. Lots of being on my knees and down on the floor for contractions, and

having the back part of the bed up, and having my hands and chest up on the bed with my legs and butt out here and just sort of leaning on that to hold for the contractions.

Karen was able to give herself up completely to her birth process, and in doing so she overcame her earlier fears and anxieties:

I just sort of relaxed and let go, and didn't really feel like I had any choice but to just go with it. There was really no turning back; there was no being afraid. There really was no fear involved, and I'm really proud of myself for that. Because for being so anxiety stricken about several things while I was pregnant, especially during my third trimester, the fear just ended when I went into labor, and that was really a powerful thing. That was really good.

Perhaps because Karen was able to be wholly integrated with her body and use it actively in her labor, she had a very powerful sensate experience of giving birth:

It felt like big waves at the beach pummeling you into the sand, you know, like when you get pushed under the sand and you're eating sand, and you're hoping that you'll survive this wave that you're being tumbled around by. That's how it was, every three or four minutes or so. I was very impressed with the force involved. I enjoyed it through the whole process of being uncomfortable. I was extremely uncomfortable, but I was still fascinated the whole time about what my body could do. I could visualize in my mind what the baby was doing and where he was going as he was coming down. So except for being extremely uncomfortable, I felt really good. I was just amazed at the force involved. It went beyond any of my expectations. I had an idea, but I guess it's one of those things that you don't really know what it's like until you get there.[12]

I felt strong. I felt very strong. I felt like my body could do the work, that it was doing its job. So he was born, and it was just great. It was probably the best thing I've ever done in my entire life; it was just super. John cried and I cried, and the baby was beautiful. You know, it was the classic magic moment, oh my God, there's this person who's really here. He's so beautiful.

Karen reflected on her birth experience afterward as being transformative:

I'd say that it was a tremendous learning experience. I think it's great. I think it's a great thing. I think that it was a great opportunity to learn about myself, my capabilities, all my fears, all my apprehensions. Now I just feel like I can do anything. I'm excited about the future, because I did this.

Birth enabled Karen to feel stronger, more confident, and more self-assured. Months after the birth, she was still feeling empowered. She had many plans for her own continuing development on the career path and was investigating an "at-home bachelor of science program in holistic medicine and nutrition." She was very excited about doing a degree at home. She and her husband were about to buy a modest home with plenty of space in a working-class neighborhood. And she still held onto her "old goal to get some used ceramic-producing equipment, get a wheel and kiln and a space, and find these resources, buy them, and start doing my artwork again."

What factors in pregnancy and birth helped move Karen toward a more positive and empowering sense of herself? How did her experience contrast with Jodie's? First, prior to becoming pregnant, Karen appeared to have had a fairly positive sense of herself and her body. While articulating many insecurities and anxieties, she also was able to talk positively about her person and her corporeal self. Jodie was only able to do this during pregnancy, when she was finally liberated from being objectified and denigrated because her large breasts and body were acceptable in a pregnant woman. Karen had a body that drew less attention and that was suitable to her but did not evoke the constant staring and the annihilation of her personhood that Jodie's did. Karen also never had a serious weight problem, and although she spoke both before and after her pregnancy of wanting to be in better shape, she basically felt good about herself. Perhaps Karen's experience of growing up in the midst of Chicano culture enabled her to appreciate bodily diversity, malleability, and fullness. She defined her body and both its capabilities and deficiencies in terms of using it—to tone up for example—rather than solely in terms of its appearance.

The different class status of Jodie and Karen at the time of the interviews might also explain some differences in their feelings about their bodies. In the United States, the higher the social class, the greater the value on thinness for women (Sobal and Stunkard 1989). Both Jodie and Karen were from working-class backgrounds, but Jodie was upwardly mobile in a profession dominated by middle- and upper-class people and values, while Karen remained in the working class. Both Jodie and Karen had full bodies related to their diverse ethnic backgrounds: southern Italian for Jodie, mixed for Karen. Neither had bodies that conformed to the wafer-thin, tall, northern European standard, but Jodie was immersed in a culture that regularly reinforced this ideal, whereas in Karen's working class milieu, there were probably more heavy women and more acceptance of greater weight range. Because neither Karen nor Jodie had "ideal" bodies, the only way they could rid themselves of bodily oppression was to reject hegemonic notions of the female body, something perhaps easier for Karen in her working-class milieu than for Jodie in her upwardly mobile profession.

A further differentiating factor between Karen and Jodie was that Karen had an extremely rewarding birth experience that augmented her positive and active sense of her body. She was in control of her own labor and had no medical interference. All too often, medical interference in normal labor, even when defined as being for the mother's own good (such as administration of pain-relieving drugs), lessens a woman's feelings of control as well as her sensations of actually *giving* birth. Although many women request pain relievers such as epidurals or drugs, they are often not aware that such interventions reduce their own control, and they have have no idea what sort of bodily sensations they may be missing other than pain. Furthermore, such interventions may slow down the labor and contribute to fear and loss of control, leading to further interventions, and so on in a vicious cycle. Many researchers have documented at length and from a variety of perspectives how the highly medicalized American way of birth robs women of power and agency but how giving birth under circumstances that prioritize the mother's experiences, desires, and sensations can make possible an integrated sense of self and can transform a woman's negative feelings about her body and herself.[13]

For example, thirty-eight-year-old Letty described the birth of her third child as different from her other two births. Because she felt more in charge of her third birth, she derived powerful satisfaction and self-confidence from it:

> When I went into labor, I stayed home most of the day. I was really pleased with myself that I read the signals about the labor and I knew what was happening. It was a real partnership between the baby's body and the baby's spirit or strength, and my body expelling the baby. And you know, it's hard, and I went through a lot of different emotions with being angry and frustrated and feeling very empowered. This time the urge to push took over me. It was an incredible feeling—I sat bolt upright in bed. It was like this thing just took over and it was the most incredible feeling I've ever had, and I was ready. It was about six, eight pushes, and the baby was out. The urge to push takes over your body, absolutely, it's like another being comes in. I didn't know. I never expected it. I hadn't experienced it before.
>
> After each birth experience I felt more confident in myself and more confident in what I can do as a person, and now, I think I transferred that feeling of confidence into validating success in my job or validating success in any kind of mothering that I do so it gave me a model of what it means to feel good about myself. This is exactly what I want to strive for, to feel that confident and that powerful, to have that feeling of power and to reach for it in other areas of my life.

Today, as a result of the many changes in birth culture inspired by the feminism of the 1960s and 1970s, growing numbers of women are giving birth without medical intervention. My research with fifteen women during pregnancy and the postpartum period supports general findings that many women still have medicated labors, but those who do not are much more likely to feel empowered by their experience. Women who give birth naturally are able to become much more fully one with their bodies as they use them to bring forth life. Emphasizing this power enables them, I believe, to care less about how their bodies look, to escape from self-abnegating objectification, and to feel empowered. As Antonia, a natural birth activist in Florence, Italy said, "I have met women who stay conscious and present at birth, helping their bodies. Afterward they seem stronger, more clear. These women have been able to realize inner wishes. . . . They have a sense of power in themselves and will not be victims again."[14]

CONCLUSION

A character in Sandra Cisneros's story "Little Miracle, Kept Promises" says, "I'm a snake swallowing its tail. I'm my history and my future. All my ancestors' ancestors inside my own belly. All my futures and all my pasts" (1991, 126).

Her words evoke the manifold ways in which women's lives and histories are wrapped up in our bodies. Through our bodies we can live out our own oppression and objectification, which are institutionalized by a patriarchal, capitalist culture that profits from our subordination. Or we can use our bodies to express our power, individuality, and creativity. We can use the transitional and creative nature of reproduction to transform our bodies and ourselves. But to do so we must continue to critique and challenge practices and ideologies that demean us and rob us of agency. We must appreciate the diversity of the female form and the beauty of all women. We must continually celebrate our work—at home, in the garden, at the factory, at the community center, and in the office—and challenge attention focused only on how we look. We must celebrate our power to give birth and link it to respect for our sexuality. And to make all this happen, we must continue to tell our stories as testimony to experience, diversity, and transformation.

Notes

CHAPTER 1

1. This essay is a revision and amalgam of "The Social and Cultural Uses of Food" (Counihan 1999) and "Food and Gender: Identity and Power" (Counihan 1998).
2. See the recipe appendix for two Florentine tomato sauce recipes.
3. The following sources treat social responses to food shortages and famine: Richards 1932, 1939; Firth 1959; Holmberg 1969 (originally 1950); Turnbull 1972, 1978; Laughlin and Brady 1978; Colson 1979; Prindle 1979; Dirks 1980; Young 1986; Vaughan 1987; Messer 1989; Newman 1990.
4. See for example Arnold 1988; Barry 1987; Hilton 1973; Kaplan 1976, 1984, 1990; Mackintosh 1989; Tilly 1971.
5. Physicians 1985; Brown and Pizer 1987; Brown 1987; Arnold 1988; Glasser 1988; Lappé and Collins 1986.
6. Some works that explore the U.S. value on thinness are: Powdermaker 1960; Bruch 1973, 1978; Boskind-Lodahl 1976; Stunkard 1977; Orbach 1978; Kaplan 1980; Styles 1980; Millman 1980; Boskind-White and White 1983; Schwartz 1986; Sobal and Stunkard 1989. See chapters 5, 6, and 7.
7. Garb, Garb, and Stunkard 1975; Stunkard 1977; Beller 1977; Massara and Stunkard 1979; Massara 1989; Sobal and Stunkard 1989.
8. Works that have abundant material on the overlap between food, sex, and gender are Tambiah 1969; Verdier 1969; Murphy and Murphy 1974; Farb and Armelagos 1980; Meigs 1984; Adams 1988; Gregor 1985; Pollock 1985; Kahn 1986; Herdt 1987; Frese 1991; Holmberg 1969; Siskind 1973.
9. Quoted in Starn 1990, 78.
10. Becker 1995; Beller 1977; Cassidy 1991; de Garine and Pollock 1995; Pollock 1992; Sobo 1997.
11. Some sources that focus explicitly on food and the power relations between men and women are Adams 1990; Charles and Kerr 1988; DeVault 1991; McIntosh and Zey 1998; and Weismantel 1988.
12. There is an enormous literature on what Kaplan (1980) has called "the special relationship between women and food." In Western culture, women have variously used compulsive eating, obesity, fasting, or the symbolic value of food as a means of expressing themselves and coping with the problems of achieving a meaningful place in a world where they are defined as subordinate. Some sources dealing with women's complicated relationship to food are Bell 1985; Beller 1977; Boskind-Lodahl 1976; Boskind-White and White 1983; Bruch 1973, 1978; Bynum 1987; Charles and Kerr 1988; Chernin 1981, 1985; Gordon 1988, 1990; Kaplan 1980; Lawrence 1984; Massara 1989; Millman 1980; Orbach 1978; Palazzoli 1971; Schwartz 1986; Styles 1980; Thoma 1977; Waller, Kaufman, and Deutsch 1940.
13. Malinowski 1961, 168–72; Kahn 1986, 1988; Young 1971, 1989.
14. Perhaps the most well-known redistributive ritual is the potlatch of the Northwest coast Indians, a feast that involves enormous conspicuous consumption between tribes to establish prestige and power relations, debts, social congress, and communion with the gods. See Benedict 1934; Codere 1950; Mauss 1967, 31–37; Piddocke 1969; and Harris 1974.
15. Frazer 1951; Goody 1962; Huntington and Metcalf 1979; Nutini 1988.

16. Some sources on feeding as a form of socialization and personality formation are Du Bois 1941, 1944; Bossard 1943; Freud 1946; Freud 1962; Mead 1963 (originally 1935), 1967 (originally 1949); Holmberg 1969; Shack 1969; Shack 1971; Bruch 1973; Farb and Armelagos 1980.

17. The following sources have material on the meaning of food through the study of symbolism, taboo, etiquette, and/or cuisine: Lévi-Strauss 1966; Lehrer 1969, 1972; Verdier 1969; Holmberg 1969, 78–81, 173–75; Firth 1973; Murphy and Murphy 1974, 162–63; Ortner 1975; C. Hugh-Jones 1979, especially chapters 5 and 6; S. Hugh-Jones 1979; Farb and Armelagos 1980; Goody 1982; Laderman 1983; Mennell 1985; Manderson 1986a, 1986b, 1986c.

18. On Jewish dietary law see Douglas 1966; Soler 1973; Alter 1979; Feeley-Harnik 1981; Fredman 1981; Harris 1985.

19. See also S. Hugh-Jones 1979 and C. Hugh-Jones 1979, especially chapter 5.

20. On food in literature see the special issue of *Mosaic* entitled *Diet and Discourse: Eating, Drinking and Literature* edited by Evelyn Hinz (1991) which contains twelve articles and an extensive annotated bibliography (Kiell 1991). M. F. K. Fisher's lifelong opus centers around food, especially her *The Art of Eating*. See also Avakian 1997, Colwin 1993; and Romer 1984; Mayes 1996.

CHAPTER 2

1. This paper was originally published in *Anthropological Quarterly* 57, 2:47–59, 1984. Fieldwork in Bosa from June 1978 through August 1979 was supported by a Fulbright-Hays Dissertation Research Grant, a grant-in-aid from Sigma Xi, the Scientific Research Society of North America, and a University Fellowship from the University of Massachusetts. A trip to Bosa in February 1980 to make the film "Looking for Giolzi: Carnival and Anthropology in the Sardinian Town of Bosa" was made possible by the film's director, Stefano Silvestrini, and production manager, Sofia Manozzi. Research in Bosa in August 1982 was made possible in part by funds from Franklin and Marshall College. To these institutions and individuals I am most grateful. I thank the following people for commenting on earlier drafts of this paper: Peter Brown, Elizabeth Mathias, James Taggart, Richard Ward, and several anonymous reviewers. Some relevant works on Sardinia and Italy published since I wrote this paper are Angioni 1989; Assmuth 1997; Bertolo 1993; Bimbi and Castellano 1993; Caldwell 1991; Clark 1996; Da Re 1990, 1995; De Gioannis and Serri 1991; Saraceno 1988; Siebert 1993; and Vargas-Cetina 1993.

2. Bread seems to be expressive of the differential impact of change in different areas of Sardinia. In Bosa, bread making has disappeared completely, whereas in the nearby mountainous village of Montresta women in almost every household regularly bake their own bread. In the central Sardinian mountain villages of Talana (Bodemann 1979) and Esporlatu (Mathias 1983) many women still make bread, while this has declined in Tonara (Gallini 1981). In the mid-1990s in the town of Baunei, many women were still making traditional bread at home and some had started a small commercial bakery as well (Assmuth 1997). Clearly many factors influence bread making and this paper attempts to outline some important ones.

3. The expression "*a cercare pane migliore di quello di grano*"—"to look for bread better than that of wheat"—is a central and recurrent expression in Satta's (1979) penetrating ethnographic novel about Nuoro, the isolated capital of the province that includes Bosa. The expression suggests that we should not challenge the order of things by looking for bread better than that made of its quintessential essence— wheat.

4. I gathered data on contemporary Bosan food habits during 1978 and 1979 through participant observation, interviews, food logs, and questionnaires. Comparative data on past food habits come from the memories of older informants, travelers' and scholars' reports (Bodio 1879; Casalis 1835; Chessa 1906; Dessì 1967; La Marmora 1839, 1860; Le Lannou 1941; Smyth 1828; Tyndale 1840; and Wagner 1928), and government statistics (ISTAT 1960, 1968). Cautious use of ethnographic analogy on contemporary data from areas more isolated than Bosa suggests a picture of how Bosa might have been in the past. See Angioni 1974, 1976; Barbiellini-Amidei and

Bandinu 1976; Cambosu 1954; Cannas 1975; Dellitala 1978; Satta 1979; and especially Cirese et al. 1977 and Mathias 1983.

5. See La Marmora 1839, 241 for a similar description of bread in nineteenth-century Sardinia and Assmuth 1997 for a portrayal of contemporary bread making.

6. *Comari* (female) and *compari* (male) are fictive kin. They are ordinarily the people who hold one's children at baptism and to whom one is thus linked by special obligation and respect.

7. For descriptions of baking in Sardinia see Angioni 1974, 266–69, Assmuth 1997, 259–61; Da Re 1995; Cirese et al. 1977; Mathias 1983; and Satta 1979, 67–68.

8. My friend Nina was from Bosa and continued to make bread for her employers at their country home where I was able to photograph her. She only made bread for wages and did not make bread for her family in Bosa, nor did any other woman I or anyone else knew.

CHAPTER 3

1 This essay was originally published in *Anthropological Quarterly* 61, 2:51–62, 1988.

2 A lacuna in my sample is the absence of young, radical, university-educated women. The political struggles of *"sessant'otto"* (1968) and beyond produced a strong streak of radical, leftist feminism in many young Italian women. However, none of my informants was "coming of age" in the late 1960s and early 1970s, and none of the younger cohort attended the university where they would have been exposed to more explicitly feminist ideals. It remains to be seen to what extent feminists are turning their ideals into changed child-rearing practices and significantly altered social policy (see Passerini 1996).

3 Although beyond the scope of this article, anorexia nervosa does occur in Italy, predominantly among upper-middle and upper-class urban teenage girls who manifest some of the same issues involved in the disorder in the United States, including the struggle for power and autonomy (see Allegranzi et al. 1994; De Clerq 1990, 1995; Palazzoli 1963; and Recalcati 1997). None of my informants showed any signs of anorexia nervosa, and few knew anyone who did. Nevertheless the existence of the disorder in Italy supports my claims about women's loss of their traditional source of identity and influence through feeding and its lack of replacement with other sources of power and prestige. In such a context, some women seek the limited and self-destructive form of power represented by self-denial and self-control.

4 See Asssmuth 1997; Cornelisen 1969; Chapman 1971; Davis 1973; Silverman 1975; Schneider and Schneider 1976; Teti 1976; Belmonte 1979; Coppi and Fineschi 1980; Falassi 1980; Feletti and Pasi 1981; Pitkin 1985; Lo Russo 1998.

5 Breast-feeding does not ruin a woman's figure, but it is interesting that Florentine women think it does and favor it anyway. Because of the calories needed to make milk, breast-feeding can help women lose weight after pregnancy. Sagging breasts come not from nursing but from failure to wear a support bra (Boston Women's Health Book Collective 1984, 400).

6 See Falassi 1980 and Silverman 1975 for descriptions of male-female power relations in premodern Tuscany.

CHAPTER 4

1. This is a slightly revised version of an essay that appeared in the special issue on "Comida" in the Brazilian journal *Horizontes Antropológicos* 2, 4:104–17, 1996.

2. See chapters 5 and 6 for further discussion of anorexic women's common antipathy to sex. See Bell 1985; Boskind-White and White 1983; Bruch 1978, 1988; Brumberg 1988, 1997; Bynum 1987; Liu 1979; Orbach 1978.

3. I do not wish to imply that all tribal societies are fundamentally alike. I choose to compare the United States to some cultures of the Amazon and New Guinea because there are good data on the overlapping relationship between eating, intercourse, and definitions of masculinity and femininity in the latter that illuminate the U.S. case. I believe that the Judeo-Christian ideology in combination with class, race, and gender inequality have affected male-female definitions and relationships in the United States in ways fundamentally different from those of nonstratified tribal societies.

4. Besides Gregor (1985), Herdt (1987), Kahn (1986), Meigs (1984), and Murphy and Murphy (1985), see also Farb and Armelagos (1980), Frese (1989), Tambiah (1969), and Verdier (1969).

5. The epidemic of AIDS has caused us to define men's bodies as vulnerable in new ways to disease and death. Interestingly, however, the stereotypical cultural view is that men's bodies are vulnerable to AIDS only when having sex with other men. They are not defined as vulnerable to women. In fact, it is women who are perceived as vulnerable to AIDS through sexual penetration by infected men.

6. Paige and Paige 1981. Initiation rituals also occur in many African and aboriginal Australian societies. Consideration of these cases is beyond the scope of this paper but would be an interesting focus of further research.

CHAPTER 5

1. This is a slightly revised and updated version of an essay originally published in *Food and Foodways*, 1:77–94, 1985. I thank Roger Haydon, Steve Kaplan, Theresa Rubin, Jolane Solomon, and anonymous reviewers for comments on earlier drafts of this chapter. Since I wrote the original essay, many, many books have been published dealing with women's relationship to food and body. Of most relevance to this chapter are Susan Bordo's (1993) *Unbearable Weight: Feminism, Western Culture, and the Body* and Becky Thompson's (1994) *A Hunger So Wide and So Deep: American Women Speak Out on Eating Problems*, which I have referred to where directly relevant in the essay. Also important is Joan Jacob Brumberg's (1988) *Fasting Girls: The Emergence of Anorexia Nervosa as a Modern Disease*, which I refer to extensively in the next chapter.

2. Today I would make a clearer distinction between compulsive eating and obesity than I did in 1985. The two may or may not overlap. Compulsive eating may be associated with bulimia and not result in obesity, for example, and obesity may result from factors other than compulsive eating. Compulsive eating may be a response to severe psychological and emotional abuse, as Thompson documents (1994). Obesity may bring on problems of its own distinct from those involved in compulsive eating.

3. For discussions of female physiology and fat see Beller 1977; Bierman and Hirsch 1981; Contento 1980; Dyrenforth, Wooley, and Wooley 1980; Hirsh 1984. For discussions of women, weight, food, and political economy, see Aronson 1980; Hacker 1980; Leghorn and Roodkowsky 1977. For personal accounts of food, see Broughton 1978; Liu 1979; Roth 1982.

4. See Sobal and Stunkard 1989; Stunkard 1977.

5. See Thompson 1994, chapter 6; Brown and Rothblum 1990.

6. On the body and beauty attitudes of African Americans see especially Collins 1990; Hughes 1997; Parker et al. 1995; Russell, Wilson, and Hall 1993; Wilson and Russell 1996; Freedman 1990a, 1990b; Gray, Ford, and Kelly 1987; and Hsu 1987. On African American cooking and identity see Angelou 1997; Beoku-Betts 1995; Harris 1994; Hughes 1997; Mintz 1997; Shange 1998; and Wade-Gayles 1997.

7. Some gay men, however, seem to be as concerned about weight as heterosexual women (Millman 1980, 245), and some lesbians seem able to reject the thinness obsession (Crowder 1993). Further consideration of both sexual preference and gender on eating disorders and attitudes toward the body is needed. On men and eating disorders, see Frasciello and Willard 1995; Garrett 1992; *Males with Eating Disorders* 1990; and Sharp et al. 1994.

CHAPTER 6

1. This is a slightly revised version of a paper originally published in *Food and Foodways*, 3, 4:357–75, 1989. For their comments, I thank Steve Kaplan, Pamela Quaggiotto, and especially Jim Taggart, who read more drafts than either of us remembers.

2. Current knowledge suggests that biological disfunction does not seem to be the cause of holy or modern anorexia (Bell 1995, 14–15; Brumberg 1988, 24–27; Bruch 1973, chap. 3). Although biological symptoms occur in medieval and modern fasters—including distorted perception, sensitivity to cold and light, lanugo, constipation, slowed metabolism, hormone imbalance, hypothalmic disfunction, and amenorrhea (Bruch 1973; Bynum 1987; Bell 1985)—they appear to be effects rather than causes. In studies of near and total starvation, neither anthropologists

(Holmberg 1969; Turnbull 1972) nor researchers on war and concentration camp victims (Bruch 1973, chap. 2; Winnick 1979) have observed that a lack of food alone causes anorexia nervosa. Bell concurs for medieval people: "Starvation alone certainly did not cause holy anorexia" (14). Furthermore, feeding does not cure the disorder; anorexics who are force-fed usually start fasting again as soon as they can (Bruch 1978, chap. 6; Lawrence 1984, chap. 5), whereas "normal" starvation victims welcome food (Firth 1959; Winnick 1979). However, some people seem to be susceptible to what Brumberg calls "an addiction to starvation" (1988, 31); some people—and there is no reason why they should exist only in Western society—seem to have a biological predisposition. But they will not become holy or anorexic fasters unless both cultural and psychological forces make food self-denial a powerful statement.

3. Geertz (1973, 43) affirms that "it may be in the cultural particularities of a people—in their oddities—that some of the most instructive revelations of what it is to be generally human are to be found."

4. The significance of exchange is so fundamental in anthropology as to be axiomatic. See, for example, Lévi-Strauss 1967; Malinowski 1922; and Weiner 1988.

5. There is an enormous literature on anorexia nervosa, which is well covered in Brumberg's book, especially in chapter 1 and its notes. Feminist approaches to eating disorders are reviewed in chapter 5 of this volume. Some important titles are Bruch 1973, 1978, 1988; Bordo 1993; Boskind-Lodahl 1976; Boskind-White and White 1983; Cauwels 1983; Chernin 1981, 1985; Dally 1969; Garfinkel and Garner 1982; Gordon 1988; Lawrence 1984; Levenkron 1982; Macleod 1981; Orbach 1978, 1982; Palazzoli 1974; Striegel-Moore, Silberstein, and Rodin 1986; and Thompson 1994.

6. The description by one of my female college students of her bout with anorexia nervosa supports claims for the cultural persistence of certain themes in extreme fasting and indicates that pursuit of religious purity and asceticism can still be a meaningful component of it: "I became a member of a holiness church. . . . I decided to practice aestheticism [asceticism] and suffered anorexia nervosa. All this was an attempt to control my life and please God. I would go on liquid fasts for days at a time and read the Bible for hours. If I began to have sexual desires, I went on a fast to put my body under subjection to the Bible—in short get rid of the sexual desire. The Bible encouraged presenting yourself as a living sacrifice unto God. And I did. I went overboard with my practices to achieve holiness" (journal, December 6, 1988).

7. On food symbolism see e.g., Barthes 1975; Douglas 1972, 1984; Kahn 1986; Lévi-Strauss 1969; Meigs 1984; Tambiah 1969; Verdier 1969; and Weismantel 1988.

8. Some well-documented examples are the Gurage of Ethiopia (Shack 1969; Shack 1971), the Kalaunans of Goodenough Island (Young 1971, 1986), the Trobriand Islanders of Melanesia (Malinowski 1922), the Siriono of Bolivia (Holmberg 1969), and the Bemba of Northern Rhodesia (Richards 1939).

9. Bell's major claim is that "a historically significant group of women exhibited an anorexic behavior pattern in response to the patriarchal social structures in which they were trapped" (xii). Medieval holy women, he claims, struggled against their subordinate social position by exerting their will to fast to circumvent male authority and establish a direct connection to God. Bynum differs from Bell in claiming that medieval holy women are not best viewed as victims of patriarchy (295). Although male hagiographers depicted them thus, Bynum (208) asserts they were seizing power and establishing a direct connection to God through fasting, not just reacting against male dominance. Brumberg desires not to reduce an array of female behaviors to opposition to men and does not explicitly characterize women's fasting as a reaction against patriarchy, for she emphasizes its diverse aims and meanings over time (37). However, her book documents the clear relations of dominance-subordination between male interpreters of fasting and female practitioners. Furthermore, her proposals for reducing the incidence of contemporary anorexia involve giving women a sense of the value of their sex and support for "their specific aspirations [and] for female creativity in general" (269), implying that their self-destructive fasting is related to their subordination.

10. Anna Freud (1946, 126) believes that the child's "conflicting behavior towards food" stems from "conflicting emotions towards the mother which are transferred on to the food which is a symbol for her. Ambivalence towards the mother may express

itself as fluctuations between over-eating and refusal of food; guilty feelings towards the mother and a consequent inability to enjoy her affection as an inability to enjoy food; obstinacy and hostility towards the mother as a struggle against being fed."

CHAPTER 7

1. This paper was originally published in *Anthropological Quarterly* 65, 2:55–66, 1992. I am grateful to Phyllis Pease Chock, Lin Emmons, Janet Fitchen, Ellen Messer, Peggy Ratcheson, Jim Taggart, and several anonymous reviewers for their thoughtful comments on earlier drafts of this paper. I thank Millersville University for travel funds to present a version of this article at the 89th Annual Meeting of the American Anthropological Association, and to my students at Stockton State College and Millersville University for sharing their intimate thoughts about the meaning of food.

2. Anthropologists of very different theoretical perspectives have studied food to determine the cultural construction of reality. See Barthes 1975; Douglas 1974; Harris 1985; Hull 1986; Kahn 1986; Laderman 1983; Lévi-Strauss 1966; Manderson 1986a, 1986b, 1986c; Meigs 1984; Reid 1986; Weismantel 1988; Young 1986.

3. See Adams 1990; Brumberg 1988; Frese 1988; Harris 1985; Kahn 1986; Laderman 1983; Manderson 1986a; Meigs 1984; Weismantel 1988. Some peoples, such as the Hua of New Guinea, make the extrinsic or contagious properties of food prevalent in their alimentary regime (Meigs 1984, 17). Because their "ideology of life" (27) centers on relationships, they base many of their food rules on beliefs about the harmful or beneficial effects one person may have on another. In the United States, college students define food mainly in terms of its intrinsic properties, and emphasize how eating constitutes the self rather than the community.

4. Whereas the journals contain a fine depiction of students' cultural constructions of food rules, they are not such a good source of information on students' actual eating behavior. Students do often write about their behavior, but these descriptions are passed through the filter of their own selection and interpretation. Certain kinds of questions would be better answered through participant-observation than through the journals, for example, questions about how students' actual consumption fits their ideal rules, about how the context of the eating event affects consumption, and about how they actually relate to eating while doing it. I also have data on student eating through food logs that they kept for two weeks, reporting everything they ingested during that time. I refer to these only in the most general terms here and recognize that like all data on food consumption, they are approximate (see Quandt and Ritenbaugh 1986).

5. African-American, Asian-American, and Hispanic students make up a very small proportion of my sample and thus I am not able to speak about their distinctiveness. This is largely due to the fact that these students are underrepresented at Millersville and Stockton in particular and in my "Food and Culture" class as well. Similarly, students belonging to other ethnic or religious minorities are also underrepresented. Most students are Christian or nonreligious. Few or none in my sample belong to Muslim, Hindu, Jewish, Buddhist, or other religious sects with significant dietary proscriptions. There is a serious dearth of studies that focus on eating habits and attitudes of America's diverse racial, ethnic, and religious populations. As Moore has argued, anthropology needs to challenge its own racism and sexism by including the experiences of women and people of color in both its data and its theory (1988). Such inclusion will improve the field's ability to generalize and will render it more true to its goal of understanding the entire human condition. There does appear to be a significant difference in the attitudes of African-American females toward food and the body from those of Euro-American females. The former diet somewhat less frequently (Emmons 1992) and may have culturally appropriate acceptance of a larger body size (Parker et al. 1995; Styles 1980). Furthermore, they appear to have a more self-reliant attitude toward their future and are less likely to conceptualize their lives as based on economic dependence on a man than white college women (Holland and Eisenhart 1990, 85). This self-reliance may then be related to their less strenuous adherence to the prevalent thinness standards. Among Puerto Ricans in Philadelphia, Massara argues that weight gain in a woman after marriage is viewed

positively (1989). It is a sign that her husband is providing for her, that she is fulfilling her role as a "good wife," and that she is content (1989, 297).

6. Data from student journals is referenced with F=female or M=male, F=Fall semester or S=Spring semester, and year.

7. See Fitchen (1987) for a discussion of how contradictions between experts on groundwater contamination led to a failure by the general public to believe in their prescriptions.

8. See chapter 5 and Brumberg 1988; Bruch 1973, 1978; Chernin 1981; Lawrence 1984.

9. In the United States in the past, as Frese has documented, male and female foods were defined on the basis of their color and ability to produce blood; red foods were male and white foods were female (1989; see also Brumberg 1988 for beliefs about proper male and female eating in the past).

10. NAAFA was originally the National Association to Aid Fat Americans and at some point changed its name to the National Association to Advance Fat Awareness.

CHAPTER 8

1. This chapter owes its evolution to the comments of several anonymous reviewers and to people who heard me present it at the 1991 Annual Meeting of the American Anthropological Association, at the 1992 Annual Meeting of the Northeastern Anthropological Association, and at the Folklore Archives of the University of California at Berkeley in 1994. I thank Alan Dundes and Stanley Brandes for inviting me to be a visiting scholar in the Anthropology Department at Berkeley, where I did much research for this paper. I thank Amy Sheldon and Linda Hughes, whose insightful comments I didn't always follow but to whom I owe much inspiration. I thank Millersville students Terri Widener and Keith Appleby for invaluable advice about the numbers. I thank the staff and children of the centers where I worked. I thank my supportive husband Jim Taggart for reading many drafts and our sons, Ben and Willie, for delighting me with their fantasies and fascinating me with their eating.

2. See Boskind-Lodahl 1976; Bruch 1973, 1978; Brumberg 1988; Charles and Kerr 1988; Chernin 1981, 1985; DeVault 1991; Kaplan 1980; Millman 1980; Orbach 1978.

3. Birch 1980; Birch, Martin, and Rotter 1984; Bruch 1973; Dietz and Gortmaker 1985; Dyrenforth, Wooley, and Wooley 1980; Freud 1946; Katriel 1987; Satter 1987; Shapiro et al. 1984.

4. The fact that my husband, Jim Taggart, has been analyzing folktales for years was a big factor in this decision.

5. In extensive searching, I could find no published story collections for children from any other cultures nor from nonwhite ethnic or racial groups in the United States except Brady's "skinwalker" collection from ten- to twelve-year old Navajo children (1984), and Minami and McCabe's stories from seventeen Japanese five- to nine-year-old children (1991). McDowell collected riddles from Chicano and European-American children in Texas and compared their structure and content, but without attention to gender (1979). Sutton-Smith refers to stories collected from African-American children by Heath, but she only includes a few in the published works I could find (Heath 1982, 1983, 1986, 1994). Both Heath and Michaels (1981) point out differences in narrative style between African-American and Euro-American children, but neither looks at gender. Iona and Peter Opie collected folklore of all kinds (e.g. riddles, jokes, rhymes, bets, jeers, pranks, and so on) from British children, but no stories (1959). Knapp and Knapp (1976) and Bronner (1988) also collected American children's folklore but no narratives. Spiro made interesting observations about differences in young boys' and girls' fantasy play on an Israeli Kibbutz, but reports no stories (1975, 1979). Steedman looks at the written stories of British working-class nine-year-old girls, analyzing one story in particular, and draws conclusions about class and gender, but offers no oral narratives (1982). Dyson and Genishi include several articles on gender and racial/ethnic diversity in children's stories (1994).

6. Sutton-Smith also included stories from 6-10 year old children, but I do not consider this age group in this study (1981).

7. Vivian Paley has come out with three more books (Paley 1996, 1998, 1999) since I first did the research for this paper.

8. See Ames 1966; Corsaro 1985; Davies 1989; Hughes 1988; Knapp and Knapp 1976; Nicolopoulou, Scales, and Weintraub 1994; Sachs 1987; Sheldon 1990; Sheldon and Rohleder 1996; Sutton-Smith 1981.
9. The following studies have some concern with gender: Cook-Gumperz and Scales 1996; Corsaro 1985; Gilbert 1994; Goodwin 1990, 1993; Goodwin and Goodwin 1987; Hendrick and Strange 1991; Hughes 1988; Kyratzis and Guo 1996; Nicolopoulou, Scales, and Weintraub 1994; Paley 1994; Pitcher and Schultz 1983; Sachs 1987; Sheldon 1990, 1992; Sheldon and Rohleder 1996; Spiro 1975, 1979; Steedman 1982; Tanz 1987. The following publications about children's fantasy utterances and language do not consider gender, although they explore race, ethnicity, or class: Allen and Bradley 1993; Britsch 1994; Brady 1984; Dickinson and Snow 1987; Feagans 1982; Heath 1982, 1983, 1986; Jewson, Sachs, and Rohner 1981; Michaels 1981; Minami and McCabe 1991; Smitherman 1994; Umiker-Sebeok 1979.
10. See especially Dyson and Genishi 1994; Slobin et al. 1996; and Tannen 1993.
11. Structuralists like Sutton-Smith and his coworkers (e.g., Abrams and Sutton-Smith 1977; Botvin and Sutton-Smith 1977; Caring 1977; Sutton-Smith, Mahony, and Botvin 1976) focus on the formation of the story, its elements, and its construction to draw conclusions about the child's cognitive and linguistic development. Brady (1984) draws attention to the importance of the story context. While interesting and important, context and structure are not my focus.
12. The names of children in my study are pseudonyms; for other studies I use the names used by the authors. In parentheses is the child's name and age in years:months and for my study the date when the story was told.
13. In "The Cannibalistic Impulses of Parents," Devereux offers the explanation that children's devouring metaphors are reflections of the genuine "cannibalistic impulses" of parents (1980).
14. Maurice Sendak's (1963) wonderful children's story *Where the Wild Things Are* uses eating themes in all of these ways (see chapter 1). This story incorporates poetically many of the symbolic messages commonly conveyed through food between children and parents; perhaps for this reason it has become a beloved and award-winning classic of children's literature.
15. See Corsaro 1985; Goodwin and Goodwin 1987; Hughes 1988; Pitcher and Schultz 1983; Sachs 1987; Sheldon 1990, 1992; Spiro 1975, 1979.
16. See Gilmore 1990; Spiro 1979; Tobin, Wu, and Davidson 1989; Whiting and Edwards 1974, 1988.
17. See Chodorow 1974, 1978; Ehrensaft 1990; Gilligan 1981, 1990; Gilligan, Lyons, and Hanmer 1990; Gilmore 1990; Greenson 1968; Rubin 1983; Taggart 1992.
18. See Bruch 1973 for a discussion of how inappropriate parental responses to infants' hunger needs produce lifelong problems with dependency and eating disorders. See also Freud 1946.

CHAPTER 9

1. An earlier, significantly shorter version of this chapter appeared in *Europaea*, 4, 1, 1998.
2. See chapter 8; Bruch 1973; Freud 1946, 1968; Freud 1962; Satter 1990; Shack 1969.
3. See Benjamin 1988.
4. Gigliola is pronounced Jeel-yol-ah.
5. As well as due to pregnancy, Elda's weight gain may have been due to the high reliance on starchy foods like chestnuts, chestnut flour, and bread. It may also have been related to the weight gains that some Germans experienced during World War II, a gain they called *"Kummerspeck"*—"the fat of sorrow." Hilde Bruch calls this "reactive obesity" and says it "seems to develop in response to an emotional trauma, frequently to . . . death or . . . the fear of death or injury" (1973, 126).
6. The Italian word is *salame* (singular), with the plural form *salami*. I have adopted the English usage of "salami" (singular) and "salamis" (plural).
7. Wet-nursing other women's babies seems to have been fairly common before, during, and after the war; several of my subjects mentioned it.

8. Recipes for dishes marked with an asterisk are listed in the recipe appendix in alphabetical order by Italian name.
9. In Florence, meat sauce is called *ragù* or *sugo*.
10. When Sandra was in high school, Italy had an educational tracking system where certain high school tracks led to a vocational diploma, but only to a limited choice of fields for university enrollment. Examples of this are the *Ragioneria* (Accounting) and *Magistrali* (Teacher Training) high schools. Other high school tracks (*Liceo scientifico, Liceo classico,* and *Liceo artistico* which I translate as Science High School, Classics High School, and Arts High School) led to a broad choice of university fields but no diploma. Very often lower-middle-class families like those of Sandra and Gigliola urged their children to follow a diploma track in high school so as to permit them direct entrance into a job.

CHAPTER 10

1. This is a substantial revision of a paper presented at the 1997 Annual Meeting of the American Anthropological Association at the session on "The Anthropology of the Body in Europe" organized by Barbara Collins.
2. See Becker 1995; Bordo 1992; Bruch 1973; Bynum 1991; Douglas 1966; Martin 1987; Meigs 1984; Mitchie 1987; Suleiman 1985.
3. Of the myriad works on the American obsession with thinness, the following are particularly relevant to anthropologists: Bordo 1992; Boskind-Lodahl 1976; Bruch 1973, 1978; Brumberg 1988; Chernin 1981; Mackenzie 1976; Millman 1980; Orbach 1978; Hughes 1997; Thompson 1994.
4. The province of Florence had 1.2 million inhabitants in 1981, the city 450,000. Prior to the Second World War, *mezzadria* peasant sharecropping dominated the countryside while high-quality, small artisanal industry and crafts predominated in the cities. Today, farming has given way to industry, artisanal industry, commerce, and tourism (Barucci 1964; Camera di Commercio 1958; Ires Toscana 1988; ISTAT 1990; Mori 1986).
5. A feminine subject is *golosa*; a masculine one is *goloso*.
6. Luisa Passerini mentioned this fact in her *Autobiography of a Generation* (1996, 16).
7. In Bosa, Sardinia, at the end of a good meal, people expressed contentment by saying, "*Consolado soe*"—"I am consoled" (Counihan 1981). See Thompson 1994 on the consoling effects of eating.
8. *Mezzadria* describes the sharecropping peasant system that dominated social and economic relations in the Tuscan countryside around Florence. See Falassi 1980; Origo 1956; Silverman 1975; Snowden 1989.
9. *Cucinare* also means "to cook."
10. The prevalence of cross-cultural linkages between food and sex would lead one to hypothesize that Florentine women may have a legitimate cultural claim to sexual pleasure on a par with men, just as they do to gustatory pleasure, but this remains to be studied. The following deal with food and sex: Freud 1918; 1962; Gregor 1985; Kahn 1986; Mead 1967; Meigs 1984; Tambiah 1969.
11. On women's economic position in Italy see Balbo and May 1975–76.
12. On anorexia nervosa in Italy, see Allegranzi et al. 1994; De Clercq 1990, 1995; *Disorders of Eating Behavior* 1986; Palazzoli 1974; and Recalcati 1997. I thank Barbara Collins for these references and Christina Miller for calling my attention to the growing Italian obsession with thinness. I thank my Italian colleague Giuseppe Lo Russo for seeking data on anorexia nervosa. He reports that official statistics are unavailable but scholars believe that eating disorders are rising and may affect as much as two percent of the adolescent population (personal communication 1999).
13. See Assmuth 1997 for recent economic statistics on women in Italy.
14. Whether the idea that women have to please men has existed "from the beginning" is debatable, but it certainly got an enormous boost during fascism through explicit policies and propaganda affirming women's duty to work long, hard, unremunerated hours to serve husbands and family (Caldwell 1986; DeGrazia 1992).

15. See DeVault 1992 for a discussion of how in the United States "feeding the family" reproduces women's subordination.

CHAPTER 11

1. I presented earlier versions of this paper at the 1995 Annual Meeting of the American Anthropological Association and the 1995 National Women's Studies Association Conference. I thank the fifteen women whom I interviewed for sharing their birth experiences with me and Millersville University Faculty Grants Committee for financial and released time support for this project.
2. Lorde 1984, 123.
3. See Bordo 1992; Boskind-Lodahl 1976; Bruch 1978; Brumberg 1997; Chernin 1981; Thompson 1994; and many other titles cited in chapters 5, 6, and 7.
4. Jean Kilbourne's video *Still Killing Us Softly* reveals this fragmentation with blunt visual clarity. See Adams 1990; Berger 1972; Bordo 1993; Collins 1990; Lorde 1984; Wolf 1993.
5. In a brilliant essay "Body Image and Self Awareness," Hilde Bruch suggests ways to develop the positive and appropriate body image that she argues is a central facet of a positive and integrated self-concept (1973, 87–105). She argues that movement is one important means through which women can come to better awareness of their bodies. She also encourages women to develop a sense of control over their own bodily functions, the ability to recognize and satisfy bodily needs, and an "affective reaction" to the body (89). On bodybuilding see Heywood 1998; Lowe 1998; Moore 1997. See Lorde 1984 on "Uses of the Erotic: The Erotic as Power."
6. On the body attitudes of NAAFA see Millman 1980. For lesbians' body attitudes see Crowder 1993; Dworkin 1989. For the attitudes of feminist fat liberationists see especially Brown and Rothblum 1990; Orbach 1978, 1982; Schoenfielder and Wieser 1983 and Wiley 1994. For information on the body attitudes of Hispanics see Massara 1989; Hiebert et al. 1988; and Garcia, Kaiser, and Dewey 1990. For those of Native Americans see Garb, Garb, and Stunkard 1975; and Rosen et al. 1988.
7. On the body and beauty attitudes of African-Americans see especially Collins 1990; Hughes 1997; Parker et al. 1995; Russell, Wilson, and Hall 1993; and Wilson and Russell 1996. See also Emmons 1992; Freedman 1990a, 1990b; Gray, Ford, and Kelly 1987; and Hsu 1987. On African-American culture, cooking, and identity see Angelou 1997; Beoku-Betts 1995; Harris 1994; Hughes 1997; Mintz 1997; Shange 1998; and Wade-Gayles 1997.
8. Regrettably, the study contains no lesbian mothers, but see Lewin 1993.
9. Women can stop commenting on friends' weight either positively or negatively to stop reproducing a system that values women on the basis of their body, whether for good or ill.
10. See Thompson 1994 for powerful descriptions of women who used food and eating as protection from severe physical, emotional, and sexual abuse, but who eventually had to deal with the problems caused by their compulsive eating and fear of fat.
11. Induced labor pains are often longer, more frequent, and more painful than natural labor pains (Jordan 1993).
12. Karen's description of labor reminds me of Enid Bagnold's fascinating novel *The Squire*, which describes the inner states of a woman who is pregnant with and gives birth to her fifth child. *The Squire* describes labor in this way: "But there comes a time, after the first pains have passed, when you swim down a silver river running like a torrent, with the convulsive, corkscrew movements of a great fish, thrashing from its neck to its tail. And if you can *marry* the movements, go with them, turn like a screw in the river and swim on, then the pain . . . becomes a flame which doesn't burn you" (Bagnold 1938, 101).
13. See Davis-Floyd 1992; Davis-Floyd and Sargent 1997; Jordan 1993; Martin 1987; Rich 1986; Rothman 1982; Van Esterik 1989; Young 1984. Several memoirs by midwives also describe the empowerment deriving from women-centered births, for example, Armstrong and Feldman 1986; Buss 1980; Logan 1989.
14. This remark is quoted by Szurek 1997, 307 from Antonia, a natural-birth activist midwife at a birthing center in Florence, Italy.
15. Cisneros 1991, 126.

Bibliography

Abrams, D. M., and Sutton-Smith, B. 1977. The Development of the Trickster in Children's Narratives. *Journal of American Folklore* 90:29–47.

Adams, Carol J. 1990. *The Sexual Politics of Meat: A Feminist-Vegetarian Critical Theory*. New York: Continuum.

Allegranzi, P., et al. 1994. La Variazione nel tempo dell'immagine corporea. Risultati di un approccio sperimentale. *Medicina Psicosomatica* 3 (4):309–19.

Allen, N. B., and G. S. Bradley. 1993. The Place of Emotion in Stories Told by Children: An Exploratory Study. *Journal of Genetic Psychology* 154 (3):397–406.

Alter, L. 1979. A New Theory of *Kashrut*. *Commentary* 68:46–52.

American Society of Plastic and Reconstructive Surgeons, Inc. 1988. *Body Fat Reduction: Suction-Assisted Lipectomy*.

Ames, Louise Bates. 1966. Children's Stories. *Genetic Psychology Monographs* 73:337–96.

Anfossi, Anna. 1968. *Socialità e organizzazione in Sardegna. Studio sulla zona di Oristano-Bosa-Macomer*. Milano: Angeli.

Angelou, Maya. 1997. New Directions. In *Through the Kitchen Window: Women Explore the Intimate Meanings of Food and Cooking*, edited by Arlene Voski Avakian. Boston: Beacon.

Angioni, Giulio. 1974. *Rapporti di produzione e cultura subalterna: Contadini in Sardegna*. Cagliari: EDES.

———. 1976. *Sa laurera: Il lavoro contadino in Sardegna*. Cagliari: EDES.

———. 1989. *I pascoli erranti. Antropologia del pastore in Sardegna*. Napoli: Liguori Editore.

Anzalone, Pasquale. 1982. Aspetti strutturali della riuscita sociale in Italia. *International Review of Sociology* 18 (1–3):181–92.

Areni, A., L. Manetti, and G. Tanucci. 1982. La condizione lavorativa della donna nella realtà rurale italiana. *International Review of Sociology* 18 (1–3):364–75.

Arens, William. 1979. *The Man-Eating Myth*. New York: Oxford University Press.

Armstrong, Penny, and Sheryl Feldman. 1986. *A Midwife's Story*. New York: Ivy Books.

Arnold, David. 1988. *Famine: Social Crisis and Historical Change*. New York: Basil Blackwell.

Aronson, Naomi. 1980. Working Up an Appetite. In *A Woman's Conflict: The Special Relationship between Women and Food*, edited by J. R. Kaplan. Englewood Cliffs, N.J.: Prentice Hall.

Assmuth, Laura. 1997. *Women's Work, Women's Worth: Changing Lifecourses in Highland Sardinia*. Transactions of the Finnish Anthropological Society no. 39. Saarijärvi: Gummerus Kirjapaino Oy.

Atkinson, Jane Monnig. 1982. Anthropology: Review Essay. *Signs* 8:232–58.

Atwood, Margaret. 1976. *Lady Oracle*. New York: Avon.

Avakian, Arlene Voski. 1997. *Through the Kitchen Window: Women Explore the Intimate Meanings of Food and Cooking*. Boston: Beacon Press.

Bagnold, Enid. 1938. *The Squire*. New York: Penguin-Virago.

Balbo, Laura. 1976. *Stato di famiglia: Bisogni, privato, collettivo*. Milano: ETAS.

Balbo, Laura and Marie P. May. 1975–76. Woman's Condition: The Case of Postwar Italy. *International Journal of Sociology* 5:79–102.

Bamberger, Joan. 1974. The Myth of Matriarchy: Why Men Rule in Primitive Society. In

Women, Culture and Society, edited by Michelle Zimbalist Rosaldo and Louise Lamphere. Stanford: Stanford University Press.

Banfield, Edward C. 1958. *The Moral Basis of a Backward Society*. Glencoe, Ill.: Free Press.

Barbiellini-Amidei, Gaspare, and Bachisio Bandinu. 1976. *Il re è un feticcio: Romanzo di cose*. Milano: Rizzoli.

Barile, Giuseppe, and Lorenza Zanuso. 1980. *Lavoro femminile e condizione familiare*. Milano: Angeli.

Barry, Tom. 1987. *Roots of Rebellion: Land and Hunger in Central America*. Boston: South End Press.

Barthes, Roland. 1975 (orig. 1961). Toward a Psychosociology of Contemporary Food Consumption. In *European Diet from Pre-Industrial to Modern Times*, edited by Elborg Foster and Robert Foster. New York: Harper and Row. Reprinted in *Food and Culture: A Reader*, edited by Carole Counihan and Penny Van Esterik. New York: Routledge, 1997.

Barucci, Piero. 1964. *Profilo economico della provincia di Firenze*. Firenze: La Nuova Italia.

Becker, Anne. 1995. *Body, Self, and Society: The View from Fiji*. Philadelphia: University of Pennsylvania Press.

Behar, Ruth. 1989. Sexual Witchcraft, Colonialism, and Women's Powers: Views from the Mexican Inquisition. In *Sexuality and Marriage in Colonial Latin America*, edited by Asunción Lavrin. Lincoln: University of Nebraska Press.

Bell, Rudolph M. 1985. *Holy Anorexia*. Chicago: University of Chicago Press.

Beller, Anne Scott. 1977. *Fat and Thin: A Natural History of Obesity*. New York: Farrar, Straus & Giroux.

Belmonte, Thomas. 1979. *The Broken Fountain*. New York: Columbia.

Benedict, Ruth. 1934. *Patterns of Culture*. Boston: Houghton-Mifflin.

Benjamin, Jessica. 1988. *Bonds of Love: Psychoanalysis, Feminism, and the Problem of Domination*. New York: Pantheon.

Bennett, John. 1943. Food and Social Status in a Rural Society. *American Sociological Review* 8 (5):561–69.

Bennett, John W., Harvey L. Smith, and Herbert Passin. 1942. Food and Culture in Southern Illinois: A Preliminary Report. *American Sociological Review* 7:645–60.

Beoku-Betts, Josephine A. 1995. We Got Our Way of Cooking Things: Women, Food and Preservation of Cultural Identity among the Gullah. *Gender and Society* 9:535–55.

Berger, John. 1972. *Ways of Seeing*. New York: Penguin.

Bertolo, Carla. 1993. Modelli culturali e pratiche sociali tra passato e presente. In *Madri e padri. Transizioni del patriarcato e cultura dei servizi*, edited by Franca Bimbi and Grazia Castellano. Milano: Franco Angeli.

Bettelheim, Bruno. 1962. *Symbolic Wounds: Puberty Rites and the Envious Male*. New York: Collier. Revised Edition.

———. 1977. *The Uses of Enchantment: The Meaning and Importance of Fairy Tales*. New York: Vintage.

Bierman, Edwin L., and Jules Hirsch. 1981. Obesity. In *Textbook of Endocrinology*, edited by Robert H. Williams. Philadelphia: Saunders.

Bimbi, Franca, and Grazia Castellano, eds. 1993. *Madri e padri. Transizioni del patriarcato e cultura dei servizi*. Milano: Franco Angeli.

Birch, Leann Lipps. 1980. Effects of Peer Models' Food Choices and Eating Behaviors on Preschoolers' Food Preferences. *Child Development* 51:489–96.

Birch, Leann Lipps, Diane Wolfe Martin, and Julie Rotter. 1984. Eating as the "Means" Activity in a Contingency: Effects on Young Children's Food Preference. *Child Development* 55:431–39.

Bleier, Ruth. 1984. *Science and Gender*. Elmsford, N.Y.: Pergamon.

Bodemann, Y. Michael. 1979. Telemula: Aspects of the Micro-Organization of Backwardness in Central Sardinia. Ph. D. diss. Department of Sociology, Brandeis University.

Bodio, Luigi. 1879. Sui contratti agrari e sulle condizioni materiali di vita dei contadini in diverse regioni d' Italia. Annali di Statistica, Ministero di Agricoltura Industria e Commerico Serie II, 8:125–206.

Bordo, Susan. 1990. Reading the Slender Body. In *Body/Politics: Women and the Discourses of Science*, edited by Mary Jacobus, Evelyn Fox Keller, and Sally Shuttleworth. New York: Routledge, Chapman and Hall.

———. 1993. *Unbearable Weight: Feminism, Western Culture, and the Body*. Berkeley: University of California Press.

Boskind-Lodahl, Marlene. 1976. Cinderella's Stepsisters: A Feminist Perspective on Anorexia Nervosa and Bulimarexia. *Signs* 2:342–56.

Boskind-White, Marlene, and William C. White. 1983. *Bulimarexia. The Binge/Purge Cycle*. New York: Norton.

Bossard, James H. S. 1943. Family Table Talk: An Area for Sociological Study. *American Sociological Review* 8:295–301.

Boston Women's Health Book Collective. 1984. *The New Our Bodies, Ourselves*. New York: Simon and Schuster.

Botvin, G. J., and B. Sutton-Smith. 1977. The Development of Structural Complexity in Children's Fantasy Narratives. *Developmental Psychology* 13:377–88.

Bouchier, A. 1917. *Sardinia in Ancient Times*. Oxford: Blackwell.

Brady, Margaret K. 1984. *"Some Kind of Power": Navajo Children's Skinwalker Narratives*. Salt Lake City: University of Utah Press.

Brink, Pamela J. 1995. Fertility and Fat: The Annang Fattening Room. In *Social Aspects of Obesity*, edited by I. de Garine and N. Pollock. Amsterdam: Gordon and Breach.

Britsch, Susan J. 1994. The Contribution of the Preschool to a Native American Community. In *The Need for Story: Cultural Diversity in Classroom and Community*, edited by Anne Haas Dyson and Celia Genishi. Urbana, IL: NCTE.

Bronner, Simon J. 1988. *American Children's Folklore*. Little Rock: August House.

Broude, Gwen J. 1988. Rethinking the Couvade: Cross-Cultural Evidence. *American Anthropologist* 90 (4):902–11.

———. 1989. A Reply to Munroe and Munroe on the Couvade. *American Anthropologist* 91 (3):735–38.

Broughton, Diane. 1978. *Confessions of a Compulsive Eater*. Nashville: Nelson.

Brown, J. Larry. 1987. Hunger in the U.S. *Scientific American* 256 (2):37–41.

Brown, J. Larry, and H. F. Pizer. 1987. *Living Hungry in America*. New York: Meridian.

Brown, Judith K. 1975. Iroquois Women: An Ethnohistorical Note. In *Toward an Anthropology of Women*, edited by Rayna R. Reiter. New York: Monthly Review.

Brown, Laura S., and Esther D. Rothblum, eds. 1990. *Fat Oppression and Psychotherapy: A Feminist Perspective*. Binghamton, N.Y.: Hayworth.

Brown, Peter J. 1979. Cultural Adaptations to Endemic Malaria and the Socio-Economic Effects of Malaria Eradication. Ph. D. diss., Department of Anthropology, State University of New York at Stony Brook.

———. 1981. Cultural Adaptations to Endemic Malaria in Sardinia *Medical Anthropology* 4:3.

Bruch, Hilde. 1973. *Eating Disorders: Obesity, Anorexia Nervosa, and the Person Within*. New York: Basic Books.

———. 1978. *The Golden Cage: The Enigma of Anorexia Nervosa*. New York: Vintage.

———. 1988. *Conversations with Anorexics*, edited by Danita Czyzewski and Melanie A. Suhr. New York: Basic Books.

Brumberg, Joan Jacobs. 1988. *Fasting Girls: The Emergence of Anorexia Nervosa as a Modern Disease*. Cambridge: Harvard University Press.

———. 1997. *The Body Project: An Intimate History of American Girls*. New York: Random House.

Burbach, Roger, and Patricia Flynn. 1980. *Agribusiness in the Americas*. New York: Monthly Review Press.

Buss, Fran Leeper. 1980. *La Partera: Story of a Midwife*. Ann Arbor: University of Michigan Press.

Bynum, Caroline Walker. 1987. *Holy Feast and Holy Fast: The Religious Significance of Food to Medieval Women*. Berkeley: University of California Press.

———. 1991. The Female Body and Religious Practice in the Later Middle Ages. In *Fragments of a History of the Human Body*, edited by Michael Feher. New York: Zone.

Caldwell, Lesley. 1986. Reproducers of the Nation: Women and Family in Fascist Policy. In *Rethinking Italian Fascism: Capitalism, Populism, and Culture*, edited by David Forgacs. London: Lawrence and Wishart.

———. 1991. *Italian Family Matters. Women, Politics and Legal Reform*. Basingstoke and London: Macmillan.

Cambosu, Salvatore. 1954. *Miele amaro*. Firenze: Valecchi.

Camera di commercio, industria, e agricoltura, Firenze. 1958. *La Provincia di Firenze e le sue caratteristiche economiche e sociali*. Firenze: Camera di commercio.

Camporesi, Piero. 1989. *Bread of Dreams: Food and Fantasy in Early Modern Europe*. Translated by David Gentilcore. Chicago: University of Chicago Press.

Cannas, Marilena. 1975. *La cucina dei sardi. 200 piatti caratteristici*. Cagliari: EDES.

Caring, M. L. 1977. Structural Parallels between Dreams and Narratives. In *Studies in the Anthropology of Play*, edited by P. Stevens. Cornwall, N.Y.: Leisure Press.

Casalis, G. 1834. Bosa. *Dizionario geografico-storico-statistico-commerciale degli stati di S. M. il Re di Sardegna*. Vol. 2:526–46. Torino.

Cassidy, Claire M. 1982. Subcultural Prenatal Diets of Americans. In *Alternative Dietary Practices and Nutritional Abuses in Pregnancy*. Washington, D.C.: National Academy Press.

———. 1991. The Good Body: When Big Is Better. *Medical Anthropology* 13:181–213.

Catasto Agrario. 1929. *Compartimento della Sardegna*. Vol. 8, fascicolo 91:120.

Cauwels, Janice M. 1983. *Bulimia: The Binge-Purge Compulsion*. Garden City, N.Y.: Doubleday.

Chapman, Charlotte Gower. 1971. *Milocca: A Sicilian Village*. Cambridge: Schenkman.

Charles, Nickie, and Marion Kerr. 1988. *Women, Food and Families*. Manchester: Manchester University Press.

Chernin, Kim. 1981. *The Obsession: Reflections on the Tyranny of Slenderness*. New York: Harper and Row.

———. 1985. *The Hungry Self*. New York: Times Books.

———. 1987. *Reinventing Eve: Modern Woman in Search of Herself*. New York: Times Books.

Chessa, Federico. 1906. Le condizioni economiche e sociali dei contadini dell' agro di Sassari. Due monografie di famiglia. *La Riforma Agraria*, January–April.

Chiavola Birnbaum, Lucia. 1986. *Liberazione della Donna*. Middletown, Conn.: Wesleyan.

Chodorow, Nancy. 1974. Family Structure and Feminine Personality. In *Women, Culture and Society*, edited by Michelle Zimbalist Rosaldo and Louise Lamphere. Stanford: Stanford University Press.

———. 1978. *The Reproduction of Mothering: Psychoanalysis and the Sociology of Gender*. Berkeley: University of California Press.

Cirese, Alberto Maria, Enrica Delitala, Chiarella Rapallo, and Giulio Angioni. 1977. *Pani tradizionali, arte efimera in Sardegna*. Cagliari: EDES.

Cisneros, Sandra. 1991. Little Miracles, Kept Promises. In *Woman Hollering Creek and Other Stories*. N.Y.: Vintage.

Clark, Martin. 1996. Sardinia: Cheese and Modernization. In *Italian Regionalism: History, Identity and Politics*, edited by Carl Levy. Oxford and Washington, D.C.: Berg.

Codacci. Leo. 1981. *Civiltà della tavola contadina: 190 "ricette" e tanti buoni consigli*. Firenze: Sansoni.

Codere, Helen. 1950. *Fighting with Property: A Study of Kwakiutl Potlatches and Warfare*. Monographs of the American Ethnological Society, 18.

Cohen, R., R. C. Klesges, M. Summerville, and A. W. Meyers. 1989. A Developmental Analysis of the Influence of Body Weight on the Sociometry of Children. *Addictive Behaviors* 14 (4):473–76.

Collins, Patricia Hill. 1990. *Black Feminist Thought: Knowledge, Consciousness, and the Politics of Empowerment*. London: Unwin Hyman.

Colson, Elizabeth. 1979. In Good Years and Bad: Food Strategies of Self-Reliant Societies. *Journal of Anthropological Research* 35:18–29.

Colwin, Laurie. *Home-Cooking*. New York: Harper and Row.

Contento, Isobel. 1980. The Nutritional Needs of Women. In *A Woman's Conflict: The Special Relationship between Women and Food*, edited by J. R. Kaplan. Englewood Cliffs, N.J.: Prentice Hall.

Cook-Gumperz, Jenny, and Barbara Scales. 1996. Girls, Boys, and Just People: The Interactional Accomplishment of Gender in the Discourse of the Nursery School. In *Social Interaction, Social Context, and Language*, edited by Dan Slobin, Julie Gerhardt, Amy Kyratzis, and Jiansheng Guo. Mahwah, N.J.: Lawrence Erlbaum Associates Publishers.

Coppi, Mirna, and Gianna Fineschi. 1980. La donna contadina: Riflessioni sulla condizione della donna nella famiglia mezzadrile toscana. In *Mezzadri , letterati, padroni nella Toscana dell'Ottocento*, edited by Clemente, Coppi, Fineschi, Fiesta and Pietrelli. Palermo: Sellerio.

Corea, Gina. 1989. *The Mother Machine: Reproductive Tehcnologies from Artificial Insemination to Artificial Wombs*. New York: Harper and Row.

Cornelisen. Ann. 1969. *Torregreca: Life, Death, Miracles*. New York: Delta.

Corsaro, William A. 1985. *Friendship and Peer Culture in the Early Years*. Norwood, N.J.: Ablex.

Costantini, Costante. 1976. *Con poco o nulla: Ricette di cucina popolare toscana*. Firenze: Libreria Editrice Fiorentina.

Counihan, Carole M. 1981. Food, Culture and Political Economy: An Investigation of Changing Food Habits in the Sardinian Town of Bosa. Ph. D. diss., University of Massachusetts, Amherst.

———. 1998. Food and Gender: Identity and Power. In *Food and Gender: Identity and Power*, edited by Carole Counihan and Steven Kaplan. Newark: Gordon and Breach.

———. 1999. The Social and Cultural Uses of Food. Forthcoming in *The Cambridge World History of Food and Nutrition*, edited by Kenneth F. Kiple and Conee Kriemhild Ornelas-Kiple. New York and Cambridge: Cambridge University Press.

———. n. d. *Food at the Heart: Gender and Family in Florence, Italy, 1908–1984*. In progress.

Counihan, Carole M., and Debra Tarbert. 1988. Attitudes toward Hunger and Fasting in the U. S.: Cultural Value and Problem. Paper presented at the 87th Annual Meeting of the American Anthropological Association, Phoenix Ariz.

Crowder, Diane Griffin. 1993. Lesbians and the (Re/De)Construction of the Female Body. In *Reading the Social Body*, edited by Catherine B. Burroughs and Jeffrey David Ehrenreich. Iowa City: University of Iowa Press.

Dalla Costa, Mariarosa, and Marina Schenkel. 1983. Forma-famiglia e lavoro femminile: Indagine su donne insegnanti e infermieri nel Veneto. *La Critica Sociologica* 66:138–44.

Dally, Peter. 1969. *Anorexia Nervosa*. New York: Grune & Scratton.

D'Andrade, Roy. 1974. Sex Differences and Cultural Institutions. In *Culture and Personality: Contemporary Readings*, edited by Robert A. Levine. New York: Aldine.

Da Re, Maria Gabriella. 1990. *La casa e i campi. Divisione sessuale del lavoro nella Sardegna tradizionale*. Cagliari: CUEC Editrice.

———. 1995. But What is Bread? *Europaea* 1 (1):219–25.

Dash, Julie. 1997. Rice Culture. In *Through the Kitchen Window: Women Explore the Intimate Meanings of Food and Cooking*, edited by Arlene Voski Avakian. Boston: Beacon.

Davies, Bronwyn. 1989. *Frogs and Snails and Feminist Tales: Preschool Children and Gender*. Sydney: Allen and Unwin.

Davis, J., and R. Oswalt. 1992. Societal Influences on a Thinner Body Size in Children. *Perceptual and Motor Skills* 74 (3):697–98.

Davis, John. 1973. *Land and Family in Pisticci*. London: Athlone.

———. 1977. *People of the Mediterranean. An Essay in Comparative Social Anthropology*. London: Routledge and Kegan Paul.

Davis, William N. 1985. Epilogue. In *Holy Anorexia*, by Rudolph M. Bell. Chicago: University of Chicago Press.

Davis-Floyd, Robbie. 1992. *Birth as an American Rite of Passage*. Berkeley: University of California Press.

Davis-Floyd, Robbie E., and Carolyn F. Sargent. 1997. *Childbirth and Authoritative Knowledge: Cross-Cultural Perspectives*. Berkeley: University of California Press.

De Clercq, Fabiola. 1990. *Tutto il pane del mondo*. Milano: Bompiani.

———. 1995. *Donne invisibili. L'anoressia, la sofferenza, la vita*. Milano: Rizzoli.

de Garine, Igor. 1995. Sociocultural Aspects of the Male Fattening Sessions among the Massa of Northern Cameroon. In *Social Aspects of Obesity*, edited by Igor de Garine and Nancy J. Pollock. Amsterdam: Gordon and Breach.

de Garine, Igor, and Nancy J. Pollock. 1995. *Social Aspects of Obesity*. Amsterdam: Gordon and Breach.

De Gioannis, Paola, and Giuseppe Serri. 1991. *La Sardegna: Cultura e Società. Antologia storico-letteraria*. Firenze: La Nuova Italia Editrice.

De Grazia, Victoria. 1992. *How Fascism Ruled Women: Italy, 1922–1945*. Berkeley: University of California Press.

Delaney, Janice, Mary Jane Lupton, and Emily Toth. 1988. *The Curse: A Cultural History of Menstruation*. Revised edition. Urbana: University of Illinois Press.

Delitala, Enrica. 1978. *Come fare ricerca sul campo. Esempi di inchiesta sulla cultura subalterna in Sardegna*. Cagliari: EDES.

deMan, Anton F. 1987–88. Familial Factors and Relative Weight in Children. *Psychology and Human Development* 2 (1):27–32.

De Simone, Roberto, and Annabella Rossi. 1977. *Carnevale si chiamava Vincenzo*. Roma: De Luca.

Dessí, Giuseppe, Ed. 1967. *Scoperta della Sardegna. Antologia di testi di autori italiani e stranieri*. Milano: Il Polifilo.

Détienne, Marcel, and Jean-Pierre Vernant. 1989. *The Cuisine of Sacrifice among the Greeks*. Translated by Paula Wissing. Chicago: University of Chicago Press.

DeVault, Marjorie L. 1991. *Feeding the Family: The Social Organization of Caring as Gendered Work*. Chicago: University of Chicago Press.

Devereux, George. 1980. The Cannibalistic Impulses of Parents. In *Basic Problems of Ethnopsychiatry*. Chicago: University of Chicago Press.

Dietz, William H., and Steven Gortmaker. 1985. Do We Fatten Our Children at the Television Set? Obesity and Television Viewing in Children and Adolescents. *Pediatrics* 75 (5):807–12.

Dickinson, K. D., and C. E. Snow. 1987. Interrelationships among Prereading and Oral Language Skills in Kindergartners from Two Social Classes. *Early Childhood Research Quarterly* 2:1–25.

Di Giorgi, Umberto, and Roberto Moscati. 1980. The Role of the State in the Uneven Spatial Development of Italy: The Case of the Mezzogiorno. *Review of Radical Political Economics* 12 (3):50–63.

di Leonardo, Micaela. 1991. Introduction. In *Gender at the Crossroads of Knowledge: Feminist Anthropology in the Postmodern Era*, edited by Micaela di Leonardo. Berkeley: University of California Press.

Dinnerstein, Dorothy. 1977. *The Mermaid and the Minotaur: Sexual Arrangements and Human Malaise*. New York: Harper and Row.

Dirks, Robert. 1980. Social Responses during Severe Food Shortages and Famine. *Current Anthropology* 21 (1):21–44.

Disorders of Eating Behavior. 1986. A Psychoneuroendocrine Approach: Proceedings of the International Symposium held in Pavia, Italy, September, 1985. New York: Pergamon Press.

Douglas, Mary. 1966. *Purity and Danger*. London: Routledge & Kegan Paul.

———. 1972. Deciphering a Meal. *Daedalus* 101:61–82.

———. 1973. *Natural Symbols: Explorations in Cosmology*. New York: Pantheon.

———. 1974. Food as an Art Form. *Studio International* 188, 969:83–88.

———. 1975. *Implicit Meanings*. London: Routledge & Kegan Paul.

———, ed. 1984. *Food in the Social Order: Studies of Food and Festivities in Three American Communities*. New York: Russell Sage Foundation.

Du Bois, Cora. 1941. Attitudes towards Food and Hunger in Alor. In *Language, Culture, and Personality: Essays in Memory of Edward Sapir*, edited by L. Spier, A. I. Hallowell, and S. S. Newman. Menasha, Wis.

———. 1960. *The People of Alor*. Cambridge: Harvard University Press.

Dworkin, Sari H. 1989. Not in Man's Image: Lesbians and the Cultural Oppression of Body Image. *Women and Therapy* 8 (1–2):27–39.

Dyrenforth, Sue R., Orland W. Wooley, and Susan C. Wooley. 1980. A Woman's Body in a Man's World: A Review of Findings on Body Image and Weight Control. In *A*

Woman's Conflict: The Special Relationship between Women and Food, edited by J. R. Kaplan. Englewood Cliffs, N.J.: Prentice Hall.

Dyson, A. H., and C. Genishi. 1994. *The Need for Story.* Urbana: NCTE.

Ehrensaft, Diane. 1990. *Parenting Together: Men and Women Sharing the Care of Their Children.* Urbana: University of Illinois Press.

Eitzen, D. Stanley. 1985. *In Conflict and Order: Understanding Society*, 3d ed. Boston: Allyn and Bacon.

Eliot, T. S. 1961. *Selected Poems.* London: Faber and Faber.

Emmons, Lillian. 1986. Food Procurement and the Nutritional Adequacy of Diets in Low-Income Families. *Journal of the American Dietetic Association* 86 (12):1684–93.

————. 1987. Relationship of Participation in Food Assistance Programs to the Nutritional Quality of Diets. *American Journal of Public Health* 77:856–58.

————. 1992. Dieting and Purging Behavior in Black and White High School Students. *Journal of the American Dietetic Association* 92:3306–12.

————. 1994. Predisposing Factors Differentiating Adolescent Dieters and Nondieters. *Journal of the American Dietetic Association* 94 (7):725–31.

Esquivel, Laura. 1989. *Like Water for Chocolate.* New York: Doubleday.

Falassi, Alessandro. 1980. *Folklore by the Fireside: Text and Context of the Tuscan Veglia.* Austin: University of Texas Press.

Farb, Peter, and George Armelagos. 1980. *Consuming Passions: The Anthropology of Eating.* New York: Houghton-Mifflin.

Fausto-Sterling, Anne. 1985. *Myths of Gender: Biological Theories about Women and Men.* New York: Basic Books.

Feagans L. 1982. The Development and Importance of Narratives for School Adaptation. In *The Language of Children Reared in Poverty*, edited by L. Feagans and D. Farran. New York: Academic Press, 95–118.

Feeley-Harnik, Gillian. 1981. *The Lord's Table: Eucharist and Passover in Early Christianity.* Philadelphia: University of Pennsylvania.

Feletti, Maria Grazia, and Santino Pasi. 1981. *La memoria del pane. Vicende alimentari di un paese: Sant'Alberto di Ravenna.* Bologna: Capelli.

Ferguson, Ann. 1989. *Blood at the Root: Motherhood, Sexuality and Male Dominance.* London: Pandora.

Firth, Raymond. 1959. *Social Change in Tikopia: Restudy of a Polynesian Community after a Generation.* New York: Macmillan.

Fisher, M. F. K. 1992. *To Begin Again: Stories and Memoirs, 1908–1929.* New York: Pantheon.

Fitchen, Janet M. 1987. Cultural Aspects of Environmental Problems: Individualism and Chemical Contamination of Groundwater. *Science, Technology and Human Values* 12 (2):1–12.

————. 1988. Hunger, Malnutrition and Poverty in the Contemporary United States: Some Observations on their Social and Cultural Context. *Food and Foodways* 2:309–33. Reprinted in *Food and Culture: A Reader*, edited by Carole Counihan and Penny Van Esterik. New York: Routledge, 1997.

————. 1990. Letter to Carole Counihan. November 1990.

Frank, G. C. 1991. Taking a Bite out of Eating Behavior: Food Records and Food Recalls of Children. *Journal of School Health* 61 (5):198–200.

Frasciello, Lauren M., and Susan G. Willard. 1995. Anorexia Nervosa in Males: A Case Report and Review of the Literature. *Clinical Social Work Journal* 23 (1):1–47.

Frazer, James G. 1951. Adonis, Attiris, Osiris. In *The Golden Bough: A Study in Magic and Religion* vol II, part IV. New York: Macmillan.

Fredman, Ruth Gruber. 1981. *The Passover Seder: Afikoman in Exile.* Philadelphia: University of Philadelphia Press.

Freedman, Alix M. 1990a. Deadly Diet: Amid Ghetto Hunger, Many More Suffer Eating Wrong Foods. *Wall Street Journal*, 18 December, p. 1+.

————. 1990b. Poor Selection: An Inner City Shopper Seeking Healthy Food Finds Offerings Scant. *Wall Street Journal*, 20 December, p. 1+.

Frese, Pamela. 1989. The Food of Life: Gendered Food, Reproduction, and the Life-Cycle. Paper presented at the 1989 Annual Meeting of the American Anthropological Association, Washington D.C.

————. 1991. The Union of Nature and Culture: Gender Symbolism in the American Wedding Ritual. In *Transcending Boundaries: Multi-Disciplinary Approaches to the Study of Gender*, edited by P. R. Frese and J. M. Coggeshall. New York: Bergin and Garvey.

Freud, Anna. 1946. The Psychoanalytic Study of Infantile Feeding Disturbances. *The Psychoanalytic Study of the Child. An Annual*. vol. 2. Reprinted in *Food and Culture: A Reader*, edited by Carole Counihan and Penny Van Esterik. New York: Routledge, 1997.

————. 1968 [1947]. The Establishment of Feeding Habits. In *Indications for Child Analysis and Other Papers, 1945–56*. New York: International Universities Press.

Freud, Sigmund. 1918. *Totem and Taboo*. New York: Vintage.

————. 1950. *The Interpretation of Dreams*. Translated by A. A. Brill. New York: Modern Library.

————. 1962. *Three Contributions to the Theory of Sex*. New York: Dutton.

Friedlander, Judith. 1978. Aesthetics of Oppression: Traditional Arts of Women in Mexico. *Heresies* 1 (4):3–9.

Gallini, Clara. 1971. *ll consumo del sacro: feste lunghe in Sardegna*. Bari: Laterza.

————. 1973. *Dono e malocchio*. Palermo: Flaccovio.

————. 1981. *Intervista a Maria*. Palermo: Sellerio.

Garb, Jane L., J. R. Garb, and A. J. Stunkard. 1975. Social Factors and Obesity in Navajo Children. *Proceedings of the First International Congress on Obesity*. London: Newman, pp. 37–39.

Garcia, S. E., L. L. Kaiser, and K. G. Dewey. 1990. Self-Regulation of Food Intake among Rural Mexican Preschool Children. *European Journal of Clinical Nutrition* 44 (5):371–80.

Garfinkel, Paul E., and David M. Garner. 1982. *Anorexia Nervosa: A Multidimensional Perspective*. New York: Brunner/Mazel.

Garrett, Catherine. 1992. *Men and Anorexia Nervosa: A Challenge to Current Theory*. Kingswood, NSW: University of Western Sydney: Working Papers in Women's Studies 9.

Geertz, Clifford. 1973. *The Interpretation of Cultures*. Selected essays. New York: Basic Books.

————, ed. 1974. *Myth, Symbol, and Culture*. New York: Norton.

————. 1975. On the Nature of Anthropological Understanding. *American Scientist* 63:47–53.

Gianini Belotti, Elena. 1975. *Little Girls: Social Conditioning and Its Effects on the Stereotyped Role of Women during Infancy*. London: Writers and Readers Publishing Cooperative.

Gilbert, Pam. 1994. "And They Lived Happily Ever After": Cultural Storylines and the Construction of Gender. In *The Need for Story: Cultural Diversity in Classroom and Community*, edited by Anne Haas Dyson and Celia Genishi. Urbana: NCTE.

Gilligan, Carol. 1981. *In a Different Voice: Psychological Theory and Women's Development*. Cambridge: Harvard University Press.

————. 1990. Joining the Resistance: Psychology, Politics, Girls and Women. *Michigan Quarterly Review* 29 (4):501–36.

Gilligan, Carol, Nona P. Lyons, and Trudy J. Hanmer, eds. 1990. *Making Connections: The Relational Worlds of Adolescent Girls at Emma Willard School*. Cambridge: Harvard University Press.

Gilmore, David D. 1990. *Manhood in the Making: Cultural Constructions of Masculinity*. New Haven: Yale University Press.

Ginatempo, Nella, ed. 1993. *Donne del Sud. Il prisma femminile sulla questione meridionale*. Palermo: Gelka Editori.

Ginsborg, Paul. 1990. *A History of Contemporary Italy: Society and Politics, 1943–1988*. New York: Penguin.

Glasser, Irene. 1988. *More Than Bread: Ethnography of a Soup Kitchen*. Tuscaloosa: University of Alabama Press.

Goddard, Victoria. 1996. *Gender, Family and Work in Naples*. Oxford and Washington, D.C.: Berg Publishers.

Goddard, Victoria A., Joseph P. Llobera, and Chris Shore, eds. *Anthropology of Europe: Identities and Boundaries in Conflict*. Oxford and Providence: Berg Publishers.

Good, Kenneth. 1991. *Into the Heart: One Man's Pursuit of Love and Knowledge among the Yanomama*. With David Chanoff. New York: Scribners.

Goodwin, Marjorie Harness. 1990. *He-Said-She-Said: Talk as Social Organization among Black Children*. Bloomington: Indiana University Press.

———. 1993. Tactical Uses of Stories: Participation Frameworks Within Girls' and Boys' Disputes. In *Gender and Conversational Interaction*, edited by Deborah Tannen. New York: Oxford University Press.

Goodwin, Marjorie Harness, and Charles Goodwin. 1987. Children's Arguing. In *Language, Gender and Sex in Comparative Perspective*, edited by Susan U. Philips, Susan Steele, and Christine Tanz. New York: Cambridge University Press.

Goody, Jack. 1962. *Death, Property and the Ancestors: A Study of the Mortuary Customs of the Lodagaa of West Africa*. Stanford: Stanford University Press.

———. 1982. *Cooking, Cuisine and Class: A Study in Comparative Sociology*. New York: Cambridge University Press.

Gordon, Richard A. 1988. A Sociocultural Interpretation of the Current Epidemic of Eating Disorders. In *The Eating Disorders*, edited by B. J. Blinder, B. F. Chaiting, and R. Goldstein. Great Neck, N.Y.: PMA Publishing.

———. 1990. *Anorexia and Bulimia: Anatomy of a Social Epidemic*. Cambridge: Basil Blackwell.

Gould, Rosalind. 1972. *Child Studies through Fantasy: Cognitive-Affective Patterns in Development*. New York: Quadrangle Books.

Gramsci, Antonio. 1955. *Il materialismo storico, e la filosofia di Benedetto Croce*. Torino: Einaudi. (Opere di Antonio Gramsci, 2.)

———. 1957. *The Modern Prince and Other Writings*. New York: International Press.

Graziani, A. 1977. Il mezzogiorno nell' economia italiana oggi. *Inchiesta* 29:3–18.

Gray, James J., Kathryn Ford, and Lily M. Kelly. 1987. The Prevalence of Bulimia in a Black College Population. *International Journal of Eating Disorders* 6 (6): 733–40.

Great Britain Naval Intelligence Division. 1945. *Italy*. Geographical Handbook Series, B. R. 517. Vol. 4.

Greenson, Ralph R. 1968. Dis-Identifying from Mother: Its Special Importance for the Boy. *International Journal of Psycho-Analysis* 49:370–74.

Gregor, Thomas. 1985. *Anxious Pleasures: The Sexual Lives of an Amazonian People*. Chicago: University of Chicago Press.

Hacker, Sally. 1980. Farming Out the Home: Women and Agribusiness. In *A Woman's Conflict: The Special Relationship between Women and Food*, edited by J. R. Kaplan. Englewood Cliffs, N.J.: Prentice Hall.

Harris, Jessica B. 1994. Celebrating Our Cuisine. *The Black Woman's Health Book: Speaking for Ourselves*, edited by Evelyn C. White. Seattle: Seal Press.

Harris, Marvin. 1974. *Cows, Pigs, Wars and Witches*. New York: Vintage.

———. 1985. *Good to Eat: Riddles of Food and Culture*. New York: Simon and Schuster.

Harrison, G. C. 1980. Culture and Ethnic Influences on Food Intake and Nutritional Requirements. In *Nutrition in Pregnancy*, edited by E. A. Wilson. Lexington: University of Kentucky Press.

Heath, Shirley. 1982. Questioning at Home and at School: A Comparative Study. In *Doing the Ethnography of Schooling: Educational Anthropology in Action*, edited by George Spindler. New York: Holt, Rinehart, and Winston.

———. 1983. *Ways with Words: Language, Life and Work in Communities and Classrooms*. New York: Cambridge University Press.

———. 1986. Taking a Cross-Cultural Look at Narratives. *Topics in Language Disorders* 7 (1):84-94.

———. 1994. Stories as Ways of Acting Together. In *The Need for Story: Cultural Diversity in Classroom and Community*, edited by Anne Haas Dyson and Celia Genishi. Urbana: NCTE.

Hellman, Judit Adler. 1987. *Journeys among Women. Feminism in Five Italian Cities*. Cambridge: Polity Press.

Hendrick, Joanne, and Terry Strange. 1991. Do Actions Speak Louder than Words? An Effect of Functional Use of Language on Dominant Sex Role Behavior in Boys and Girls. *Early Childhood Research Quarterly* 6:565–76.

Herdt, Gilbert. 1987. *The Sambia: Ritual and Gender in New Guinea*. New York: Holt, Rinehart, Winston.

Hess, John L., and Karen Hess. 1977. *The Taste of America*. New York: Penguin.

Heywood, Leslie. 1998. *Bodymakers: A Cultural Anatomy of Women's Body Building*. New Brunswick, N.J.: Rutgers University Press.

Hiebert, Kathleen A., Marianne E. Felice, Deborah L. Wingard, Rodrigo Munoz, and James M. Ferguson. 1988. Comparison of Outcome in Hispanic and Caucasian Patients with Anorexia Nervosa. *International Journal of Eating Disorders* 7 (5):693–96.

Hightower, Jim. 1975. *Eat Your Heart Out: Food Profiteering in America*. New York: Crown.

Hilton, Rodney. 1973. *Bond Men Made Free: Medieval Peasant Movements and the English Rising of 1381*. New York: Viking.

Hinz, Evelyn J., ed. 1991. *Diet and Discourse: Eating, Drinking and Literature*. A Special issue of *Mosaic*. Winnnipeg: University of Manitoba.

Hirsch, Jules. 1984. Hypothalamic Control of Appetite. *Hospital Practice* (February): 131–38.

Holland, Dorothy C., and Margaret A. Eisenhart. 1990. *Educated in Romance: Women, Achievement, and College Culture*. Chicago: University of Chicago Press.

Holmberg, Allan R. 1969. *Nomads of the Long Bow: The Siriono of Eastern Bolivia*. Prospect Heights, Ill.: Waveland.

Homans, Hilary. 1984. A Question of Balance: Asian and British Women's Perceptions of Food during Pregnancy. In *The Sociology of Food and Eating*, edited by Anne Murcott. Aldershot, England: Gower.

Horn, David G. 1994. *Social Bodies: Science, Reproduction, and Italian Modernity*. Princeton: Princeton University Press.

Horowitz, Helen Lefkowitz. 1987. *Campus Life: Undergraduate Cultures from the End of the Eighteenth Century to the Present*. Chicago: University of Chicago Press.

Howe, Louise Kapp. 1977. *Pink Collar Workers: Inside the World of Women's Work*. New York: Avon.

Hrdy, Sarah Blaffer. 1981. *The Woman That Never Evolved*. Cambridge: Harvard University Press.

Hsu, L. K. George. 1987. Are Eating Disorders Becoming More Common in Blacks? *International Journal of Eating Disorders* 6 (1):113–24.

Hughes, Linda A. 1988. "But That's Not Really Mean": Competing in a Cooperative Mode. *Sex Roles* 19 (11–12):669–87.

Hughes, Marvalene. 1997. Soul, Black Women, and Food. In *Food and Culture: A Reader*, edited by Carole Counihan and Penny Van Esterik. New York: Routledge. (Previously published as Styles 1980).

Hugh-Jones, Christine. 1979. *From the Milk River: Spatial and Temporal Processes in Northwest Amazonia*. Cambridge: Cambridge University Press.

Hugh-Jones, Stephen. 1979. *The Palm and the Pleiades: Initiation and Cosmology in Northwest Amazonia*. Cambridge: Cambridge University Press.

Hull, Valerie. 1986. Dietary Taboos in Java: Myths, Mysteries and Methodology. In *Shared Wealth and Symbol. Food. Culture and Society in Oceania and Southeast Asia*, edited by Lenore Manderson. New York: Cambridge University Press.

Humphrey, Theodore C., and Lin T. Humphrey. 1988. *"We Gather Together": Food and Festival in American Life*. Ann Arbor: University of Michigan Press.

Huntington, Richard, and Peter Metcalf. 1979. *Celebrations of Death. The Anthropology of Mortuary Ritual*. Cambridge: Cambridge University Press.

L'Industria Alimentare. 1978. *Mondo Economico* 33, 42:34–66.

L'Informatore del Lunedí. 1979. "Morte de fame a Bosa." April 4, 1979, 1.

Ires Toscana. 1988. *Toscana che cambia. Economia e società nella Toscana degli anni '80*. Milano: Angeli.

ISTAT (Istituto Centrale di Statistica). 1960. Indagine statistica sui bilanci di famiglie non agricole negli anni 1953–54. *Annali di statistica* 3, 2. Roma.

———. 1968. Indagine statistica sui bilanci delle famiglie italiane, anni 1963-64. *Annali di statistica*, 8, 21. Roma.

———. 1972. *Secondo censimento generale dell'agricoltura*, 25/x/70, 2, 93. Roma.

———. 1985. *Annuario statistico italiano*. Roma.

———. 1990. *Censimento della popolazione*. Roma.

Jacobus, Mary, Evelyn Fox Keller, and Sally Shuttleworth, eds. 1990. *Body/Politics: Women and the Discourses of Science*. New York: Routledge, Chapman and Hall.

Jewson, Jan, Jacqueline Sachs, and Ronald P. Rohner. 1981. The Effect of Narrative Context on the Verbal Styles of Middle Class and Lower Class Children. *Language in Society* 10:201–15.

Jordan, Brigitte. 1993. *Birth in Four Cultures: A Cross-Cultural Investigation of Childbirth in Yucatan, Holland, Sweden and the United States*. 4th ed. Revised and expanded by Robbie Davis-Floyd. Prospect Heights, Ill.: Waveland.

Kahn, Miriam. 1986. *Always Hungry, Never Greedy: Food and the Expression of Gender in a Melanesian Society*. New York: Cambridge University Press.

———. 1988. "Men Are Taro" (They Cannot Be Rice): Political Aspects of Food Choices in Wamira, P. N. G. *Food and Foodways* 3 (1–2):41–58.

Kaplan, Jane Rachel, Ed. 1980. *A Woman's Conflict: The Special Relationship between Women and Food*. Englewood Cliffs, N.J.: Prentice Hall.

Kaplan, Steven L. 1976. *Bread, Politics and Political Economy in the Reign of Louis XV*. The Hague: Martinus Nijhoff.

———. 1984. *Provisioning Paris: Merchants and Millers in the Grain and Flour Trade during the Eighteenth Century*. Ithaca, N.Y.: Cornell University Press.

———. 1990. The State and the Problem of Dearth in Eighteenth-Century France: The Crisis of 1738–41 in Paris. *Food and Foodways* 4 (2):111–41.

Katona-Apte, Judit. 1975. Dietary Aspects of Acculturation in South Asia. In *Gastronomy: The Anthropology of Food Habits*, edited by Margaret L. Arnott. The Hague: Mouton.

Katriel, Tamar. 1987. "Bexibùdim!": Ritualized Sharing among Israeli Children. *Language and Society* 16:305–20.

Kaufman, Lois. 1980. Prime-Time Nutrition. *Journal of Communication* (Summer): 37–46.

Keats, John. 1976. *What Ever Happened to Mom's Apple Pie?* Boston: Houghton Mifflin.

Kelly, Raymond C. 1976. Witchcraft and Sexual Relations: An Exploration in the Social and Semantic Implications of the Structure of Belief. In *Man and Woman in the New Guinea Highlands*, edited by Paula Brown and Georgeda Buchbinder. Washington, D.C.: American Anthropological Association.

Kertzer, David I. 1980. *Comrades and Christians: Religion and Political Struggle in Communist Italy*. Cambridge: Cambridge University Press.

———. 1993. *Sacrificed for Honor: Italian Infant Abandonment and the Politics of Reproductive Control*. Boston: Beacon Press.

Kertzer, David I., and Richard P. Saller, eds. 1991. *The Family in Italy from Antiquity to the Present*. New Haven: Yale University Press.

Khare, R. S., and M. S. A. Rao. 1986 *Food, Society and Culture: Aspects of South Asian Food Systems*. Durham, N.C.: Carolina Academic Press.

Kiell, Norman. 1991. Food in Literature: A Selective Bibliography. In *Diet and Discourse: Eating, Drinking and Literature*, edited by Evelyn J. Hinz. Winnipeg: University of Manitoba.

King, Russell. 1975. *Sardinia*. Newton Abbot: David and Charles.

Knapp, Mary, and Herbert Knapp. 1976. *One Potato, Two Potato, The Folklore of American Children*. New York: Norton.

Kyratzis, Amy, and Jiansheng Guo. 1996. "Separate Worlds for Girls and Boys"? View from U. S. and Chinese Mixed-Sex Friendship Groups. In *Social Interaction, Social Context, and Language*, edited by Dan Slobin, Julie Gerhardt, Amy Kyratzis, and Jiansheng Guo. Mahwah, N.J.: Lawrence Erlbaum Associates Publishers.

Laderman, Carol. 1983. *Wives and Midwives: Childbirth and Nutrition in Rural Malaysia*. Berkeley: University of California Press.

La Leche League International. 1981. *The Womanly Art of Breastfeeding*. 3rd ed. New York: Plume.

La Marmora, Alberto Ferrero Della. 1839. *Voyage en Sardaigne*. 2nd edition. Paris: Arthus Bertrand.

———. 1860. *Intineraire de l'île de Sardaigne pour faire suite au voyage en cette contrée*. 2 vols. Turin: Fratelli Brocca.

Lappé, Frances Moore, and Joseph Collins. 1978. *Food First: Beyond the Myth of Scarcity*. New York: Ballantine.

Lappé, Frances Moore, and Joseph Collins. 1986. *World Hunger: Twelve Myths*. New York: Grove Press.

Laughlin, Charles, and Ivan Brady, eds. 1978. *Extinction and Survival in Human Populations*. New York: Columbia University Press.

Lawrence, Marilyn. 1984. *The Anorexic Experience*. London: Women's Press.

Leach, Edmund. 1964. Anthropological Aspects of Language: Animal Categories and Verbal Abuse. In *New Directions in the Study of Language*, edited by E. H. Lennenberg. Cambridge, Mass.: MIT Press.

Leach, Penelope. 1987. *Babyhood*. 2d ed. New York: Knopf.

Lee, Richard B. 1979. *The !Kung San: Men, Women and Work in a Foraging Society*. New York: Cambridge University Press.

———. 1984. *The Dobe !Kung*. New York: Holt, Rinehart & Winston.

Leghorn, Lisa, and Mary Roodkowsky. 1977. *Who Really Starves? Women and World Hunger*. New York: Friendship Press.

Lehrer, Adrienne. 1969. Semantic Cuisine. *Journal of Linguistics* 5:39–56.

———. 1972. Cooking Vocabularies and the Culinary Triangle of Lévi-Strauss. *Anthropological Linguistics* 14 (5):144–71.

Le Lannou, Maurice. 1941. *Pâtres e paysans de la Sardaigne*. Tours: Arrault et C.

Lelli, Marcello. 1975. *Proletariato e ceti medi in Sardegna, una società dipendente*. Bari: De Donato.

Levenkron, Steven. 1978. *The Best Little Girl in the World*. New York: Warner.

———. 1982. *Treating and Overcoming Anorexia Nervosa*. New York: Scribners.

Lévi-Strauss, Claude. 1963a. *Totemism*. Translated from the French by Rodney Needham. Boston: Beacon Press.

———. 1963b. The Structural Study of Myth. In *Structural Anthropology*, New York: Anchor Books, 202–28.

———. 1966. The Culinary Triangle. *Partisan Review* 33:586–95.

———. 1967. *The Elementary Structures of Kinship*. Boston: Beacon.

———. 1969. *The Raw and the Cooked: Introduction to a Science of Mythology*. New York: Harper & Row.

———. 1971. *From Honey to Ashes: Introduction to a Science of Mythology*. New York: Harper & Row.

———. 1975. *Tristes tropiques*. New York: Atheneum.

Lewin, Ellen. 1993. *Lesbian Mothers: Accounts of Gender in American Culture*. Ithaca, N.Y.: Cornell University Press.

Lewin, Kurt. 1943. Forces behind Food Habits and Methods of Change. In *The Problem of Changing Food Habits*, Bulletin no. 108. Washington, D.C.: National Academy of Sciences.

Liu, Aimee. 1979. *Solitaire*. New York: Harper & Row.

Logan, Onnie Lee. 1989. *Motherwit: An Alabama Midwife's Story*. As told to Katherine Clark. New York: Plume.

Lorde, Audre. 1984. *Sister Outsider*. Freedom, Calif.: The Crossing Press.

Lo Russo, Giuseppe. 1998. *L'Antigastronomo: breve ideario di gastronomia, cucina e altro*. Firenze: Tipografia Coppini.

Lowe, Maria. 1998. *Women of Steel: Female Bodybuilders and the Struggle for Self-Definition*. New York: New York University Press.

Mable, Harriet M., William D. G. Balance, and Richard Galgan. 1986. Body Image Distortion and Dissatisfaction in University Students. *Perceptual and Motion Skills* 63:907–11.

Macintyre, Sally. 1984. The Management of Food in Pregnancy. In *The Sociology of Food and Eating*, edited by Anne Murcott. Aldershot, England: Gower.

Mackenzie, Margaret. 1976. Self-Control, Moral Responsibility, Competence, and Rationality: Obesity as Failure in American Culture. *Obesity/Bariatric Medicine* 5 (4):132–33.

Mackintosh, Maureen. 1989. *Gender, Class and Rural Transition: Agribusiness and the Food Crisis in Senegal*. London: Zed.

Macleod, Sheila. 1981. *The Art of Starvation: A Story of Anorexia and Survival*. New York: Schocken.

Magliocco, Sabina. 1993. *The Two Madonnas. The Politics of Festival in a Sardinian Community.* American University Studies, series. Vol. 61. New York: Peter Lang.

Mahler, Margaret S., Fred Pine, and Anni Bergman. 1975. *The Psychological Birth of the Human Infant: Symbiosis and Individuation.* New York: Basic Books.

Males with Eating Disorders. 1990. New York: Brunner/Mazel.

Malinowski, Bronislaw. 1922. *Argonauts of the Western Pacific.* New York: Dutton.

———. 1927. *Sex and Repression in Savage Society.* Chicago: University of Chicago Press.

———. 1929. *The Sexual Life of Savages.* Boston: Beacon.

———. 1961. *Argonauts of the Western Pacific.* New York: Dutton.

Manderson. Lenore, ed. 1986a. *Shared Wealth and Symbol: Food, Culture and Society in Oceania and Southeast Asia.* New York: Cambridge University Press.

———. 1986b. Introduction: The Anthropology of Food in Oceania and Southeast Asia. In *Shared Wealth and Symbol: Food, Culture and Society in Oceania and Southeast Asia*, edited by Lenore Manderson. New York: Cambridge University Press.

———. 1986c. Food Classification and Restriction in Peninsular Malaysia: Nature, Culture, Hot and Cold. In *Shared Wealth and Symbol: Food, Culture and Society, in Oceania and Southeast Asia*, edited by Lenore Manderson. New York: Cambridge University Press.

March, Kathryn S. 1998. Hospitality, Women, and the Efficacy of Beer. In *Food and Gender: Identity and Power*, edited by Carole Counihan and Steven Kaplan. Amsterdam: Gordon and Breach. (Originally published in *Food and Foodways* 1(4):351–87, 1987).

Marshall, Lorna. 1976. *The !Kung of Nyae Nyae.* Cambridge: Harvard University Press.

Martin, Emily. 1987. *The Woman in the Body: A Cultural Analysis of Reproduction.* Boston: Beacon.

Marx, Karl. 1967. *Writings of the Young Marx on Philosophy and Society.* Translated and edited by Lloyd D. Easton and Kurt H. Guddat. Garden City, N.Y.: Doubleday Anchor.

Marx, Karl, and Frederick Engels. 1970. *The German Ideology.* New York: International Press.

Massara, Emily Bradley. 1989. *Que Gordita. A Study of Weight among Women in a Puerto Rican Community.* New York: AMS Press.

Massara, Emily B., and Albert J. Stunkard. 1979. A Method of Quantifying Cultural Ideals of Beauty and the Obese. *International Journal of Obesity* 3:149–52.

Mathias, Elizabeth Lay. 1979. Modernization and Changing Patterns in Breastfeeding: The Sardinian Case. In *Breastfeeding and Food Policy in a Hungry World*, edited by Dana Raphael. New York: Academic.

———. 1983. Sardinian Born and Bread. *Natural History* 1/83:54–62.

Mauss, Marcel. 1967 (orig. 1925). *The Gift: Forms and Functions of Exchange in Archaic Societies.* New York: Norton.

Mayes, Frances. 1996. *Under the Tuscan Sun: At Home in Italy.* San Francisco: Chronicle Books.

McDowell, John H. 1979. *Children's Riddling.* Bloomington: Indiana University Press.

McIntosh, William Alex, and Mary Zey. 1998. Women as Gatekeepers of Food Consumption: A Sociological Critique. In *Food and Gender: Identity and Power*, edited by Carole Counihan and Steven Kaplan. Amsterdam: Gordon and Breach. (Originally published in *Food and Foodways* 3 (4):317–22, 1989).

McKnight, David. 1973. The Sexual Symbolism of Food among the Wik-Mungkan. *Man* 8 (2):194–209.

Mead, Margaret. 1935. *Sex and Temperament in Three Primitive Societies.* New York: Morrow.

———. 1967. *Male and Female: A Study of the Sexes in a Changing World.* New York: Morrow.

Meigs, Anna S. 1984. *Food, Sex, and Pollution: A New Guinea Religion.* New Brunswick, N.J.: Rutgers University Press.

Mennell, Stephen. 1985. *All Manners of Food: Eating and Taste in England and France from the Middle Ages to the Present.* Oxford: Blackwell.

Merelli, Maria. 1985. *Protagoniste di se stesse. Un'indagine tra le ragazze di Fiorano Modenese.* Milano: Franco Angeli.

Messer, Ellen. 1984. Anthropological Perspectives on Diet. *Annual Review of Anthropology* 13:205–49.

———. 1989. Small But Healthy? Some Cultural Considerations. *Human Organization* 48 (1):39–52.

Messina, Maria. 1988. The Odour of Piety. Paper presented at the 87th Annual Meeting of the American Anthropological Association.

Michaels, Sarah. 1981. "Sharing Time": Children's Narrative Styles and Differential Access to Literacy. *Language in Society* 10:423–42.

Miller, T. M., J. G. Coffman, and R. A. Linke. 1980. Survey on Body Image, Weight, and Diet of College Students. *Journal of the American Dietetic Association* 77:561–66.

Millman, Marcia. 1980. *Such a Pretty Face: Being Fat in America*. New York: Norton.

Minami, Masahiko, and Allyssa McCabe. 1991. Haiku as a Discourse Regulation Device: A Stanza Analysis of Japanese Children's Personal Narratives. *Language in Society* 20:577–99.

Mintz, Sidney W. 1985. *Sweetness and Power: The Place of Sugar in Modern History*. New York: Penguin.

———. 1997. *Tasting Food, Tasting Freedom: Excursions into Eating, Culture and the Past*. Boston: Beacon.

Minuchin, Salvador, Bernice L. Rosman, and Lester Baker. 1978. *Psychosomatic Families: Anorexia Nervosa in Context*. Cambridge: Harvard University Press.

Mitchie, Helena. 1987. *The Flesh Made Word: Female Figures and Women's Bodies*. New York: Oxford University Press.

Moffatt, Michael. 1989. *Coming of Age in New Jersey. College and American Culture*. New Brunswick N.J.: Rutgers University Press.

Moore, Henrietta L. 1988. *Feminism and Anthropology*. Minneapolis: University of Minnesota Press.

Moore, Pamela L., ed. 1997. *Building Bodies*. New Brunswick, N.J.: Rutgers University Press.

Mori, G., ed. 1986. *La Toscana*. Torino: Einaudi.

Munroe, Robert L., and Ruth H. Munroe. 1989. A Response to Broude on the Couvade. *American Anthropologist* 91 (3):730–35.

Munroe, Robert L., Ruth H. Munroe, and John W. M. Whiting. 1973. The Couvade: A Psychological Analysis. *Ethos* 1:30–74.

Murphy, Yolanda, and Robert F. Murphy. 1985. *Women of the Forest*. 2d ed. New York: Columbia University Press.

Murru Corriga, Giannetta. 1990. *Dalla montagna ai Campidani: Famiglia e mutamento in una comunità di pastori*. Cagliari: EDES.

Musio, Gavino. 1969. *La cultura solitaria. Tradizione e acculturazione nella Sardegna arcaica*. Bologna: Il Mulino.

Newman, Lucile, ed. 1990. *Hunger in History: Food Shortage, Poverty, and Deprivation*. New York: Blackwell.

Nicolopoulou, Angelika, Barbara Scales, and Jeff Weintraub. 1994. Gender Differences and Symbolic Imagination in the Stories of Four-Year-Olds. In *The Need for Story*, edited by A. H. Dyson and C. Genishi. Urbana: NCTE.

Nochlin, Linda. 1988. *Women, Art, and Power and Other Essays*. New York: Harper & Row.

Nutini, Hugo. 1988. *Todos Santos in Rural Tlaxcala: A Syncretic, Expressive, and Symbolic Analysis of the Cult of the Dead*. Princeton: Princeton University Press.

Oakley, Ann. 1980. *Women Confined: Towards a Sociology of Childbirth*. New York: Schocken.

———. 1984. *The Captured Womb: A History of the Medical Care of Pregnant Women*. New York: Basil Blackwell.

Opie, Iona, and Peter Opie. 1959. *The Lore and Language of Schoolchildren*. Oxford: Clarendon Press.

Oppo, Anna, ed. 1990. *Famiglia e matrimonio nella società sarda tradizionale*. Cagliari: La Tarantola Edizioni.

———. 1992. Ruoli femminili in Sardegna: rotture e continuità. *Inchiesta*, (luglio–dicembre) 112–28.

Orbach, Susie. 1978. *Fat Is a Feminist Issue: The Anti-Diet Guide to Permanent Weight Loss*. New York: Berkeley Books.
———. 1982. *Fat Is a Feminist Issue, II: A Program to Conquer Compulsive Eating*. New York: Berkeley.
Origo, Iris. 1956. *War in Val D'Orcia: A Diary*. Harmondsworth: Penguin.
Orlando, Giuseppe, Fabrizio de Filippis, and Mauro Mellano. 1977. *Piano alimentare o politica agraria alternativa?* Bologna: Il Mulino.
Ortner, Sherry B. 1975. Gods' Bodies, Gods' Food: A Symbolic Analysis of a Sherpa Ritual. In *The Interpretation of Symbolism*, edited by Roy Willis. New York: John Wiley and Sons.
Pagliari, Marcella Pompili. 1982. Condizione femminile e organizzazione familiare nell'Italia meridionale: Ipotesi per una ricerca sulla soggettività della donna nel lavoro. *International Review of Sociology* 18 (1–3):396–410.
Paige, Karen Ericksen, and Jeffrey M. Paige. 1981. *The Politics of Reproductive Ritual*. Berkeley: University of California Press.
Palazzoli, Maria Selvini. 1963. *L'anoressia mentale*. Milano: Feltrinelli.
———. 1971. Anorexia Nervosa. In *The World Biennial of Psychiatry and Psychotherapy*, edited by Silvano Arieti. Vol. 1. New York: Basic Books.
———. 1974. *Self-Starvation; From the Intrapsychic to the Transpersonal Approach to Anorexia Nervosa*. London: Chaucer. (Originally published as *L'anoressia mentale*. 1963. Milano: Feltrinelli).
Paley, Vivian Gussin. 1981. *Wally's Stories: Conversations in the Kindergarten*. Cambridge: Harvard University Press.
———. 1984. *Boys and Girls: Superheroes in the Doll Corner*. Chicago: University of Chicago Press.
———. 1986. *Mollie Is Three: Growing Up in School*. Chicago: University of Chicago Press.
———. 1988. *Bad Guys Don't Have Birthdays: Fantasy Play at Four*. Chicago: University of Chicago Press.
———. 1990. *The Boy Who Would Be a Helicopter*. Cambridge: Harvard University Press.
———. 1992. *You Can't Say You Can't Play*. Cambridge: Harvard University Press.
———. 1994. Princess Annabella and the Black Girls. In *The Need for Story*, edited by A. H. Dyson and C. Genishi. Urbana: NCTE.
———. 1996. *Kwanzaa and Me: A Teacher's Story*. Cambridge: Harvard University Press.
———. 1998. *The Girl with the Brown Crayon*. Cambridge: Harvard University Press.
———. 1999. *The Kindness of Children*. Cambridge: Harvard University Press.
Pandian, Jacob. 1985. *Anthropology and the Western Tradition: Toward an Authentic Anthropology*. Prospect Heights, Ill.: Waveland.
Parker, Seymour. 1960. The Wiitiko Psychosis in the Context of Ojibwa Personality and Culture. *American Anthropologist* 62:603–23.
Parker, Sheila, Mimi Nichter, Mark Nichter, Nancy Vuckovic, Colette Sims, and Cheryl Rittenbaugh. 1995. Body Image and Weight Concerns among African American and White Adolescent Females: Differences That Make a Difference. " *Human Organization* 54 (2):103–14.
Parsons, Anne. 1969. *Belief, Magic and Anomie*. New York: Free Press.
Passerini, Luisa. 1996. *Autobiography of a Generation: Italy 1968*. (Translation of *Autoritratto di gruppo*.) Hanover, N.H.: University Press of New England.
Paul, Lois. 1974. The Mastery of Work and the Mystery of Sex in a Guatemalan Village. In *Women, Culture and Society*, edited by Michelle Zimbalist Rosaldo and Louise Lamphere. Stanford: Stanford University Press.
Peacock, James L. 1986. *The Anthropological Lens: Harsh Light, Soft Focus*. New York: Cambridge University Press.
Physicians Task Force on Hunger in America. 1985. *Hunger in America: The Growing Epidemic*. Middletown, Conn.: Wesleyan University Press.
Piaget, Jean. 1962. *Play, Dreams and Imitation in Childhood*. New York: Norton.
Piddocke, Stuart. 1969. The Potlatch System of the Southern Kwakiutl: A New Perspective. In *Environment and Cultural Behavior*, edited by Andrew P. Vayda. Austin: University of Texas Press.

Pinna, Luca. 1971. *La famiglia esclusiva, parentela e clientelismo in Sardegna*. Bari: Laterza.
———. 1978. *Convegno regionale sul piano agricolo-alimentare*. Cagliari: Mulas.
Piquereddu, Paolo, ed. 1991. *In nome del pane: forme, techniche, occasioni della panificazione tradizionale in Sardegna*. Nuoro: Istituto Superiore Regionale Etnografico, e Sassari: Carlo Delfino Ed.
Pitcher, Evelyn Goodenough, and Ernst Prelinger. 1963. *Children Tell Stories: An Analysis of Fantasy*. New York: International Universities Press.
Pitcher, Evelyn Goodenough, and Lynn Hickey Schultz. 1983. *Boys and Girls at Play: the Development of Sex Roles*. South Hadley, Mass.: Bergin and Garvey.
Pitkin, Donald. 1985. *The House That Giacomo Built: History of an Italian Family. 1898–1978*. New York: Cambridge.
Pollitt, Katha. 1990. "Fetal Rights": A New Assault on Feminism. *The Nation* (26 March): 409–18.
Pollock, Donald K. 1985. Food and Sexual Identity among the Culina. *Food and Foodways* 1 (1):25–42. Reprinted in *Food and Gender: Identity and Power*, edited by Carole M. Counihan and Steven L. Kaplan. Amsterdam: Gordon and Breach, 1998.
Pollock, Nancy J. 1992. *These Roots Remain: Food Habits in Islands of the Central and Eastern Pacific since Western Contact*. Honolulu: Institute for Polynesian Studies.
———. 1995. Social Fattening Patterns in the Pacific: The Positive Side of Obesity—A Nauru Case Study. In *Social Aspects of Obesity*, edited by I. de Garine and N. Pollock. Amsterdam: Gordon and Breach.
Powdermaker, Hortense. 1960. An Anthropological Approach to the Problem of Obesity. *Bulletin of the New York Academy of Medicine* 36:286–95. Reprinted in 1997 in *Food and Culture: A Reader*, edited by Carole Counihan and Penny Van Esterik. New York: Routledge, 1997.
Pratt, Jeff C. 1986. *The Walled City: A Study of Social Change and Conservative Ideologies in Tuscany*. Aachen: Edition Herodot im Rader-Verlag.
Prindle, Peter H. 1979. Peasant Society and Famine: A Nepalese Example. *Ethnology* 18:49–60.
Quaggiotto, Pamela. 1987. On the Nature of Women through Sicilian Ritual: The Symbolic Correlates of Capitalism. Paper read at the 1987 Annual Meeting of the American Anthropological Association.
Quandt, Sara A., and Cheryl Ritenbaugh. 1986. *Training Manual in Nutritional Anthropology*. Washington D.C.: American Anthropological Association.
Randall, Margaret. 1997. *Hunger's Table: Women, Food and Politics*. Watsonville, Calif.: Papier Mache Press.
Recalcati, M. 1997. *L'ultima cena: anoressia e bulimia*. Milano: Bruno Mondadori.
Reid, Janice. 1986. "Land of Milk and Honey": The Changing Meaning of Food to an Australian Aboriginal Community. In *Shared Wealth and Symbol: Food, Culture and Society in Oceania and Southeast Asia*, edited by Lenore Manderson. New York: Cambridge University Press.
Rich, Adrienne. 1986. *Of Woman Born: Motherhood as Experience and Institution*. 10th Anniversary Edition. New York: Norton.
Richards, Audrey I. 1932. *Hunger and Work in a Savage Tribe*. London: Routledge.
———. 1939. *Land, Labour and Diet in Northern Rhodesia: An Economic Study of the Bemba Tribe*. Oxford: Oxford University Press.
Romer, Elizabeth. 1984. *The Tuscan Year: Life and Food in an Italian Valley*. New York: North Point Press.
Rosaldo, Michelle Zimbalist. 1974. Women, Culture and Society: A Theoretical Overview. In *Women, Culture and Society*, edited by Michelle Zimbalist Rosaldo and Louise Lamphere. Stanford: Stanford University Press.
Rosen, Lionel W., Christine L. Shafer, Gail M. Dummer, Linda K. Cross, Gary W. Deuman, and Steven R. Malmberg. 1988. Prevalence of Pathogenic Weight-control Behaviors among Native American Women and Girls. *International Journal of Eating Disorders* 7 (6):807–11.
Roth, Geneen. 1982. *Feeding the Hungry Heart: The Experience of Compulsive Eating*. New York: Signet.
Rothman, Barbara Katz. 1982. *In Labor: Women and Power in the Birthplace*. New York: Norton.

———. 1989. *Recreating Motherhood: Ideology and Technology in Patriarchal Society*. New York: Norton.

Rubin, Lillian. 1983. *Intimate Strangers: Men and Women Together*. New York: Harper and Row.

Russell, Kathy, Midge Wilson, and Ronald Hall. 1993. *The Color Complex: The Politics of Skin Color among African Americans*. New York: Harcourt Brace Jovanovich.

Sachs, Jacqueline. 1987. Preschool Boys' and Girls' Language Use in Pretend Play. In *Language, Gender and Sex in Comparative Perspective*, edited by Susan U. Philips, Susan Steele, and Christine Tanz. New York: Cambridge University Press.

Sacks, Karen. 1979. *Sisters and Wives: The Past and Future of Sexual Equality*. Westport, Conn.: Greenwood.

Sahlins, Marshall. 1972. *Stone Age Economics*. Hawthorne, N. Y. : Aldine.

———. 1976. *Culture and Practical Reason*. Chicago: University of Chicago Press.

Sanday, Peggy Reeves. 1981. *Female Power and Male Dominance: On the Origins of Sexual Inequality*. New York: Cambridge University Press.

———. 1986. *Divine Hunger: Cannibalism as a Cultural System*. New York: Cambridge University Press.

Saraceno, Chiara. 1984. Shifts in Public and Private Boundaries: Women as Mothers and Service Workers in Italian Day-Care. *Feminist Studies* 10:7–29.

———. 1988. *Pluralità e mutamento: Riflessioni sull'identità femminile*. Milano: Franco Angeli Editore.

Satta, Salvatore. 1979. *Il giorno del giudizio*. Milano: Adelphi.

Satter, Ellyn. 1987. *How to Get Your Kid to Eat . . . But Not Too Much*. Palo Alto: Bull.

———. 1990. The Feeding Relationship: Problems and Interventions. *Journal of Pediatrics* 117 (2):181–89.

Saunders, George. 1981. Men and Women in Southern Europe: A Review of Some Aspects of Cultural Complexity. *Journal of Psychoanalytic Anthropology* 4 (4):435–66.

Schneider, Jane and Peter Schneider. 1976. *Culture and Political Economy in Western Sicily*. New York: Academic.

Schneider, Peter, Jane Schneider, and Edward Hansen. 1972. Modernization and Development: The Role of Regional Elites and Noncorporate Groups in the European Mediterranean. *Comparative Studies in Society and History* 14 (3):328–50.

Schoenfielder, Lisa, and Barb Wieser, eds. 1983. *Shadow on a Tightrope: Writings by Women on Fat Oppression*. San Francisco: Aunt Lute Books.

Schwartz, Hillel. 1986. *Never Satisfied: A Cultural History of Diets, Fantasies and Fat*. New York: Free Press.

Science and Education Administration. 1980. *Food*. U. S. Department of Agriculture Home and Garden Bulletin no 228. Washington D.C.: Government Printing Office.

Sendak, Maurice. 1963. *Where the Wild Things Are*. New York: Harper Collins.

Sgritta, Giovanni B. 1983. Recherches et familles dans la crise de l'état-providence (le cas italien). *Revue Française des affaires sociales* 37:167–72.

Shack, Dorothy N. 1969. Nutritional Processes and Personality Development among the Gurage of Ethiopia. *Ethnology* 8 (3):292–300. Reprinted in *Food and Culture: A Reader*, edited by Carole Counihan and Penny Van Esterik. New York: Routledge, 1997.

Shack, William A. 1971. Hunger, Anxiety, and Ritual: Deprivation and Spirit Possession among the Gurage of Ethiopia. *Man* 6 (1):30–45. Reprinted in *Food and Culture: A Reader*, edited by Carole Counihan and Penny Van Esterik. New York: Routledge, 1997.

Shange, Ntozake. 1998. *If I Can Cook, You Know God Can*. Boston: Beacon.

Shapiro, Leona R., Patricia B. Crawford, Marjorie J. Clark, Dorothy L. Pearson, Jonathan Raz, and Ruth L. Huenemann. 1984. Obesity Prognosis: A Longitudinal Study of Children from the Age of 6 months to 9 Years. *American Journal of Public Health* 74:968–72.

Sharp, C. W., S. A. Clark, J. R. Duncan, D. H. R. Blackwood, and C. M. Shapiro. 1994. Clinical Presentation of Anorexia Nervosa in Males: 24 New Cases. *International Journal of Eating* Disorders 15 (2):125–34.

Sheldon, Amy. 1990. Pickle Fights: Gendered Talk in Preschool Disputes. *Discourse Processes* 13:5–31.

———. 1992. Conflict Talk: Sociolinguistic Challenges to Self-Assertion and How Young Girls Meet Them. *Merrill Palmer Quarterly* 38 (1):95–117.

———. 1993. Pickle Fights: Gendered Talk in Preschool Disputes. In *Gender and Conversational Interaction*, edited by Deborah Tannen. New York: Oxford University Press.

Sheldon, Amy, and Lisa Rohleder. 1996. Sharing the Same World, Telling Different Stories: Gender Differences in Co-Constructed Pretend Narratives. In *Social Interaction, Social Context, and Language: Essays in Honor of Susan Ervin-Tripp*, edited by D. I. Slobin, J. Gerhardt, A. Kyratzis, J. Guo. Mahwah, N.J.: Lawrence Erlbaum Associates.

Shostak, Marjorie. 1981. *Nisa, the Life and Words of a !Kung Woman*. New York: Vintage.

Sidel, Ruth. 1990. *On Her Own. Growing Up in the Shadow of the American Dream*. New York: Penguin.

Siebert, Renate. 1993. *"E' femmina però è bella": tre generazioni di donne al sud*. Torino: Rosenberg and Sellier.

Silverman, Sydel. 1975. *Three Bells of Civilization: The Life of an Italian Hill Town*. New York: Columbia University Press.

Siskind, Janet. 1973. *To Hunt in the Morning*. New York: Oxford.

Slobin, D. I., J. Gerhardt, A. Kyratzis, J. Guo, eds. 1996. *Social Interaction, Social Context, and Language: Essays in Honor of Susan Ervin-Tripp*. Mahway, N.J.: Lawrence Erlbaum Associates.

Smitherman, Geneva. 1994. "The Blacker the Berry, the Sweeter the Juice": African American Student Writers. In *The Need for Story*, edited by A. Dyson and C. Genishi. Urbana, Ill.: NCTE.

Smyth, William Henry. 1828. *Sketch of the Present State of the Island of Sardinia*. London: Murray.

Snowden, Frank M. 1989. *The Fascist Revolution in Tuscany 1919–1922*. New York: Cambridge University Press.

Sobal, Jeffrey, and Albert J. Stunkard. 1989. Socioeconomic Status and Obesity: A Review of the Literature. *Psychological Bulletin* 105 (2):260–75.

Sobal, Jeffrey, and Claire Monod Cassidy. 1987. Dieting Foods: Conceptualizations and Explanations. *Ecology of Food and Nutrition* 20:89–96.

Sobo, Elisa J. 1997. The Sweetness of Fat: Health, Procreation, and Sociability in Rural Jamaica. In *Food and Culture: A Reader*, edited by Carole Counihan and Penny Van Esterik. New York: Routledge.

Soler, Jean. 1973. Sémiotique de la nourriture dans la Bible. *Annales: Economies, Sociétés, Civilisations* 28 (4):943–55.

Somogyi, Stefano. 1973. L' alimentazione nell' Italia unita. *Storia d'Italia* 5:1.

Spiro, Melford E. 1975. *Children of the Kibbutz*. With the Assistance of Audrey Spiro. Revised edition. Cambridge: Harvard University Press.

———. 1979. *Culture and Gender: Kibbutz Women Revisited*. New York: Schocken.

Stack, Carol B. 1974. *All Our Kin: Strategies for Survival in a Black Community*. New York: Harper & Row.

Starn, Frances. 1990. *Soup of the Day: A Novel*. New York: Dell.

Stasch. A. R., M. M. Johnson, and G. S. Spangler. 1970. Food Practices and Preferences of Some College Students. *Journal of the American Dietetic Association* 57, 523–27.

Steedman, Carolyn. 1982. *The Tidy House: Little Girls Writing*. London: Virago.

Steiner-Adair, Catherine. 1990. The Body Politic: Normal Female Adolescent Development and the Development of Eating Disorders. In *Making Connections: The Relational Worlds of Adolescent Girls at Emma Willard School*, edited by Carol Gilligan, Nona P. Lyons, and Trudy J. Hanmer. Cambridge: Harvard University Press.

Striegel-Moore, Ruth H., Lisa R. Silberstein, and Judith Rodin. 1986. Toward an Understanding of the Risk Factors for Bulimia. *American Psychologist* 41 (3):246–63.

Stunkard, Albert J. 1977. Obesity and the Social Environment. Current Status. Future Prospects. *Annuals of the New York Academy of Science* 300:298–320.

Styles, Marvalene H. 1980. Soul, Black Women and Food. In *A Woman's Conflict, the Special Relationship between Women and Food*, edited by J. R. Kaplan. Englewood Cliffs, N.J.: Prentice-Hall. (Reprinted as Hughes 1997.)

Suleiman, Susan Rubin. 1985. *The Female Body in Western Culture: Contemporary Perspectives*. Cambridge: Harvard University Press.

Sutton-Smith, Brian. 1972. *The Folkgames of Children*. Austin: University of Texas Press.

———. 1979. *Play and Learning*. New York: Gardner Press.

———. 1981. *The Folkstories of Children*. Philadelphia: University of Pennsylvania Press.

Sutton-Smith, Brian, D. H. Mahony, and G. J. Botvin. 1976. Developmental Structures in Fantasy Narratives. *Human Development* 19:1–13.

Szurek, Jane. 1997. Resistance to Technology-Enhanced Childbirth in Tuscany: The Political Economy of Italian Birth. In *Childbirth and Authoritative Knowledge: Cross Cultural Perspectives*, edited by Robbie E. Davis-Floyd and Carolyn F. Sargent. Berkeley: University of California Press.

Taggart, James M. 1983. *Nahuat Myth and Social Structure*. Austin: University of Texas Press.

———. 1986. "Hansel and Gretel" in Spain and Mexico. *Journal of American Folklore* 99 (394):435–60.

———. 1992. Fathering and the Cultural Construction of Brothers in Two Hispanic Societies. *Ethos* 20:421–52.

———. 1997. *The Bear and His Sons: Masculinity in Spanish and Mexican Folktales*. Austin: University of Texas Press.

Tambiah, S. J. 1969. Animals Are Good to Think and Good to Prohibit. *Ethnology* 8 (4):423–59.

Tannen, Deborah, ed. 1993. *Gender and Conversational Interaction*. Ithaca, N.Y.: Cornell University Press.

Tanz, Christine. 1987. Introduction to Part 2—Gender Differences in the Language of Children. In *Language, Gender and Sex in Comparative Perspective*, edited by Susan U. Philips, Susan Steele and Christine Tanz. New York: Cambridge University Press, 163–77.

Teti, Vito. 1976. *Il pane, la beffa e la festa: Cultura alimentare e ideologia dell'alimentazione nelle classi subalterne*. Firenze: Guaraldi.

———. 1995. Food and Fatness in Calabria. In *Social Aspects of Obesity*, edited by I. de Garine and N. Pollock. Amsterdam: Gordon and Breach.

Thelen, Mark H., Anne L. Powell, Christine Lawrence, and Mark E. Kuhnert. 1992. Eating and Body Image Concerns among Children. *Journal of Clinical Child Psychology* 21 (1):41–46.

Thoma, Helmut. 1977. On the Psychotherapy of Patients with Anorexia Nervosa. *Bulletin of the Menninger Clinic* 41 (5):437–52.

Thomas, Elizabeth Marshall. 1959. *The Harmless People*. New York: Knopf.

Thompson, Becky W. 1994. *A Hunger So Wide and So Deep: American Women Speak Out on Eating Problems*. Minneapolis: University of Minnesota Press.

Tilly, Louise. 1971. The Food Riot as a Form of Political Conflict in France. *Journal of Interdisciplinary History* 2 (1):23–57.

Tobin, Joseph J., David Y. H. Wu, and Dana H. Davidson. 1989. *Preschool in Three Cultures: Japan, China and the United States*. New Haven: Yale University Press.

Treichler, Paula A. 1990. Feminism, Medicine and the Meaning of Childbirth. In *Body/ Politics: Women and the Discourses of Science*, edited by Mary Jacobus, Evelyn Fox Keller, and Sally Shuttleworth. New York: Routledge, Chapman and Hall.

Turnbull, Colin M. 1972. *The Mountain People*. New York: Simon & Schuster.

———. 1978. Rethinking the Ik: A Functional Non-Social System. In *Extinction and Survival in Human Populations*, edited by C. Laughlin and I. Brady. New York: Columbia University Press.

Turner, Victor W. 1969. *The Ritual Process: Structure and Anti-Structure*. Chicago: Aldine.

Tylor, Sir Edward Burnett. 1958 (orig. 1871). *Primitive Culture*. New York: Harper & Row, vol. 1.

Tyndale, John Warre. 1840. *The Island of Sardinia*. 3 volumes. London: Richard Bently.

Umiker-Sebeok, Jean. 1979. Preschool Children's Intraconversational Narratives. *Journal of Child Language* 6:91–109.

Van Esterik, Penny. 1989. *Beyond the Breast-Bottle Controversy*. New Brunswick, N.J.: Rutgers University Press.

————. 1998. Feeding Their Faith: Recipe Knowledge among Thai Buddhist Women. In *Food and Gender: Identity and Power*, edited by Carole Counihan and Steven Kaplan. Amsterdam: Gordon and Breach. (Originally published in *Food and Foodways* 1(2):197–215, 1986.)

Van Gennep, Arnold. 1960. *The Rites of Passage*. Chicago: University of Chicago Press.

Vargas-Cetina, Gabriella. 1993. Our Patrons Are Our Clients: A Shepherds' Cooperative in Bardia, Sardinia. *Dialectical Anthropology* 18 (3/4):337–62.

Vaughn, Megan. 1987. *The Story of an African Famine: Gender and Famine in Twentieth Century Malawi*. New York: Cambridge University Press.

Veauvy, Christiane. 1983. Le mouvement féministe en Italie. *Peuples Méditerranéens/ Mediterranean Peoples* 22–23:109–30.

Verdier, Yvonne. 1969. Pour une ethnologie culinaire. *L'Homme* 9 (1):49–57.

Wade-Gayles, Gloria. 1997. "Laying On Hands" through Cooking: Black Women's Majesty and Mystery in Their Own Kitchens. In *Through the Kitchen Window: Women Explore the Intimate Meanings of Food and Cooking*, edited by Arlene Voski Avakian. Boston: Beacon.

Wagner, Max Leopold. 1928. *La vita rustica della Sardegna rispecchiata nella sua lingua*. Translated by Valentino Martelli. Cagliari: Società Editoriale Italiana.

Walens, Stanley. 1981. *Feasting with Cannibals: An Essay on Kwakiutl Cosmology*. Princeton: Princeton University Press.

Waller, J. V., R. Kaufman and F. Deutsch. 1940. Anorexia Nervosa: A Psychosomatic Entity. *Psychosomatic Medicine* 2:3–16.

Warren, Kay B., and Susan C. Bourque. 1991. Women, Technology, and International Development Ideologies: Analyzing Feminist Voices. In *Gender at the Crossroads of Knowledge: Feminist Anthropology in the Postmodern Era*, edited by Micaela di Leonardo. Berkeley: University of California Press.

Weiner, Annette. 1988. *The Trobrianders of Papua New Guinea*. New York: Holt, Rinehart & Winston.

Weingrod, Alex, and Emma Morin. 1971. "Post-peasants": The Character of Contemporary Sardinian Society. *Comparative Studies in Society and History* 13(3):301–24.

Weismantel, M. J. 1988. *Food, Gender and Poverty in the Ecuadorian Andes*. Philadelphia: University of Pennsylvania Press.

Whiting, Beatrice, and Carolyn P. Edwards. 1974. A Cross-Cultural Analysis of Sex Differences in the Behavior of Children Aged Three through Eleven. In *Culture and Personality: Contemporary Readings*, edited by Robert A. LeVine. New York: Aldine.

————. 1988. *Children of Different Worlds*. Cambridge, Mass.: Harvard University Press.

Wiley, Carol. 1994. *Journeys to Self-Acceptance: Fat Women Speak*. Freedom, Calif.: The Crossing Press.

Wilhelm, Maria de Blasio. 1988. *The Other Italy: Italian Resistance in World War II*. New York: Norton.

Willis, Susan. 1991. *A Primer for Daily Life*. New York: Routledge.

Wilson, Midge, and Kathy Russell. 1996. *Divided Sisters: Bridging the Gap between Black Women and White Women*. New York: Anchor Books.

Winnick, Myron. 1979. *Hunger Disease: Studies by the Jewish Physicians in the Warsaw Ghetto*. New York: Wiley.

Wolf, Eric. 1974. *Anthropology*. New York: Norton.

Wolf, Naomi. 1993. *The Beauty Myth*. New York: Bantam, Doubleday, Dell.

Young, Iris Marion. 1984. Pregnant Embodiment: Subjectivity and Alienation. *Journal of Medicine and Philosophy* 9:45–62.

Young, Michael W. 1971. *Fighting with Food: Leadership, Values and Social Control in a Massim Society*. Cambridge: Cambridge University Press.

————. 1986. "The Worst Disease": The Cultural Definition of Hunger in Kalauna. In *Shared Wealth and Symbol: Food, Culture and Society in Oceania and Southeast Asia*, edited by Lenore Manderson. New York: Cambridge University Press.

Zaslow, Jeffrey. 1986. Fat or Not, Fourth Grade Girls Diet Lest They Be Teased or Unloved. *Wall Street Journal*, 11 February, p. 28.

Zelman, E. C. 1977. Reproduction, Ritual, and Power. *American Ethnologist* 4:714–33.

Recipes

The following recipes were given to me by the women and men I knew in Florence between 1970 and 1984. These are home-cooking recipes and bear the distinct stamp of their originator. Another woman would insist on a different way of making the same delicious dishes. These recipes yield enough to serve about four people.

BACCALÀ ALLA LIVORNESE (Dried codfish, Leghorn style)

1 pound soaked dried codfish
Flour for dredging
$^1/_4$ cup olive oil
Small bunch of parsley, chopped

3 cloves garlic
Crushed red pepper flakes
1 (28-ounce) can or three fresh
   tomatoes, chopped

Dredge the fish in flour. Fry in the oil until almost cooked through. Remove the fish and add the parsley, garlic, and red pepper. Sauté for 5 minutes. Add the tomatoes and simmer for 10 minutes. Return the fish to the skillet and simmer for 5 more minutes. As Elda says, "It's superlative!"

FRITELLE (Rice fritters)

Fritelle are traditional in Florence for the Feast of St. Joseph, March 19, when many women make them at home and all the pastry shops sell them.

1 cup rice
1 pint milk
$^1/_2$ cup raisins
$^1/_2$ cup sugar
1 teaspoon vanilla extract

1 tablespoon rum
3 eggs, separated
1 to 2 tablespoons flour
3 to 4 tablespoons vegetable oil
$^1/_2$ cup powdered sugar

Boil the rice in the milk until it is cooked. Let it cool. Add the raisins, sugar, vanilla, and rum. Stir in the egg yolks. Whip the egg whites until they form stiff peaks, and fold them into the rice mixture. Add a little flour until the batter is dense, but not too thick. Heat the oil in a large frying pan and drop tablespoonsful of batter into the hot oil; cook for about 2 minutes on each side, until the fritters are golden brown. Transfer them to absorbent paper and sprinkle with powdered sugar.

MINESTRONE (Hearty vegetable soup)

There are as many minestrone recipes are there are women with kitchens. Most vegetables go well in this soup: try using any fresh seasonal vegetables. If you choose not to add pasta, serve this minestrone with lots of good bread.

1 onion
1 carrot
1 stalk celery
Small bunch of parsley
3 tablespoons olive oil
1 zucchini, sliced
1 cup sliced green cabbage

$^1/_2$ cup string beans, chopped
2 to 3 medium potatoes, chopped
2 cups Swiss chard or spinach,
  washed and trimmed
1 cup cooked or canned white
  beans, such as great northern
  beans

4 ounces pasta such as spaghetti broken
into 1 to 2-inch pieces (optional)

Chop the onion, carrot, celery, and parsley. In a soup pot, sauté these in the oil until soft. Add 3 to 4 cups water, the zucchini, cabbage, and string beans, and bring to a boil. Lower the heat to maintain a simmer, and cook about 1 hour. Add the potatoes and Swiss chard and simmer for 30 minutes. Add the white beans and bring the soup to a boil. Drop in the pasta, if using, and cook until done, about 15 more minutes.

ELDA'S POMAROLA (Tomato sauce)

There are many ways to make *pomarola*, and every Italian cook has her own "right" way. Here is Elda's recipe for the "true" *pomarola*.

1 onion
2 to 3 tablespoons olive oil

3 to 4 large fresh tomatoes, chopped
4 or 5 fresh basil leaves

Chop the onion and sauté it in 2 tablespoons olive oil. When the onion is translucent, add the tomatoes and basil and cook until thick. Pass the sauce through a food mill, add a tablespoon or so of oil, and cook a few minutes more.

VANNA'S POMAROLA

The following recipe was given to me by Vanna and is quite different from Elda's recipe above. This sauce makes a good base for additional ingredients such as cooked bacon, meat, sausage, sardines, and so on.

1 medium onion	Pinch of crushed red pepper (optional)
1 carrot	2 tablespoons olive oil
1 stalk celery	4 to 5 fresh tomatoes, chopped or
A few basil leaves	1 (28- or 32-ounce) can
Small bunch of parsley	Salt
2 cloves garlic (optional)	Black pepper

Make a *battuto* (finely chopped mass) of the onion, carrot, celery, basil, and parsley, with the garlic and red pepper if you desire (Vanna uses garlic and onion together only in a meat sauce, and most Florentines agree with this practice). Sauté the *battuto* lightly in the oil for a few minutes until soft. Add the tomatoes and cook briefly until the whole mass forms a sauce. Pass the sauce through a food mill. Add salt and pepper to taste. One can then add a variety of other ingredients to the *pomarola* sauce to make different pasta recipes.

STRACOTTO ("The over-cooked," i.e., Pot-roast)

1 (2- to 4-pound) cut of beef for pot roast	Small bunch of parsley
A few sprigs fresh rosemary	1 (32-ounce) can or 3 to 4
5 to 6 cloves garlic	fresh tomatoes, chopped
Salt	2 to 3 tablespoons olive oil
1 teaspoon black pepper	Flour for dredging
Chopped onion, celery, and carrot (optional)	

Push bits of rosemary and half the garlic with salt and pepper into the meat. Chop the rest of the garlic and the parsley (with the celery, onion, and carrot if desired) and sauté in oil until soft. Dredge the meat lightly in flour, and brown in the hot oil on all sides. Add the tomatoes and enough water to cover. Bring to a boil, lower the heat to a simmer, and cook for 2 to 3 hours until the meat is tender and the water has reduced to a thick sauce. Serve the sauce with pasta as the first course, and the meat as the second course with salad.

Index